"YOU
CAN FOOL
ALL OF THE
PEOPLE
ALL THE
TIME"

ALSO BY ART BUCHWALD

ART BUCHWALD

"YOU CAN FOOL ALL OF THE PEOPLE ALL THE TIME"

Illustrated by
Steve Mendelson

FAWCETT COLUMBINE • NEW YORK

A Fawcett Columbine Book

Published by Ballantine Books

Library of Congress Catalog Card Number: 86-90742

ISBN: 0-449-90200-5

This edition published by arrangement with
G. P. Putnam's Sons

Front cover photograph © 1985 by Diana Walker

Back cover photograph © 1985 by Donal Holway

Manufactured in the United States of America

First Ballantine Books Edition: October 1986

10 9 8 7 6 5 4 3 2 1

CONTENTS

CONTENTS

CONTENTS

CONTENTS

CONTENTS

LIST OF ILLUSTRATIONS

"YOU
CAN FOOL
ALL OF THE
PEOPLE
ALL THE
TIME"

What
Introduction?

Alas. The manuscript was delivered, neatly typed and paged, when the call came in the middle of the night from the EDITOR.

"Where is the introduction to the book?" she demanded.

"What introduction?"

"Every book has to have an introduction to whet the reader's appetite."

"Why should the reader's appetite be whetted? After all, he or she has plunked down the money and is stuck with it."

"You're wrong. Potential book buyers first read the introduction before they decide whether to purchase it or not."

"I thought they read the cover flap," I said.

"They do read the flap first, and then if they are still curious they go on to the introduction. That's where most book sales are closed," she said.

"What should I say in the introduction?"

"You have to tell the reader what the work is about."

"If I do that he or she won't buy the book. They'll fake they read it just to impress their friends."

"There are people like that," my editor admitted. "But at the same time there are many indecisive readers who can get hooked if you just give a hint in your introduction of what they can expect."

"There's some juicy stuff in there about Nancy and Ronald Reagan," I said.

"That's good. People always like to read juicy stuff about the Reagans."

"Should I mention I've included a piece on my impoverished sex life as a US Marine?"

"Impoverished sex lives of Marines don't sell books."

"I've blown the whistle on banks, the Pentagon, the Japanese, and the phone company."

"There's a big market for books on greed."

"What about the pieces on the Mafia, prayers in school, taxes, and Little Red Riding Hood on Wall Street?"

"Can you go into more detail?"

"I'd rather not. I've given away too much already."

"But the introduction isn't long enough!" she protested.

"Perhaps I'll write a short note to the reader so he'll think I'm his friend."

"You can try. At this stage you have nothing to lose."

"What about this?" I said.

" 'Dear Reader,

" 'I believe you've read far enough. Now just take this book over to the cashier and give her your credit card or the cash, and get the hell out of here before we arrest you for loitering in a public building. We've been watching you for some time. Don't look around AND DON'T PUT THE BOOK BACK. Who wants to buy it after you've turned the pages with your dirty fingers?

Compliments of the Author'

"How does that sound?" I asked her.

"It's not quite what I had in mind when I said I wanted an introduction. Couldn't you soften it up for those people who don't have too much of a sense of humor?"

"If they don't have a sense of humor I don't want them reading this book. After all, I've got feelings too."

"Perhaps we might skip the introduction," my editor suggested. "If the tone isn't right we could scare off more readers than we could attract."

"Suits me," I said. "It's probably better not to have one."

PART ONE

THE WORLD'S
GREATEST HUGGER

The World's
Greatest Hugger

As if we didn't have enough to worry about, there is trouble in America's bedrooms. The information comes from syndicated columnist Ann Landers who, in conducting a reader survey, discovered that 72 percent of her women readers would rather be hugged and treated tenderly by men than have sexual intercourse with them.

Although the figure came as a shock to many people, it did not come as a surprise to me. Ever since I reached puberty a few years back, I have been dealing with nothing but the group that would rather be hugged.

In my high school years, the figure was more like 99 percent, and even those girls who only agreed to be hugged and treated tenderly thought *that* was a very big deal.

When I went from high school to the US Marine Corps, I was hoping the odds would change in my favor. After all, I did have a uniform, and was going off to fight for my country. Either I attended the wrong USO clubs, or the wrong Salvation Army canteens, but I could never meet the women who preferred "the act" to the hug. This was very frustrating, because while my buddies came off leave with happy smiles on their faces, I dragged myself in at four in the morning, my arms dead from hugging my dates all night long.

You would expect in a wartime situation that you could find some women who enjoyed both being hugged and the ultimate experience as well. I never did.

I would hug and hold them tenderly till the sun came up, but every time I suggested we go one more step they would reply, "I'm not that kind of girl."

"What kind of girl *are* you?" I would ask.

"I'm the kind of girl who just likes to be held in someone's arms."

If I got angry enough I would reply, "You don't need a boy-friend—you need a nanny."

Okay, the conflict was over, and according to my US Marine discharge papers, I was now a man entitled to all veterans' bene-fits as well as the adulation of a grateful nation which had been spared the horrors of war.

Surely the University of Southern California coeds would un-derstand that man cannot live by hugs alone. But once again the odds were stacked against me. A survey on campus revealed that 85 percent of the women said they would rather be hugged and held tenderly, while only 15 percent admitted that they would "go further," provided either the person was on the first-string football team, or his father owned the Bank of America.

In no time I developed a reputation at USC. The word was out on sorority row that if you wanted to have a tender evening, go out with Buchwald. But if you wanted the earth to move, date somebody else.

After three years of hugging and frustrating tenderness, I de-cided to go to Paris, where women were noted for pleasing themselves by pleasing their men. They considered hugging just the soup course to a wonderful night.

As with most legends of love, this one turned out to be slightly exaggerated.

I hugged under the bridges of Notre-Dame, I hugged under the

4

Eiffel Tower, I hugged in the streets of Montmartre, and I treated French women as tenderly as the filet mignon they had ordered in a restaurant I couldn't afford. And all they ever did when I took them home was thank me at the door and say, "You're not like other Americans who only want French girls to make love."

Well that was some time ago, and I forgot all about such things until the Ann Landers survey was splashed over the front pages. I showed the article to my wife, and thought she would laugh. But all she said when she finished was, "Why don't you ever hug me?"

"Because," I screamed, "I've been doing it all my life and it never got me anywhere!"

America the Great

The following conversation was overheard in a Dallas bar at two o'clock in the morning during the Republican convention:

"You know what makes America great?"

"What?"

"It's being able to turn on your TV set and listen to a politician tell you how great America really is."

"I'll tell you what makes America great. It's winning a gold medal at the Olympics and thanking President Reagan, even if he didn't have a darn thing to do with it."

"Nah, that's not what makes America great. What makes America great is the American family."

"Whose family?"

"Your family."

"I'm divorced. I'm supporting two families."

"That's my point. Only in America are we rich enough to support more than one family at a time."

"It wasn't my idea. It was the judge's."

"Right. That's because we have justice for all."

"I wouldn't say that. He took her side against mine. What kind of justice is that?"

"The greatness of our country is that no matter how rich or how poor you are, you can always appeal an injustice."

"You tried to hire a lawyer lately?"

"Forget your personal problems. I'll tell you what makes America great. It's living in a Christian country."

"I'm not a Christian."

"Well then, it's living in a Judeo-Christian country."

"I'm not Judeo. I'm Voodeo."

"That's exactly what I said. What makes America great is living in a Judeo-Christian-Voodeo country—where you can practice the faith of your choice whether in a school, a church, or at an airport."

"How about this? What makes America great is that 'you' can be outraged at Miss America posing in the nude for *Penthouse* magazine, but nobody can stop 'me' from buying it just to see what all the fuss is about."

"I thought of one. What's great about America is that we can get our clothes whiter than any country in the world."

"And according to Cliff Robertson, AT&T is working twice as hard to gain our trust."

"I'll tell you what is great. Our children, who will be the future leaders of America."

"Not to mention our women. They're really great."

"And getting greater all the time."

"You better believe it!"

"Let's not forget the minorities who want their share of the greatness of America."

"No one would forget them in an election year."

6

"At the same time we do have faults."

"That in itself is the great thing about America. We recognize our faults and have the ability to correct them without endangering our national security."

"Or shortchanging the people on the bottom of the ladder."

"I'll tell you another thing that's great about America. The Dallas Cowboys."

"What's so great about the Dallas Cowboys?"

"They're America's team."

"I hate the Dallas Cowboys."

"That's what I mean. You can either love them or hate them, and as long as you don't live in Dallas, no one is going to arrest you."

"Well, it's been great talking to you."

"It's been great talking to you—but not nearly as great as talking about America."

Forget Sally
and Anya

In President Reagan's "I'm Not Really Mad at the Russians" speech, he ended by saying, "Just suppose with me for a moment that an Ivan and an Anya could find themselves, oh, say, in a waiting room or sharing a shelter from the rain or a storm with a Jim or a Sally, and there was no language barrier to keep them from getting acquainted.

"Would they then debate the differences between their respective governments? Or would they find themselves comparing notes about their children and what each other did for a living? . . . And as they went their separate ways, maybe Anya would be saying to Ivan, 'Wasn't she nice? She also teaches music.' And Jim would be telling Sally what Ivan did or didn't like about his boss. They might even have decided they were all going to get together for dinner sometime soon."

Mr. Reagan's point, I believe, was that if people got to know each other one on one, they wouldn't want to go to war.

While getting Jim and Sally and Ivan and Anya together is a very nice scenario for peace, I think it's more important for Ronnie and Nancy and Mikhail and his wife to find themselves sharing shelter from the rain or storm.

"Hi, my name's Ronnie Reagan and this is my wife Nancy. We're originally from California."

"My name is Mikhail Gorbachev and this is my wife, Raisa. We are hard-line communists."

"That's neat. We're rock-ribbed conservative Republicans. What do you do for a living?"

"I used to be Secretary for Agriculture, but now I am leader of the Soviet Union."

"Hey, how about that, Nancy? Mikhail here is the President of a superpower just like me. We have a lot in common."

Nancy turns to Raisa. "Do you have to give a lot of state dinners?"

Raisa replies, "Every night I have to give a state dinner. I never have enough china."

"It seems that's my problem, too. Who makes your clothes?"

"Oscar of Belorussia. Who makes yours?"

"Adolfo of New York. Here is a photo of the latest suit he designed for me."

"It is very beautiful. But then you are a beautiful lady . . ."

"She's darling, Ronnie."

Ronnie says, "Tell me, Mikhail, what bugs you the most about being the President of the USSR?"

"The Party bosses. They are always telling me I'm doing something wrong."

"Isn't that funny? That's what bugs me the most about being President of the United States. I don't mind the opposition. But I sure get mad when my own people keep telling me I'm screwing up."

Nancy says to Raisa, "How do you get along with your children?"

Raisa replies, "Don't ask."

Nancy laughs. "Me, too. I guess we'll never close the generation gap."

Ronnie says to Mikhail, "So what's the toughest thing about your job?"

"Balancing the budget, providing jobs, and keeping the USSR Number One."

"I can't believe it. Here we are, strangers caught in the storm, and we have the same common problems, interests, and aspirations. How about the four of us getting together for dinner sometime and working out a plan to avoid blowing up the world?"

"I'd like that very much, Ronnie. Here is my hotline number. Call me day or night."

"Great. And here's my card. If I'm not at the White House, try the Camp David number. We're always there on weekends."

That night as Ronnie and Nancy are getting out of their soaking clothes, Nancy says, "Wasn't she a lovely person? Did you know she also plays the balalaika?"

And Ronnie says, "He's a first-class guy. He told me that before he became Secretary for Agriculture, his real ambition was to be a movie actor."

Reagan's
Running Mate

The President and his chief political advisers were watching the Democratic National Convention in the upstairs sitting room of the White House.

After seeing the reception Geraldine Ferraro got, one of the aides said, "Well, are you now convinced, Mr. President, that we still have a gender gap?"

The President said, "I've done more for women than any president in history."

"You know that and we know that. But the country doesn't know it. You've got to fight fire with fire."

"You mean dump George Bush as my running mate?"

"Not necessarily. Can we get him over here?"

The President picked up the phone and said to the operator, "Is Vice President Bush in town? B-U-S-H—as in burning. Good, ask him to come over." The President hung up.

"I appointed the first woman to the Supreme Court. The women didn't hold a twenty-minute demonstration in Moscone Hall when I did that," Reagan said.

"The problem with having a woman Supreme Court justice is you can't hold up her arm like Mondale's doing and say, 'How do you like my running mate?' "

Vice President Bush came into the room, wearing tennis whites.

"Sorry about the way I'm dressed, sir. But you told me you didn't want to see me until next Tuesday."

"It's all right, George. I'm glad to see you anytime."

Bush looked around at the grim faces of the President's staff. "Oh no—don't tell me I have to go to another state funeral."

"It's nothing like that, George," the President said. "Have you been watching the Democratic National Convention?"

"On and off. They're in a mess, aren't they?"

"Yes and no," the President said. "The boys are very concerned about Geraldine Ferraro on Mondale's ticket. It could upset our entire campaign strategy."

"Don't worry about that, sir. I can handle Rep. Ferraro. Hey, I heard a very funny joke in the tennis locker room about Geraldine and Fritz."

"Cool it, George. We can't tell any Ferraro-Fritz jokes in the White House. If just one leaks out to the press, we're dead."

"Well, what do you want me to do?"

Mike Deaver cleared his throat. "George, would you have any objection to showing up at the Republican Convention in drag?"

"You've got to be kidding!" Bush said. "Mr. President, they are kidding, aren't they?"

The President said, "The boys think it might help us with the women voters."

Deaver said, "We have the guy from Hollywood who did Dustin Hoffman's makeup in *Tootsie*, and he'll do a wonderful job on you. There isn't a woman in America who will recognize you."

"I won't do it," George said. "I don't care how many votes it brings to the party. Besides, I have nothing to wear."

Jim Baker said, "Just try on one of Nancy Reagan's Adolfo suits. If it doesn't look good on you, we'll be the first to say."

"How long do I have to go in drag?" George said as he slipped on a skirt.

"Only until November," Deaver told him. "After that, you'll be your own man."

Testing,
9-8-7-6-

"Mr. President, can I have a voice level please? We go on the air in a few minutes."

"My fellow Americans, I'm pleased to tell you today that I've signed legislation that would outlaw Russia forever. We begin bombing in five minutes."

"Mr. President, you're not coming through very well. What I'm getting on my earphones is that you said we were going to begin bombing the Russians in five minutes."

"You heard me correctly. There is nothing wrong with the sound."

"Mr. President, you're not serious, are you?"

"Of course not. It's just a joke, like 9-8-7-6-5-4-3-2-1."

"I don't know that joke."

"Well, there are two guys on this American nuclear submarine and they start wondering what would happen if they both put their keys into the missile computer at the same time."

"Mr. President, you're fading on me. Could you speak up just a little?"

"How's this? I'm sick and tired of the commies turning down all my disarmament plans. I say let's nuke 'em and get it over with. How was that?"

"Your voice was loud and clear, but I'm not sure I heard the message correctly. Did you say something about nuking the Russians?"

"I'm just having a little fun with the mike test. We're not on the air, are we?"

"Not yet, sir. But we're awfully close. Could we try it once more? Why don't you recite 'Mary had a little lamb'?"

"I don't know that one. How about 'Give my regards to the Kremlin, say hello to the Big Red Square. Tell all the folks on Gorky Street that we'll soon be there.'"

"That was good, Mr. President. Are you comfortable with the volume?"

"Why shouldn't I be comfortable with the volume? Are you taping all these tests?"

"Yes, sir."

"Good. You never can tell when I might want to use one. How much time do we have?"

"Two minutes. Would you like to try another test?"

"How's this? I never saw a mushroom cloud. I never hope to see one. But if I did, I know that I would rather see than be one."

"Mr. President, I hope I'm not out of line, but do you know something I don't know?"

"How's that?"

"Well, all these voice tests indicate there seems to be something on your mind. A lot of guys in the control room are calling their wives."

"Don't be ridiculous. I'm just trying to make the voice tests more interesting. They have no right to call their wives, because anything I say before my radio broadcast is off the record."

"Yes, sir. But suppose the Russians pick up on the tests and think it's the real thing?"

"Just let them try it and see how far they get."

"That's not the point, sir. I think when we're going for a voice level we ought to stick to safer subjects such as Mondale and taxes."

"I'm the President and I can say anything I want to when I'm testing. It's my mike and I paid for it."

13

Bullish
on America

It was revealed some time ago that William J. Casey, the CIA Director, bought and sold millions of dollars in stocks and other securities as the market took off.

A lot of people might think that there is some conflict of interest in doing this sort of thing when you're heading up one of the most sensitive organizations in the United States. But I'm not one of them. Mr. Casey is still a private citizen and can invest his own money as he sees fit.

I admire anyone who can run a superpower's intelligence agency and also have time to keep his finger in the stock market.

I can just imagine how he did it.

An aide comes in with a top-secret cable.

"Our man in Havana says that Castro is shipping concrete to Grenada to build an airfield."

"Let me see that. Do you know what this means?"

"War?"

"Not yet. It means if Grenada goes ahead with its airfield, we'll boycott them, and there will be a nutmeg shortage in the United States."

"Do you want to speak to the President?"

"No, I want to speak to my broker at E. F. Hutton. I have to find out what company handles nutmeg in the US."

"This is just in from Tokyo. The Japanese are coming out with a new microcomputer chip which could blow California's silicon valley off the face of the earth."

14

"I was afraid of this. If the Soviets can get their hands on Japanese hi-tech, they can go ahead with their SS-64 missile and we'll have to develop the Pershing Three."

"What's the answer?"

"I'm going to get out of Hewlett-Packard and into Sony-American. Tell our station chief that as soon as the first microchip comes off the line I want to hear about it. We can't afford to be caught napping. What else have you got?"

"One of our undercover agents in Libya says that Quaddafi is planning to overthrow the Royal Family of Saudi Arabia."

"This could mean the end of the oil glut. I better get back into Standard Oil of New Jersey right away."

"Should we do anything to prevent the coup?"

"What do you suggest?"

"Get word to Quaddafi he's a dead man if he ever tries it."

"Good idea. I'll hold off on Standard Oil until we get his reply."

"By the way, the White House called and wants to know if we have anything out of Israel concerning their work with lasers. It could be a big factor in our new Star Wars strategy."

"They haven't come up with anything yet. If they did I would have bought United Laser, which is putting up the money for the research. Tell the White House that if they see some heavy trading in United Lasers then the Israelis will have made a breakthrough."

"Our man in East Germany says his mole indicates that the East Germans have developed an infrared instant camera which Moscow is going to issue to all KGB agents in the fall."

"It doesn't bother me. I've been out of Polaroid since last summer. How are the Soviets doing with their gas line to Western Europe?"

"They're on schedule."

"I was afraid of that. This means the Baton Rouge Shipping Company is going to be stuck with twenty liquid gas tankers that the West Germans ordered."

"I'm sorry about that, sir."

"No one can call every stock right. Did you find out the names of the subcontractors on the MX missile yet?"

"The Air Force is being very cagey about giving out any names."

"Oh, they are, are they? Get me Cap Weinberger on the line right away. How can I run a decent intelligence operation if our own people are going to keep secrets from me?"

Moonlight on the Teachers

When educational scores plummet in the United States, everyone tends to blame the schoolteachers. But this is too easy. The average salary for a teacher, after four years of college and taking special courses, is $17,000 a year. Because many schoolteachers have to moonlight at another job to stay alive, they're not getting enough sleep to be sharp in the classroom.

I became aware of this when I took my nephew to dinner the other night.

"Look," he said, "there's my English teacher."

"Where?" I asked.

"The man coming over in the waiter's uniform."

"He's your English teacher?"

"Sure. Hi, Mr. Peterson."

"Hello, Michael," Peterson said to my nephew. "What brings you here on a school night?"

"My uncle is taking me out for my birthday. How did I do on my English test today?" Michael asked.

"I haven't been able to mark it yet. We had a big party of lobbyists from the American Bankers Association and they've kept me running. What would you like to order?"

Michael studied the menu and said, "What gives with the Oysters Rockefeller?"

"Nothing gives with the Oysters Rockefeller, Michael. Oysters Rockefeller cannot give. You should say, 'How are the Oysters Rockefeller?' "

"Well, how are they?"

"I would recommend them."

"Okay, I'll take a shot at them."

"You can't shoot Oysters Rockefeller. You can only eat them."

"Come on, Mr. Peterson. Don't ruin my birthday."

"I'm sorry, Michael, I forgot my place. As a waiter, I shouldn't correct you."

"Hey, Mr. Peterson. Is that Mr. Alfredo, our science teacher, in the white jacket carrying all those dirty dishes?"

"That's correct. He's a busboy here, but as soon as he gets his masters degree in biophysics, I'm sure he'll become a waiter. The manager of this restaurant has had very good luck with the teaching staff of Warren Harding High School. As an alumnus, he tries to hire as many of us as he can. Miss Bellows, your math teacher, is the hatcheck girl, and Mr. Fallows of the Phys. Ed. department is the bouncer in the bar."

"Is it degrading to work as a waiter at night and a school-teacher in the daytime?" I asked Peterson.

"Oh, I don't ever tell anyone I moonlight in the daytime as a teacher. If you let people know you're a teacher, they tend to think you're wasting the taxpayers' money. But if you tell them you're a waiter, they feel you're doing something worthwhile."

"You teachers have a tough life," I said.

"It could be worse. Most of the staff at Herbert Hoover High School work the night shift at National Airport for Federal Express. They never get any tips."

We gave our order, and after Peterson left I said to Michael, "Is he a good teacher?"

"Better than most. You know John Hanrahan, the kid I play

football with? Well, he and his parents discovered that his French teacher, Mr. Dubois, was working in a gas station. Dubois forgot to put the gas cap back on their tank, and John's parents were so angry when they got home, they called the principal of the school and demanded that Dubois be fired, because they said they didn't want their son to be taught French by someone who didn't even know how to pump gas."

"Was Dubois fired?"

"No, because fortunately the principal had done the same thing at the gas station where he was working the night before."

We finished our dinner and asked Peterson if he could call us a cab.

He told us it would be no problem. "I'll call Mrs. Thompson, Michael's homeroom teacher. She hasn't had a fare all night long."

No Taxes
for the People

Now that he has been reelected President, Ronald Reagan has miles to go and promises to keep.

The promise that voters will remember the best is that Mr. Reagan said he could see no situation where he would raise the people's taxes. The President was not just whistling "Dixie"—he really meant it.

Therefore, you can imagine how aghast I was when I walked into the Treasury Department cafeteria and found a fellow at a table studying a top-secret manual titled, "Death and Taxes for the '80s."

"That's an interesting book you have there," I said.

"We've all been instructed to memorize it," he said confidentially. "It provides the guidelines to interdicting the deficit during the next four years."

"You're not going to increase taxes?"

"Of course not," he said. "President Reagan promised that, if elected, he would kill them, not raise them."

"Then how are you going to cut the deficit?"

"It says in the book we're going to add revenue enhancers."

"Aren't they the same as taxes?"

"Wait a minute," he said, leafing through the pages. "No, they're just the opposite. We are going to reform the code so that people will pay less instead of more taxes."

"How do you plan to do that?"

"Here it is on page twelve: 'One way to keep the tax base from rising is to stop people from deducting their state and city income taxes from their federal tax.' By doing this the government should be able to make thirty billion dollars on the deal."

"If people can't deduct state and city income taxes from their federal returns, they'll still be paying more than they did before."

"Yes, but they'll get mad at the state and city officials and not at us. They can't fault the President just because he wants to close a notorious tax loophole."

"I should hope not."

"It says here that one of the ways to win the hearts and minds of the people is to withhold revenue on unemployment insurance."

"You're going to tax unemployment insurance?"

"No, we going to enhance it, so that people entitled to it will give a portion of it back to the government."

"It still sounds like a tax to me."

"It will only affect those out of work. If you have a job, it won't cost you anything."

"Do they have any other revenue enhancers in the book?"

"Here's one we'll take a shot at. We are going to simplify everyone's taxes so even if they start spiraling up in the first five years, they will go down in the next six, providing inflation stays at four percent and the Gross National Product goes up to seven."

"Do you think you can get away with that?"

"We can't, but the President can. That's why people elected him."

"What else is in the manual?"

"There is a chapter devoted to how to conduct covert lobbying operations behind congressional lines, as well as how to neutralize anyone who accuses the President of raising taxes when he said he wouldn't."

"What exactly do you mean by neutralize? You're not thinking of assassinating anyone who accuses President Reagan of going back on his campaign promises?"

"Are you crazy? We're not the CIA. When we say neutralize, we mean to reinforce our tax base so that we won't be confronted with a fiscal window of vulnerability."

"So what's the bottom line?"

"The bottom line is that no matter how you cut it, the American people are going to have to pay more money to the government in eighty-five than they did in eighty-four. In spite of that, the people still won't get mad at Ronald Reagan."

"Why not?"

"Because everyone knows that Ronald Reagan is a nice guy, and nice guys don't raise people's taxes."

Buy This
Man a Drink

It used to be that if you went into a bar you could always find an argument over the merits of a pro-football team. But now, thanks to Ronald Reagan's constant drumbeat concerning defense weapons, he's got the whole country talking about whether we can win a nuclear war or not.

I dropped by Dumbarton's Bar & Grill the other afternoon for a beer. The man on the next stool said, "How do you think we'll do against the Russians this year?"

I couldn't tell which side he was on, so I played it cool.

"It's too early to tell. It depends on whether we can harden our Minuteman silos in time to put our MX missiles in place."

"Exactly what I was thinking," he said. "Of course the commies could still crawl through our window of vulnerability."

"Yeah, but if we get the B-1 bomber built, set up our Pershing and cruise missiles in Europe, and develop a tricky Star Wars defense, we can zap their land-based air attack before it gets off the ground," I added.

"How many nuclear warheads do you think we need to smash them back if they launch a first-strike attack?"

"We've got about ten thousand now. I'd say we could use another five thousand just to be on the safe side. Even if they knock out seven thousand, we could pulverize them with the other eight."

"You know where I think we're making our big mistake?" he said. "We're trying to match the Soviets missile for missile.

21

What we should do is go ahead with single-warhead Midgetmen that the Russians couldn't hit because we'd spread them all over the country. There's something to be said for not putting all your MXs in one dense-pack."

Dumbarton, who was washing glasses, said, "A guy was in here yesterday, and he had heard from a friend at the Pentagon that the Soviets were violating the SALT Two treaty when it came to underground testing."

"I wouldn't put it past them," I said, ordering another beer.

"You know what we have to do?" said the guy on the next stool. "We have to rethink MAD, the Mutual Assured Destruction strategy we've been using for the past twenty years. It's not working anymore. I say we sit down with the Soviets, offer them a zero option, and if they don't take it, tell them to buzz off."

"How do you feel about a limited nuclear war?" I asked him.

"I'm not against it, as long as we don't kill more than forty or fifty million people on each side. What about you, Dumbarton?"

"It's an option," said Dumbarton, "and I don't want to take away our bargaining chips. The Soviets have got us outnumbered when it comes to conventional war, so if we up the ante and announce we're prepared to fight a limited nuclear war, it will give them something to chew on."

I said, "What really gets me sore is that Congress is dragging its feet when it comes to spending money for a good defense. Reagan knows what the country needs better than anybody."

The guy next to me said, "You better believe it. I saw him in *Hellcats of the Navy* the other night on TV, and the man really has the guts to stand up to the Russians."

Dumbarton refilled our glasses. "I think Reagan has what it takes. But I'm not too sure about Cap Weinberger."

"Why not?"

"He's too light. He could be knocked over by one SS-19 intermediate-range missile. You need a big guy in that position who can take a lot of punishment when he gets hit by an ICBM."

Someone at the end of the bar asked, "Anybody hear the Baltimore Orioles' score?"

Dumbarton said to him angrily, "Watch your language, buddy. There are ladies in this bar, and if you want to talk dirty you can go drink somewhere else."

Dear Diary

I'm not saying I have enough evidence yet to back it up, but just suppose that Adolf Hitler were still alive and living in a nursing home in East Germany.

He is visited by his literary agent.

"Adolf, we need more diaries."

"I wrote sixty for you already. How many can I produce?"

"I can sell as many as you can write. There seems to be an insatiable appetite for them in the West."

"My arm hurts. Why can't I dictate them to a secretary and have them typed up?"

"Because they have to be in your own handwriting. The publishers at *Stern* are not fools. Here's a brand-new black book with your seal on it. Start writing."

"What should I write?"

"Write something nice about Winston Churchill."

"Who is Winston Churchill?"

"He was the Prime Minister of Great Britain during World War Two."

"I don't remember him. Was he the fellow with the umbrella?"

"No, that was Neville Chamberlain. Churchill was the chubby one with the cigar. You hated him."

"Why should I write something nice about him if I hated him?"

"Because we're using the diaries to change your image. We want the world to think you were really a nice person."

"Who says I wasn't a nice person?"

"There are a lot of people who didn't know the real you. Historians have been painting you as a maniac."

"Have them shot."

"Look, Adolf, I don't have much time. Here's an old pen, just like the one you used in 1944. Think of something nice to say about Churchill."

"What about this? 'Churchill is up to his old tricks again, chasing women. I can't have people like this in the Party.' "

"No, Adolf. I don't think the historians will buy that. Why don't you say you admired Churchill as a war leader, and you have to give him credit for the way he handled Roosevelt."

"Who's Roosevelt?"

"He was the President of the United States."

"Was he a Jew?"

"No, he wasn't."

"I never liked Jews."

"The world knows that, Adolf. But don't put it in your diary. It will only add to the bad things they've been saying about you. In order for these diaries to really sell, we've got to show a different Adolf Hitler from the one the public knows. We want history to think of Hitler as a person who loved his dog and his mistress, and had contempt for the Nazis who surrounded him. Now let's see you write something in the notebook."

"I'm tired. I want to take a nap."

"You can sleep later, Adolf. I need these notebooks. We're talking about millions of German marks—West German marks. You and Eva will never have to worry about your old age again. If you don't want to write about Churchill, write something about Hermann Göring."

"I haven't seen Hermann in years. How is the fat slob?"

"He's dead. He committed suicide at Nuremberg."

"It serves him right. He didn't know beans about running a Luftwaffe."

24

"Write that. The historians will be fascinated about what you really thought of Göring."

"I don't want to write about Göring. He was such a dumm-kopf."

"Then write about Eva. It wouldn't hurt to get a little sex in the diaries."

"What's sex?"

"Oh, for heaven's sakes, Adolf! I don't care what you write. Just fill up the pages with gibberish. Those people at *Stern* don't care as long as it's in your own handwriting."

"Ach. It's a waste of time. If you're such a hot-shot agent, how come I haven't been invited to appear on the Phil Donahue show?"

"He wants you badly, Adolf, but after the Klaus Barbie public-ity, the CIA is still arguing about whether or not to slip you a visa."

55 MPH

I was driving down the highway the other day at a respectable 55 miles per hour when I got a call on my CB radio from the man in the car behind me.

"Come on, Chicken Little, speed it up. If you can't drive, get the hell off the road," he said.

"It might interest you to know that I am within the established speed limit as posted along this US highway."

"No one pays any attention to the fifty-five-mile-per-hour speed limit anymore," he said.

"That's where you're wrong. There are many God-fearing citizens who still observe the law of the land. It is people like you who are a menace to society."

"Get out of the left lane so I can pass you, you numbskull."

"If I did that, sir, you would only start speeding and I would become an accessory to a crime. Why are you in such a hurry to get to your destination anyway?" I asked him.

"What business is that of yours?"

"I'm curious to know what you're going to do with all the time you save going twenty miles an hour faster than I."

"I'm trying to get to Culpeper, Virginia, to have dinner with my mother."

"What kind of mother do you have who won't give you dinner if you arrive twelve minutes late?"

"It's not just me. My brother-in-law and sister and their kids are also coming."

"I'm glad they're going to be there," I told him.

"You don't even know my brother-in-law and sister."

"I'm just happy your mother won't be alone when they come for her, after you hit the wall at eighty miles per hour."

"How do you know I'm going to do eighty miles an hour?"

"From the make of your car. People don't buy sports cars unless they can do eighty miles an hour. I never trust anyone who drives an automobile with only two seats. He tends to be spoiled by his mother."

"What does my mother have to do with your hogging the left lane?"

"I'm not just thinking of your mother, but of all the mothers who will suffer because of your disregard for the speeding laws. If it were only your life I wouldn't be concerned how fast you drive. But somewhere up ahead is an innocent family, probably going home for Christmas, and I want them to get there in one piece."

"It's not the people who drive fast, but idiots like you who cause accidents on the highways!" he shouted.

"Statistics show that the fifty-five-mile speed limit has lowered the death rate by over fifteen percent. Good heavens, man, if you don't care for yourself, you could have some regard for the insurance companies. They have mothers, too."

"Pull over to the side of the road and we can discuss this like men."

"I know that trick. I'm wearing a safety belt and I can see in the mirror you're not. You'll probably start beating up on me before I can get mine unbuckled."

"One more time, will you pull out of the left lane so I can pass you?"

"I would, except that I could never enjoy my holidays if something happened to that lovely family up ahead. But I'll do you a favor."

"What's that?"

"If you give me your mother's number in Culpeper, I'll call her up on my cellular phone and ask her to hold up dinner until you get there."

Just One
Little Gun

At the National Rifle Association Convention in Phoenix, Arizona, President Reagan addressed a cheering audience of gun enthusiasts.

Wearing a bulletproof vest and surrounded by a phalanx of Secret Service men and local police officers, the President decried those who would take guns away from the American people.

Signs all over the hall where Mr. Reagan spoke warned the audience not to bring their guns to the rally. As a further precaution, all those entering the building had to pass through metal-detector booths to make sure they were not armed.

The President said he would never disarm decent, law-abiding citizens, as plainclothesmen kept a careful eye on the audience in the convention center.

He alluded to John W. Hinckley and said, "It is a nasty truth, but those who seek to inflict harm are not fazed by gun-control laws. I happen to know this from personal experience."

The President failed to mention that Hinckley bought his gun from a Texas pawnshop in a state that has no gun-control laws.

Let us assume, for Mr. Reagan's sake, that Mr. Hinckley went into the Texas pawnshop, and stiff federal gun laws were in effect.

"Can I help you, sir?"

"Yes, I'd like to buy a handgun that I could fit in my pants pockets."

"May I ask you why you want the gun?'"

"I want to impress Jodie Foster."

"She's a very fine actress. Do you know her personally?"

"Sort of. She knows me. She'll know me better in a couple of weeks."

"There's nothing like a nice little handgun to impress the girl you love."

"I want a couple of boxes of ammunition to go with it."

"Certainly. Why would anyone buy a gun without ammunition? Here's a beauty. I just bought it from a man who wanted to trade up for something larger. It's only been fired once, at a neighbor."

"I'll take it."

"I can't give it to you right now. I have to take your particulars, and then, if everything checks out, you can come back in two weeks and I'll gift-wrap it for you."

"What do you mean 'checks out'?"

"We have to know if you have a police record or have suffered from a mental illness."

"What do you think—I'm crazy or something?"

"Of course not, sir. You look perfectly sane to me. But unfortunately the federal law no longer permits the dealer to decide who should have a gun and who shouldn't. Certainly a law-abiding citizen like yourself can wait two weeks before impressing your girlfriend."

"That's how much you know. Jodie isn't the type of girl who has all the time in the world to be impressed. I could lose her in the next two weeks."

"I understand, sir, but if I sold you this gun without checking you out, I could be fined and sent to jail. Believe me, it isn't easy for us dealers. I have many customers who come in here and when I tell them they have to be checked out before I can sell them a gun, I never see them again. It's killing my business."

"What do you want to know?"

"Why are you purchasing this handgun?"

"I told you. I want to impress my girlfriend."

"Couldn't you give me a better reason?"

"I'm going to Washington and I need it to protect myself against all the nuts walking the streets."

"That's better. Do you promise to use it only in self-defense?"

"Do I have to?"

"It makes it easier to get a permit."

"Aw, the heck with it. I'm not going to answer a lot of damn-fool questions just because I need a gun."

"I'm sorry, sir, but if you don't, I can't sell it to you."

"Stuff the gun. I'll skip Washington and think of another way of impressing Jodie Foster."

The Company
Never Lies

"I saw your advertisement in the Sunday newspaper and I wish to join the CIA."

"We're happy to have you. Please repeat after me, 'I swear to uphold the Constitution, and all the laws of the land.' "

"I do."

"Sorry, you can't have the job."

"Why not?"

"Because sometimes in the agency it becomes impossible to uphold all the laws of the land and still do the mission."

"Then why did you make me take the oath?"

"Just to test you to see if you had what it takes to be a member of the company."

"Give me another chance. I'd be willing to say no to the oath in a shot."

"How do you feel about congressional watchdog committees who are always prying into our covert affairs?"

"I guess they're a necessary evil in a democracy."

"You can leave now. We don't think we have an opening."

"That wasn't the answer you wanted?"

"Covert activities are too serious to be left to the politicians."

"I agree one hundred percent, sir. Congressmen and senators should stop poking their noses into our business."

"What do you mean, our?"

"I just meant our in case you changed your mind and gave me the job. I assure you, sir, that if I become a member of the company, I'll lie to Congress through my teeth."

"The agency doesn't *officially* approve of lying."

"Neither does my mother, but I lie to her all the time."

"That's a good answer. Maybe you have the makings of a CIA agent after all. As you know, we have two functions here. One is to gather intelligence information from all over the world, and the other is to instigate covert operations to destabilize governments which threaten our national security. Is there any particular branch that you would prefer to work for?"

"I'd like to get into covert operations. I've always wanted to see Nicaragua."

"How do you know we're in Nicaragua?"

"The President said we are, and he's real mad that the Senate will only let us stay there for a few more months."

"That information happens to be classified."

"I read it in *The Washington Post.*"

"If you work for us, everything you read in *The Washington Post* is classified. Is that understood?"

"Yes, sir. I'll shred it every morning after I read it."

"Let's say we sent you to Nicaragua, and we weren't able to destabilize the Sandinista government within four months. What would you do?"

"Come back to Langley."

"No, you wouldn't. You would become a member of the US Agricultural Mission in Honduras."

"I don't know anything about agriculture."

"You don't have to know anything about agriculture. Your job would be to smuggle arms to the Nicaraguan freedom fighters."

"I get it, sir. The agriculture title is my cover. Boy, whoever thought of that one was a genius."

"Now, sooner or later, some smart-aleck newspaperman is going to get wind of what you're up to, at which point we will have to deny to Congress any knowledge of having agents in Nicaragua after the four months is up. We'll have to say that you were a former CIA agent who left the agency in disgrace and you were acting on your own. We might even get the Justice Department to try you for gun-running."

"It sounds like a neat job. When can I start?"

"As soon as you take the oath to uphold the Constitution and the laws of the land. By the way, when I give it to you, the answer is, 'yes and no.' "

"What do you mean, 'yes and no'?"

" 'Yes' for your personnel files, to which Congress has access, and 'no' to reassure the people you will be working for."

Hi-Tech Jobs

Apparently, the job market for college graduates is still in the hi-tech industries. The trouble is that most graduates don't know how to apply for a hi-tech job.

When Rod Beaver came home from an interview the other day he was very discouraged.

"The personnel director only spent three minutes with me and then said I wasn't qualified."

"Of course you weren't qualified," his uncle, who works for IBM, told him. "Look at the way you're dressed. You're wearing a dark-blue suit, a white shirt, and a conservative tie. And you shaved. Is that any way to apply for a position in a hi-tech industry?"

Beaver said, "I don't understand. I wanted to make a good impression."

"You don't make a good impression in hi-tech by wearing a shirt and tie."

"But I thought everyone at IBM had to wear a dark suit, shirt, and tie."

"That was in the old days when it was important to look nice.

If you want to be a salesman you can dress like that, but if you're going for the big money in programming and research, they don't trust you if you're too well dressed."

"What should he have worn?" Beaver's mother asked.

"A sport shirt, blue jeans, and open sandals. You have to look like a crazy genius before they take any interest in you. You kids think you can just walk into a hi-tech company all dressed up and they'll be impressed with you. But it isn't so. They want people who look as if they know something about computers."

"I've got an outfit in my closet I can wear, and I'll go out for an interview this afternoon."

"Don't go out until you grow a beard. Hi-tech executives hate people who are clean-shaven. And don't get a haircut for a while. You want to look like a gorilla if you hope to get the personnel director's attention."

"Does he have to grow a beard?" his mother said.

"It could make the difference between twenty-five thousand and forty-five thousand a year," his uncle replied.

"What do I say to the personnel director?" Rod asked.

"You don't say much. Look, I'll be the personnel man. Now, the first question I'll ask you is if you think you would be happy working for the company."

"Yes, sir. It's always been my dream to work for a company like this."

"That's not the correct reply. You say you have no idea, but you're willing to give it a try. But you don't want to be bugged about how long it takes you to come up with something. And you won't want anyone checking on how many hours you put in."

"Does he have to be that surly?" his mother asked.

"There are hundreds of kids waiting out there for jobs in hi-tech, and all the companies are looking for are surly loners who don't want to be told what to do."

"If Rod is going to look unkempt and be surly, how is he going to impress the hi-tech clients?" his mother wanted to know.

"If he gets the job, he'll never see a customer. The people they hire for research and development are kept in a separate building in cages and they get a banana once or twice a day."

Rod thanked his uncle for the advice, and came back the next month to announce that he had landed a job with the Apple Corporation. "I did everything you told me, and they were so impressed with the way I looked, and how surly I was, that they selected me over two guys from the Stanford Business School and gave me a surfboard so I wouldn't get bored in my office."

How Goes the Summit?

How did the economic summit conference in Williamsburg get along?

No better and no worse than anyone expected.

When French President François Mitterrand checked in, he asked what kind of bed did they have for him. The room clerk told him that he had been provided with a large, American colonial king-sized one. Mitterrand said that that was out of the question. He only had $275 worth of French francs to spend, and he could just afford an army cot. He said that his austerity measures at home would be threatened if it were reported that he was sleeping in a king-sized bed.

The flustered clerk told him that there were no army cots available in Williamsburg.

The Japanese Prime Minister, who was waiting to check in after Mr. Mitterrand, slipped off quietly to a telephone and called Tokyo. He informed his Minister of Commerce that there was a shortage of army cots in the United States and ordered the Sony Company to start manufacturing them at once. The Minister assured Mr. Nakasone that the cots would be in Williamsburg by Monday.

Canadian Prime Minister Pierre Trudeau was the next to check in. He was wearing a heavy yellow slicker and carrying an umbrella to make his point that the only reason he had come to the conference was to discuss acid rain. When told that the hotel would not accept Canadian dollars, Mr. Trudeau threatened to go home.

Fortunately, the West German Chancellor, Helmut Kohl, was in the lobby and offered to lend Mr. Trudeau German marks, which could be charged against Canada's drawing rights to the International Monetary Fund.

Italy's Prime Minister, Amintore Fanfani, was asked to pay in advance, and when he produced traveler's checks from the Vatican Bank, the cashier said he couldn't honor them. Mr. Fanfani said the traveler's checks were now backed by the Bank of Italy, and the cashier replied, "That's why we can't take them."

The Italian Prime Minister was prepared to leave the conference in a huff when a representative of the American Express Credit Card Company asked Mr. Fanfani if he might be interested in doing a TV commercial. All he had to say was, "You don't know me, but I am the Prime Minister of Italy. The only reason they let me attend an economic summit conference is because I carry an American Express Credit Card."

Mr. Fanfani did the commercial in the hotel lobby and then was immediately shown to his room.

Margaret Thatcher had no problem at the desk. President Reagan had left orders that she could pay in British pounds to strengthen her chances of winning reelection in Great Britain.

In the meantime, the Japanese Prime Minister, Nakasone, was taking photographs of all the colonial furniture in the Williamsburg Inn so that his people back in Tokyo could copy it and flood the American market.

The German chancellor, Kohl, was shown to his room, where he found a bowl of fruit on the table and a Pershing II missile placed in a champagne bucket with a note, "There's plenty more where these came from. —Love, Ronnie and Nancy."

After everyone washed up, they all came down to dinner, which President Reagan was hosting.

President Mitterrand got down to business right away.

He said that the worldwide recession was caused by high American interest rates and enormous US budget deficits. President Reagan replied that he had inherited them from forty years of wasteful Democratic spending and couldn't change them overnight.

Mrs. Thatcher said that high unemployment in her country was caused by French farmers flooding the Common Market with cheap poultry and artichokes.

The German Chancellor said that the British were subsidizing coal and steel exports to the United States and taking jobs away from the West Germans.

The Italian Prime Minister accused the French of refusing to drink Italian wine and dumping it into the streets.

Prime Minister Trudeau refused to take off his yellow slicker during dinner, and warned all the other heads of state not to drink the water.

While everyone bickered through the meal, Prime Minister Nakasone kept taking photographs of the Williamsburg china and glassware. As soon as he got back, he planned to show them to the Mitsubishi Company, to see if they could reproduce them at half the price.

Making of a
Best Seller

I was walking past my son's room the other day and heard him typing.

"What are you up to?" I asked.

"I'm writing my memoirs telling what it was like to be your son."

This pleased me, and I said, "I hope I come out all right in the book."

"I'm sure you will," he said. "Hey, Dad, how many times should I say you took me out to the barn and whipped me with your belt?"

"I never took you out to the barn and beat you with a belt! We don't even have a barn."

"My editor said that in order for the book to sell, I'm going to have to write a lot of stuff about how you beat me up and locked me in my closet when I did something wrong."

"I didn't lock you up when you did anything wrong."

"I know that, but he wants a story like the ones Gary Crosby and Christina Crawford wrote about their parents. He says that the reading public wants to know about the private life you lead, as opposed to the public image you have. All the kids are writing one now, and they're best sellers. Would you mind if I portrayed you as a rotten father?"

"Do you have to?"

"Of course. I got a ten-thousand-dollar advance, and they don't put up that kind of money unless you really blow the whistle on your parents. You should read Chapter Two. I tell how you made everyone laugh at a speaking engagement, and then you came home drunk and dumped us all out of our beds and made us scrub the floor."

"I didn't do that and you know it."

"Gosh, Dad, it's only a book. My editor loves it—almost as much as Chapter Three, where I have you beating up Mom."

"You've got me beating up your mother?"

"I don't say that you really hurt her. But I tell how we kids used to hide under the blankets so we couldn't hear her screaming."

"I never laid a hand on her."

"I can't say that. My editor said that people are not going to plunk down $15.95 to read *Rebecca of Sunnybrook Farm.*"

"Okay, so I strapped you with a belt and I beat up your mother. What else did I do to you?"

"I'm just getting into the sex stuff in Chapter Four. Do you think that if I wrote you used to bring show girls home at three o'clock in the morning people would believe it?"

"I'm sure they would, but don't you think that's going a bit far, even for a best seller?"

"My editor suggested it. You don't have a big reputation for messing around, and this would really come as a surprise to the reader. It can't hurt."

"It can't hurt you, but it sure as hell can hurt me!" I yelled at him. "Don't you have anything good to say about me in the book?"

"I had a chapter on how you bought me my first bicycle, but my editor made me take it out. He said people might get confused after the stuff I wrote about your dumping a bowl of mashed potatoes on my head at Christmastime because I gave you some lip."

"Why didn't you write that I threw you in a cold shower with all your clothes on because you only got a B in math?"

"Hey, that's good! I'll say that I got pneumonia and you didn't even bother to visit me in the hospital."

"You'd sell out your own father for ten thousand dollars?"

"It's not just the money, Dad. My editor says that if I let it all hang out, Barbara Walters might even interview me on '20/20.' I wouldn't have to live in your shadow anymore."

"Well, if it means that much to you, go right ahead with the book. Is there any way I can help?"

"Yeah, there is one thing. Could you buy me a word processor? If I could speed up my typing, I could have it out by Christmas. I'll pay you back as soon as my agent sells the book rights to the movies."

Evil Men and Damned Souls

Journalism is becoming a very dangerous profession. In libel suits, lawyers for the plaintiffs are now demanding that journalists not only turn over all their notebooks to courts, but are also demanding that a reporter and his or her editors testify about what was going on in their *minds* when they were producing the story. Many judges have decided to let the lawyers pry into the heads of journalists and editors to try to prove that there was malice in their thinking.

There are reporters who object to this line of questioning as a threat to the First Amendment. But I'm not one of them. I'd like to confess how I arrive at a column and what goes through my mind when I'm doing it.

Not long ago I read that the Supreme Court had ruled 8 to 1 against Bob Jones University in a tax case. Bob Jones U. apparently was practicing racial discrimination, and the court said that the IRS was correct in deciding that the fundamentalist school was not entitled to a US tax exemption.

Then I read that Bob Jones III, the president of the university, commented after the ruling, "This is the same court who has decided to murder innocent babies, and takes prayers—the word of God—out of our public schools. I have pity for the heathens who sit on the Supreme Court, pity for their damned souls and their blighted minds. . . . We're in a bad fix in America when eight evil old men and one vain and foolish woman can speak a verdict on American liberties."

Well, this sounded like a good story. The first thing that went through my mind is that President Jones had been unfair to at least one Justice. William Rehnquist was the only one on the court who had voted to give the school its exemption despite its racial policies, so he shouldn't have been included as one of the eight evil old men with damned souls and blighted minds.

Besides not being evil, he isn't *that* old.

The next thing that went through my head was that I know most of the Supreme Court Justices, including the Chief, and while I've questioned some of their decisions, I haven't noticed any one of them possessing a damned soul or a blighted mind. But who am I to judge? Maybe it takes a fundamentalist preacher to be able to see evil in someone's soul, especially when he loses a big case to the Supremes.

What made the decision an interesting subject for a column was that the Reagan Justice Department, instead of defending the IRS, decided to come out on the side of Bob Jones University.

I looked back in my old notebooks, which I keep in case a judge wants to subpoena them, and discovered that the President said he didn't have the authority to take away a tax exemption from a school that practices racial discrimination.

He ordered the Attorney General not to go into the Supreme Court and defend the President's own Internal Revenue Service. With no one to speak for the government, the court appointed an outside lawyer, the distinguished former Secretary of Transportation, William Coleman, to argue the case for the IRS.

So what you finally wound up with was the US Justice Department and Bob Jones University vs. the IRS and the people of the United States.

After reading my notes, the next thing that went through my head was how lucky we were that the Supreme Court voted the way they did, or we would never know how Bob Jones III felt about those sinners who didn't see things the way he did, particularly when it came to money matters. I frankly was on the fence about the case, but after Jones proved to be such a bad loser, I am now glad, as a citizen, that my taxes aren't going to hell.

President Jones, as a man of God, can look for heathens wherever he wants to. But I don't want him to do it with my money. I might even ask the Lord to forgive him for what he said about the eight evil old men on the court. But when he calls Justice Sandra O'Connor a vain and foolish woman, I have to take umbrage. It was an uncalled-for sexist remark about a very fine lady, and is unworthy of a man who is now head of the leading non-tax-exempt institution of higher learning in the land.

"Holy Father"

The Polish Central Committee had an emergency meeting as soon as the Pope's plane took off from Krakow to return to Rome.

"All right," one of the high officials said. "Who came up with the smart idea to have the Pope visit Poland?"

Someone pointed his finger at Panowski.

Panowski threw up his hands. "I thought it would be good for tourism. You have to admit we got great press all over the world."

"Especially in Moscow," one of the members said. "Do you realize what you've done, Panowski? You brought all the Solidarity people back together again, you allowed them to have demonstrations in the street, and we may have to lift martial law."

"How did I know there were that many Catholics in the country?"

"You could have asked us, Panowski. Would you mind telling us exactly how you got us into this mess?"

"Well, last winter I got a call from the Vatican, and the man said that the Pope would like to visit his homeland. I thought he wanted to go to the village where he was born and have a few days' rest at a monastery. I didn't know he was going to use the trip to bring a message to the Polish people."

"You think the Pope just goes around the world looking for a place to take a vacation?"

"I expected him to say Mass, but I didn't realize anybody would show up for it."

"Only ten million people showed up, Panowski."

"But they didn't all take communion."

"I think you're missing the point, Panowski. Until the Pope's visit we had the unions under control, the people were dispirited and had lost their will to fight us, and we looked as if we were in control. Now everything is changed and we're back where we started. The Pope gave everyone a shot in the arm, which is something we didn't need at this time."

"So I underestimated his appeal as a spiritual leader. We all make mistakes."

"Is that what you want us to tell Moscow?"

"Why do we have to tell Moscow anything? We're an independent country."

"No reason except they have six million troops on our border. You better come up with a good story when the Kremlin calls us, which should be any minute now."

"Why don't we say he came here on a trade mission to buy Polish hams, in exchange for Vatican wheat?"

"I'm not sure the Soviets will buy that one; not after the speeches he made from the pulpit."

"We could say that the Western press exaggerated the visit and made it into a political spectacle to further their warlike intentions toward the Warsaw Pact nations."

"That's better, but it's still not good enough. The Soviets are going to ask why we let him come in the first place."

"Because we needed the hard currency to buy oil from the Russians?"

"It won't fly, Panowski."

The phone started ringing.

"It's them, Panowski. Why don't you answer it?"

"Hello, yes, Comrade. This is the Central Committee. Before you say anything, he's gone. We kicked him out of the country before he could do any damage. . . . No, no. Everything's quiet in Poland. Do you think that one priest could be a threat to the great Polish Communist Party? . . . Who told you the whole country turned out to hear him? . . . That's disinformation put out by the CIA. The man didn't even fill up one small church. A few old ladies came out to see him. You have my word for it. . . . Listen to me. . . . We don't need any troops. . . . He didn't influence any of us . . . so help me God!"

PART TWO

THE SECRET OF DEFICITS

FEDERAL DEFICIT

1985
1984
1983
1982
1981

The Secret of
Deficits

I climbed to the top of the Washington Monument the other morning to speak to the Great Economic Oracle. I placed a perfumed bowl of jelly beans at his feet.

The Master put one in his mouth. "They are very tasty."

"I grew them myself," I told him as I knelt on the dirt floor.

"What brings you all this distance, my son?" he asked.

"I am confused," I told him. "I came to find the secret of budget deficits."

The Master stroked his bald head. "There is no secret to budget deficits. If one spends more than one earns, then one must borrow what one owes."

"I know that. But the question I came to ask is, what does one do about a deficit that is so large that all the wise men of the land cannot agree how to cut it?"

"When the highest type of men see deficits they recoil at them. When the average type of men see deficits they half believe them. When the lowest type of men see deficits they laugh heartily at them."

"But how does one get the lowest type of men to become the highest?"

"It can't be done during an election year," the Master said, popping another jelly bean into his mouth.

"Why not, oh wise one?"

"Because those who are responsible for the deficits will not admit they are bad, and those who take no responsibility need them to attack those who made them. It is written in the *Book of Politics* that in an election year one talks about deficits, but one does not do anything about them."

"Why is that, Master?"

"Because to do something about deficits is to cause pain. And if one wants to rule, one must promise not to cause anyone pain."

"If one does not do anything about deficits will there not be greater pain later on?" I asked.

"A wise ruler never mentions future pain when his throne is at stake."

"How long can one live with deficits before they cause pain?"

"Depending on the size of them, one year, maybe two, perhaps forever."

"Doesn't the ruler know that?"

"Yes, he does. But true words are not beautiful. And beautiful words are not true. Ruling a big country is like cooking a small fish."

"What does that mean?"

"I have no idea, but I like the sound of it."

"Master, can we get back to deficits? There are those who say that in order to reduce them one must raise taxes and cut back on military spending. There are others who say one must cut out domestic spending and do nothing more to tax the people. Who is right?"

"It is this simplicity that makes the uneducated more effective than the educated when addressing popular audiences during an election year. You didn't bring enough licorice jelly beans."

"I'm sorry, Master. So it is your opinion that nothing can be done about deficits when a country is contesting for a new ruler?"

"Nothing of substance. One must think of the budget as a lovely river. The deficits are like the snow in the mountains that no one sees. Once spring comes, the snow melts and becomes a torrent of water and the river becomes a flood washing away everything that man has built, and there is nothing left but a depression in the land."

"You sound like Martin Feldsteen," I said.

"It's Feldstein, not Feldsteen," the Master said angrily. "And don't you forget it."

Advancing the President

"Okay, you guys, hold it down. We have to work on the President's trip to the Midwest. Harry, what have you got lined up for Detroit?"

"We have the President sitting on the stage with a Green Beret Medal of Honor winner, two Korean orphans who have just had kidney transplants, a lady astronaut, an Hispanic Nobel Prize winner, and a hundred-twenty-five-year-old former black slave from Georgia."

"If we use them all up in Detroit, what have we got left for St. Louis?"

"Eddie's working on that now. He's lined up a one-armed Little League baseball player, a Polish fireman who pulled six Irish kids out of a burning house, and a teacher who beats up kids who give her any back talk."

"Where does that leave us in Madison, Wisconsin?"

"Larry thinks we're in pretty good shape in Madison. We have a former unemployed steel worker who was retrained to become a nuclear physicist, a pregnant high school girl who refused to have an abortion, a survivor of the Bataan Death March, and a great-grandmother who used part of her Social Security payments to buy up a string of Pizza Huts in the Midwest."

"Listen, Mike, don't you think we're overdoing it on this trip? We've got a long campaign ahead of us."

"What do you suggest?"

"I'd like to save the pregnant high school kid for the Fourth of July."

"You mean until after she's had her baby? What kind of TV picture do you think that's going to make?"

"I see what you mean. What about the two Korean kids with kidney transplants? We've done that one already."

"It played in Peoria and it will play in Detroit. Besides, the kids have to go back to South Korea in a couple of weeks."

"All right. But how about saving the Green Beret for September? He isn't going anywhere."

"Don't be too sure."

"You know something we don't?"

"I'm not at liberty to say. Anyone come up with somebody we haven't thought of?"

"We found a former pilot in Minneapolis who flew a B-25 in World War Two. His plane was hit in a bombing run over Dresden and caught on fire. The crew bailed out, except for the eighteen-year-old gunner, who didn't have a parachute. So the pilot gave him his and said, 'Jump, kid. I'm going down with the plane.' "

"If he did that, what's he doing living in Minnesota?"

"It turns out the fire wasn't very serious, and the guy flew his B-25 back to England."

"What the hell kind of story is that for the President to tell in Minneapolis?"

"That's what I thought. I'll tell the pilot we don't need him."

"I still have a feeling we haven't covered all our bases on this trip."

"We have a rabbi saying the invocation in Grand Rapids, a priest in Milwaukee, a Baptist minister in Cincinnati, and the football coach of Ohio State University in Columbus."

"What about the gender gap? How are we dealing with that for the nightly news?"

"We're going to get Mrs. Dole, the Secretary of Transportation, and Mrs. Heckler, the Secretary of Health and Human Services, to warm up the audiences wherever the President goes. We tried to get Justice Sandra O'Connor to come along in her black robes, but she said she couldn't do it while the court was in session."

"Okay, I guess that's as good as we can do on such short notice. Any questions?"

"Who's working on the President's speeches?"

"What speeches? He's going to stick with the State of the Union one until the end of the campaign."

Let the Buyer
Beware

The Department of Agriculture has reported that it will cost $80,260 to raise a child born this year until it reaches age eighteen.

This seemed like a lot of scratch to Carter Brown, a friend of mine, whose wife is expecting a child very soon. So he went down to the Department to see what he was going to get for his money.

"Is it really going to cost me $80,260 to raise a child until it's eighteen?" he asked the man behind the desk.

"It's a bargain," the man told him. "Eighteen months ago we projected it would cost $134,414. But that was when we included an eight-percent inflation rate. Our eighty-thousand figure is based on no-inflation dollars."

"What does the eighty thousand cost include?"

"Just the bare-bones items such as seventeen thousand for food, twenty-seven thousand for housing, thirteen thousand for transportation, and the rest for miscellaneous items such as medical costs and shoes."

"I don't imagine you included orthodontic work in your estimate?" Brown asked.

"You have to be kidding!" The man roared with laughter. "If we included what it will cost for serious dental work, no one would have a baby!"

"What other items did you fail to include in your report, so I won't be surprised?"

The man looked at his list. "Well, in the early years of the child's upbringing you'll probably be able to stay within the eighty-thousand figure. But as your offspring goes into its teens, you could get into serious financial overruns."

"Such as?"

"The Department did not include in its report the cost of such teenage necessities as stereo equipment, movie and rock concert tickets, sports equipment, computers, weekend parties, guitar lessons, Christmas, and insurance."

"Why not?" Brown asked. "They seem to be as essential as food, housing, and transportation."

"Because we have them down as options. Some parents prefer a stripped-down child and others prefer to add everything that's on the market."

"If I pay the basic price of eighty thousand dollars to raise a child for the next eighteen years, plus all the extras that you've mentioned, is there any guarantee it will turn out all right?"

"There is no warranty with the price whatsoever. You pay your money and you take your chances. We don't guarantee anymore that when the child reaches eighteen, it will be able to read and write. Frankly, you'll be lucky if it volunteers to cut your lawn or do the dishes once a week. And if you think that for eighty grand it's going to clean up its own room, you're living in a dream world."

"It sure seems like a big investment for so little in return."

"The Department of Agriculture is not recommending that you have a baby. Our job is just to report what it will cost you to raise one. The eighty thousand dollars is our official figure. The other items I tipped you off about are unofficial, based on my own experience as the father of three teenagers. I didn't include the price of collect long-distance telephone calls during the first eighteen years, because I didn't want to scare you."

"So if I add in all the extras I can easily wind up spending two hundred thousand dollars," Brown said.

"That's a good ballpark figure unless you and your wife have to seek psychiatric help while raising your child."

"Well, I guess two hundred thousand is not an unreasonable sum of money to invest until a child reaches eighteen years old."

"Actually it's a steal," the man from Agriculture said. "When your kid reaches eighteen, it's going to cost you that much just to send it to college."

Secrets of the Press

As a newspaperman I am constantly being asked by victims what their rights are when it comes to talking to members of the media.

I shall try to address the problem in question-and-answer form, though I may lose my journalistic license for doing so.

Q: When a reporter stops me in front of my house, or sticks a microphone in my face, or telephones me in the middle of the night, what is my obligation to talk to this person?

A: You have a right to remain silent, you also have a right to shove the mike in the reporter's ear, and you have the right to hang up the telephone.

Q: Won't that make me look bad if the correspondent says on TV that night, "Mr. Blue refuses to come out of his house to talk to us"? Or the reporter writes, "Efforts by this newspaper to reach Mr. Blue were unsuccessful"?

A: Not necessarily. The viewer or reader might conclude that the reporter has been negligent by failing to get you to comment.

Q: What should I be wary of when dealing with the media?

A: The friendly young male reporter with the hearty handshake, who calls you by your first name and says he's only there to get your side of the story, and the starry-eyed girl reporter who reminds you of your daughter. They'll murder you in a story, compared to a grizzly, snarling, old-timer, who has given up making a name for himself and has no ambition to become another Woodward or Bernstein.

Q: Who are the worst ones to talk to, the print people or TV reporters?

A: It's hard to say. Print reporters have more time on their hands before they write their stories, so they can spend time ingratiating themselves with you. They can lead you from your love of gardening to admitting that you know every mob leader in Cleveland. TV reporters, on the other hand, are under pressure to get their tape to the studio, so they ask tougher questions and depend more on your facial reactions to them than the answers you give. Even if you don't say anything, they'll still show you on the air fighting your way to get into your automobile while the reporters shout questions at you.

Q: If I talk to the press, will they listen to my side of the story?

A: They'll listen to it, but that doesn't necessarily mean it will get into print. You could say a hundred things and because of space limitations only three of them might appear in the newspaper. But it's still better than TV, when rarely more than one of your statements gets on the air. If the TV people give you fifteen seconds to defend yourself, you're a lucky person.

Q: How can I get more time?

A: By admitting your guilt. Then you'll get the full minute.

Q: Suppose I'm not accused of anything, but the media want to interview me about somebody who is. Should I talk to them?

A: It depends on how much you want to get on the evening news or see your name in the paper. Obviously you have a better chance of making it if you have something negative rather than positive to say about the person accused.

Q: What if I'm an anonymous source?

A: You'll be quoted but not seen on TV. As far as newspaper people are concerned, they'd prefer to use your name, but they will always go with an anonymous source if they have to.

Q: Suppose a TV station or a newspaper or magazine calls me up and says they're doing a story on one of my friends. Is it okay to talk then?

A: That depends on how much time you've got. The reporter will spend three hours with you, and then use only one quote, usually a negative one at that. People writing books are even worse, because they have no deadlines.

Q: If everything you say is true, why do people still talk to the media?

A: Because of ego, fear, or they mistakenly figure they have nothing to hide. Then there are those who feel they can manipulate the story to their own advantage.

Q: Is it true?

A: Not very often. I think it was one of our great vice presidents, Spiro Agnew, who once said, "You can manipulate some of the press all of the time, and all of the press some of the time—but you can't manipulate ALL of the press ALL of the time."

Home Computer Trouble

The home computer business is in a lot of trouble. It would be nice to blame the Japanese for it all, but they never really got into the action.

One of the reasons the business fell into difficulty is the female gender problem. Women still don't appreciate the value of a home computer and what it can do to make their lives easier.

When I set up my brand-new computer, my wife asked why I bought it.

"This is going to change our lives. We can do our taxes on it."

"H and R Block did them already."

"Well, we can do them next year," I said. "We can also compute our household expenses on this machine. Give me all our bills and I'll start programming them."

"You have to be kidding. It will take me three months to find all our bills. Would you take my word for it that we spent ten thousand dollars more than you made in 1982?"

"All right, I'll put that into the computer."

"What does the computer say about that?"

"It says we spent ten thousand dollars more than I made. Why don't I try balancing your checkbook? Give me all the stubs."

"What for?"

"The bank's computer could have made a mistake and we can take our computer printout to the president and show it to him."

She came back and threw her check stubs on my desk, and stomped out of the study.

Three hours later she came back. "How are you doing?"

"I'm up to the Lord and Taylor's stub for March. So far everything checks out. Maybe I'll make up your calendar for the week. What have you got on it for the next few days?"

"I have a hairdresser's appointment on Thursday."

"Good. Now I'll just feed that information into the computer, and then when you want to know what you've got on for Thursday, you just place this floppy disk into this slot, put your finger on CODE, then hit this button, and you'll know you have a hairdresser's appointment on Thursday."

"I already know it."

"Okay, forget the calendar. Let's take an inventory of everything we have in the house."

"At eleven o'clock at night?"

"Why not? Once we record it on a disk, and we have a fire, we'll know what was lost."

"Suppose the computer gets burned up in the fire?"

"We won't keep the disk in the house. We'll put it in my office, and a printout in the bank's safety deposit box."

"What else can your computer do?"

"I can key into a bulletin board and talk to anyone in the United States who has a compatible communications terminal."

"You can do that by phone. You still haven't told me why you bought this computer."

"If you must know, I bought it for the children. Kids have to grow up these days with computer knowledge."

"Our children are all grown up and don't live here anymore."

"You never know when they'll come back home."

The home computer is still in my study, but I don't seem to use it as much as I thought I would. I made a friend in Minneapolis with it one night, but just when we were getting to know each other, his wife made him come to bed.

Send
the Troops

The Pentagon is getting nervous. With a White House foreign policy based on a military response to every situation, there is a growing gap between the number of worldwide commitments we've decided to make and the armed services' ability to meet them.

Not long ago, the Pentagon's Joint Chief of the Day received a call from the National Security Adviser's office at the White House.

"The President wants you to send two carriers, three missile cruisers, and six B-52s as a warning to Mozambique."

"We're plumb out of aircraft carriers, cruisers, and B-52s."

"How can you be out of them? We've given you the biggest military budget in history."

"We have the money, but most of the stuff isn't built yet. You people have asked us to send aircraft carriers to Lebanon, Central America, Libya, and Southeast Asia. We don't even have one in dry dock. I wish the White House would check with us before you people do any more saber rattling."

"We're not saber rattling. Our national security is at stake in every part of the globe, and if we don't show the flag, our credibility will be zilch."

"Well, we can't send any carriers to Mozambique."

"What about nuclear submarines?"

"They're all spoken for. We have to keep them on station as our main deterrent to the Soviets until we can put the MX missiles in place."

"What can you send to Mozambique?"

"How about a World War Two destroyer? We've got a bunch of them in mothballs."

"What kind of message is that to the Russians?"

"With all due respect, one of the problems is that you keep sending messages to the Soviets with US naval ships. Why can't you people use the diplomatic pouch like every other country does?"

"The only thing the Soviets understand is strength. If we don't produce a task force for Mozambique, they'll interpret it as a sign that we are unable to police the world."

"There is just so much we can do. The Pentagon is always happy to further the aims of American foreign policy, but if you would consult with us first, we could tell you whether we can support them militarily."

"I thought the armed forces had contingency plans for every situation on the face of the earth?"

"We do have the plans. We just don't have the troops. You have to figure out a few diplomatic initiatives that don't require military muscle."

"Well, if we can't send the fleet, what about flying in the Rapid Deployment Brigade to Kenya?"

"You have already requested them for Honduras."

"Okay, then ferry over some AWACS."

"All our AWACS are spoken for."

"Then dispatch the 82nd Airborne."

"We don't have the planes to transport the 82nd Airborne. Do you want us to pull a division out of Germany?"

"No, that would be the wrong signal to the Kremlin, particularly at the moment we're putting Pershing missiles into Europe."

"Do you people really have to send a message to Mozambique at this time? Couldn't we at least wait until the dust settles over Chad?"

"The President is very concerned that if we don't show we're serious about Mozambique, they'll be laughing at us in Angola."

"So let them laugh."

"Watch yourself, General. I'm speaking for your Commander-in-Chief. What have you got in our military arsenal to warn Mozambique?"

"If you want the truth—two jeeps, a WAC, and the US Marine Corps Band. Once we ship them overseas, you people are on your own."

Anyone for Camp?

"What do you want to do this summer, son?"

"Go to camp."

"What kind of camp?"

"Just camp."

"You have to be more specific than that. Do you want to go to arts and crafts camp, music camp, baseball camp, or weight-reduction camp?"

"I just want to go to a regular camp."

"What do you mean by a regular camp?"

"You know, one that has canoeing, and volleyball, and camp-fires and stuff like that."

"And what do you expect to learn at a camp like that?"

"I wasn't thinking about learning anything at all."

"That's the darndest thing I ever heard. What kid do you know today just goes to camp to have a good time? I'm willing to send you to a math camp so you can pick up your grades, and I'll even send you to a tennis camp so you can make the school team next year. If you don't want to do that, I'll send you to a camp where they only speak Spanish. It will be great for you to learn a second language."

"I don't want to go to a camp where you have to learn something."

"That's a rotten attitude. Let's go through the ads in the back of the Sunday magazine section. This one sounds interesting—an astronaut camp. You go through the same program the astronauts do and even simulate a space lab voyage."

"I don't want to be an astronaut camper."

"All right then, what about a theater camp? You put on your own plays and musical productions and build your own scenery."

"What kind of camp did you go to when you were a kid, Dad?"

"Camp Wakitan."

"What did they specialize in?"

"They didn't specialize in anything. In my day we didn't have the opportunities you kids have of perfecting your soccer game, or learning how to build a robot, or studying the mating habits of clams. We didn't come back any smarter than when we went."

"That's the kind of camp I want to go to."

"I refuse to send you to one like that. You've got a good mind and I'm not going to allow it to go dead in the summertime. Besides, what am I going to say to my friends when they ask me what kind of camp you're specializing in?"

"I don't care what you say. I just want to go to a place where you live in a cabin and cook marshmallows outside and have pillow fights at night."

"That's enough of that kind of talk. Let's get serious. Here's a camp where you learn how to be a computer programmer in BASIC, COBOL, and PASCAL languages. In the last week you can build your own microchip. Don't shake your head—computer knowledge is essential to your generation. Okay, what about this one? It's an auto repair camp. They supply all the tools

61

and parts and you get a mechanic's certificate at the end of the summer. That doesn't appeal to you? What about a farm camp where you kill hogs and learn all about salting pork and making bacon?"

"I don't want to know how to make bacon."

"Here's one that should grab you. It's a geology camp. You gather rocks and learn the history of the earth from them."

"No way."

"Do you know what it costs to send a kid away in the summer these days? It's almost as much as tuition to a private school. I'm not going to finance sending you to camp unless it enriches your life."

"Then forget it, I don't want to go to camp."

"Now wait a minute. Here's a camp for kids who don't want to go to camp."

"What does it specialize in?"

"It doesn't say. All the ad says is that the camp director is a former Green Beret who trained mountain tribes to shoot poison darts at anyone who tried to use the Ho Chi Minh Trail at night.

Reach Out and Kill Someone

It usually comes at ten or eleven at night, maybe when you're in bed or watching TV or in the bathtub. The phone rings, and keeps ringing. You remember the kids are out, and you break your neck to answer it.

"Hello, hello!" you shout into the receiver.

And then you hear this voice (it's usually a he, though it could be a she): "This is the Blank Upholstery Company. If you are in need of having your furniture reupholstered, or new drapes hung in your living room, leave your number at the sound of the beep and one of our salesmen will call you tomorrow morning."

You have just become the victim of an obscene junk telephone call.

The obscene junk telephone caller is now getting through to every home in America. No one is safe from being wakened out of a sound sleep or being taken away from his dinner, or even making a baby, while the obscene junk telephone caller is out there in some dark room selling his services, his subscriptions, and making his pitches for charity and political contributions, insurance policies, gold coins, and even discount telephone equipment.

But it's not a person that is calling. It's an obscene computer—one that has been programmed to start speaking as soon as it hears your voice, and is prepared to dial the next number as soon as you hang up.

Getting an unlisted number will not protect you from the obscene telephone computer. It just goes from number to number with thirty or forty tapes spitting out its filthy messages.

How can you avenge yourself against this new George Orwell Frankenstein?

There is a solution. It takes patience and a little detective work, but this is how I recently got back at one of the obscene junk calls.

Instead of hanging up on the computer, I listened to the entire message. The voice wanted me to subscribe to a magazine, at the sound of the beep, which would give me a chance to win $100,-000 in their sweepstakes. I wrote down the name of the magazine.

The next day I bought it and looked up the name of the publisher. I then called the magazine's office and said that I had a gift of flowers to send to the publisher's wife and wanted his home address. The secretary gave it to me and I found his telephone number in New Rochelle.

That night I waited until midnight and made my first call.

"Hi," I said in a bright voice. "This is the Axmo Muffler Company. We would like to give you a free estimate on our latest muffler, guaranteed for the life of your car. It is an opportunity you can't pass up—" The publisher hung up on me.

I waited a half hour and called back. "I'm sorry to disturb you, but we're conducting a survey on zits for the Acne Institute. Do you have any relatives or friends in New Rochelle who have been afflicted by this disease?" He hung up on me again.

Every half hour I made another call. I told him I was selling roofing by mail; I informed him that if he could name the first President of the United States he would get a case of dog food at cost; I inquired if he needed fertilizer for his lawn; and if he was interested in Mexican tax-free bonds.

By four o'clock the man was a blithering idiot.

"Why are you doing this to me?" he cried.

"Because," I said, in my most obscene voice, "you're doing it to us. Stop your junk call computer, and I'll stop my telephone calls."

"I'll call the police!" he screamed.

"You may call them as soon as you hear the beep," I told him.

I could have sworn I heard the publisher crying at the other end of the line.

If you want to do the same thing, be my guest. And if you can't get the big shot who instigated the junk call at his home at night, keep calling him every hour at his office.

Since the government won't stop the obscene calls, the people must take justice into their own hands. It's time every free American shouted into his or her phone, "BEEP YOUR JUNK CALLS, I'M NOT GOING TO TAKE IT ANYMORE."

All Bets
Are Off

I'm not a betting man by nature, but I have this bookmaker. He works for the Reluctant Insurance Company of America. This is how we bet. Every month I give him a certain amount of money, and he takes a gamble that my house won't burn or be broken into or damaged by a falling tree. Another bet I place with him is that my car won't hit someone in an accident, or I won't be hit by somebody else. Still a third one is that my family will not be stricken with an illness that would require hospitalization.

Funnily enough, I was never anxious to win one of these bets. I didn't want to collect from the bookie on any of them. He seemed to feel the same way I did. So much so that if for some reason I forgot to send him my check for one of our bets, he would mail me a nasty letter, wanting to know where the money was. He told me he was not in the bookmaking business for his health.

Well, recently, due to an illness in my family, my bookie lost one of the bets. Since this was the first time I had won, I thought he would be happy to pay off. After all, even in Las Vegas the house expects to lose once in a while.

So I wrote him a nice letter telling him that I had won the bet with him that no one in the family would ever have to go to the hospital for surgery.

But instead of congratulating me, I got a very terse letter back telling me he refused to accept my word until I produced the facts that he had lost. What hurt was he didn't even sign the letter "Sincerely."

I sent him all the doctor and hospital bills and pointed out that I wasn't making a dime on the wager. As a matter of fact, since he covered only 80 percent of costs, I was still a loser.

His next letter arrived with fifteen green forms and twenty red forms. Each body in the hospital, I was told, had to fill out either the green or red, or both, depending on what he or she had done.

A month later, when I didn't receive a check, I called the bookie at Reluctant's offices in Des Moines. He said he had received all the forms but couldn't pay off on the bet. He had to send it to his chief bookie in Chicago.

I protested that I had made the bet with him and asked him why he couldn't send me my money. He told me that it wasn't his job to pay off bets for the Reluctant Insurance Company, but just to collect the money from me.

"Are you mad because I finally won a bet?"

"I'm not mad at you. But they are."

"Who's they?"

"The guys in Chicago. They don't like to lose, because then they can't gamble on another skyscraper or loan a billion dollars to the Chrysler Corporation."

"That's tough," I said. "But when a bookie loses he has to pay off or he won't stay in business very long."

"We'll probably pay you, but your wager has to be reviewed by our in-house betting commission."

"How long will that take?"

"As long as they can keep making fifteen-percent interest on your money."

Two months went by and I still received no word on my bet. So I decided to take action, as any professional gambler would do under the circumstances. I grabbed a hammer from the tool box.

"Where are you going?" my wife asked.

"To Chicago and break the legs of the chief bookie if he won't pay off my bet."

She wept as my plane took off from Washington.

I returned the next day.

"Did he pay you?" my wife asked.

"No," I said.

"So did you break his legs?"

"I couldn't because he didn't have legs. The chief bookie in Chicago is a computer."

Subliminal Shopping

According to newspaper reports, subliminal messages are now being inserted into music played in retail stores to get people to buy the merchandise. For their clients, several companies are producing tapes which have secret messages in them to attack the shopper's brain and unconsciously motivate him into buying something he hadn't planned to purchase.

I was very skeptical about this information until I went to a local shopping mall. The music being piped into the mall was Christmas carols, intended to get the people in a holiday mood.

I stopped to buy a chocolate chip cookie, when suddenly something possessed me. While the loudspeaker blared out, "We Wish You a Merry Christmas," I blurted out the word "Underwear." Everyone in the line looked at me. I grabbed the man behind me by the lapels and said, "I've got to have underwear."

He pushed my hands away. "So what are you standing in the chocolate chip cookie line for? Go to a men's shop."

I dashed down the mall and stopped a uniformed security guard. "Underwear!" I screamed at him. "Give me underwear."

He wasn't sure whether to arrest me or give me directions. Finally he showed me a large menswear store at the end of the mall.

Two salesmen were standing at the door smiling. One said to the other, "Here comes another one." Then he said, before I could speak, "Third counter on the left, but you have to take a number and wait your turn."

The underwear counter was jammed with people, all screaming and shouting. I said to a man next to me, "Maybe there won't be any left by the time my number is called. What am I going to do if I can't buy any underwear?"

"Do you need some that badly?" he asked.

"I didn't think so, but suddenly I got this craving for underwear while I was waiting to buy a chocolate chip cookie."

"I came into the mall to buy pizza and the same thing happened to me."

My number was called and I bought fifty Jockey shorts and fifty undershirts. That's all they would sell me.

I walked out of the store and stopped to look at an artist doing charcoal sketches of children. While I was watching, someone was singing "Jingle Bells" over the speaker.

The word "Wok" lit up in my brain. My eyes showed desperation and I started searching for a wok store. I rushed up to a lady at the information booth, but before I could blurt it out she said, "Woks can be found in the basement of the department store at the end of the building."

"How did you know I wanted a wok?"

"Everyone wants a wok when they play 'Jingle Bells.' "

"You mean you have a secret message in 'Jingle Bells'?"

"Of course. Today it's woks, tomorrow it's wax for your floor."

"I don't need a wok," I said.

"Then put your hands over your ears, and you won't get a message."

"What comes after 'Jingle Bells'?"

She looked at her schedule. " 'White Christmas' and home computers."

"I don't need a home computer either."

"Nobody thinks they do until they hear Bing Crosby sing it."

"Do I have time to buy a chocolate chip cookie?"

"It depends. After 'White Christmas' they're playing 'Silent Night,' and there's going to be an awful crush for hand-knotted Chinese rugs at the end of the mall."

The Candidate's Husband

As more women go into politics, the public becomes increasingly curious about their spouses. I found Horace Manley, the husband of Agatha Manley, who was running for Congress for the second time, at home the other day.

He was flustered. "I wish I had known you were coming," he said. "The house is a mess."

"Don't worry, Mr. Manley. I'm not here to write about your housekeeping. Is the candidate home?"

"No, she's out talking to the United Metalworkers Union. She told me I could have a day off."

"Is it hard to be the husband of a political figure?"

"It has its pluses and minuses. But I've known ever since Agatha finished law school that she wanted to go into politics, and as long as she's happy I'm willing to put up with our public life."

"What's the toughest part of it for you?"

"Smiling all the time, and being nice to people because Agatha says they're important to her. I also have to worry about my appearance and wonder if I'm wearing the right suit and if my shoes are shined."

"You mean the voters care what the husband of a candidate looks like?"

"Oh, definitely. A husband plays a very important role in a candidate's election. Agatha says even though she does the talking, the electorate is always studying me."

"What do they ask you?"

"They want to know if Agatha is a good mother, and what she is really like at home. I always say she is a real peachy wife."

"You don't sound as if you mean it."

"There are times when I get discouraged. I would like Agatha all to myself, and it would be nice if she could spend more time with the children. But I never nag or bother her with family problems because I know she's got too many important things on her mind. When she comes home and we can squeeze in a few hours together, the children and I want her to relax."

"Does Agatha depend on you for political advice?"

"Yes, she's very good about that. She lets me sit in on staff meetings at our house after I've served everyone a buffet dinner. She's told me many times that I have a better reading on the public pulse than she does, because people say things to me that they're afraid to say to her."

"Could you give me an example of the kind of advice you give her?"

"Well, Agatha, being a woman, is against nerve gas."

"And you're not?"

"There are a lot worse things than nerve gas. But even if she doesn't agree with me, she's very interested in what the male gender is thinking. I wish I could say the same thing for her staff."

"They don't like you to talk to Agatha about politics?"

"They treat me like a dodo."

"How is that?"

"When I'm out campaigning someone is always afraid I'll make a slip if I extemporize, so they insist I stick with the script they've written for me. It's an awful speech, but every time I want to change it they say I could lose the election."

"Are you jealous of the men around Agatha?"

"Not really. I know they are only attracted to her for her power. I can put up with a lot as long as she doesn't humiliate me or the children in public."

"But at least as a politician's husband, you get invited to a lot of parties. That must be fun."

"It would be if someone knew my name. Agatha always introduces me by saying, 'I'd like you to meet my better half.' "

"I notice you're darning your wife's pantyhose."

Horace said bitterly, "Have you ever tried to live on a congresswoman's salary?"

The Big
Cover-Up

NEW YORK —Well, they've finally come up with a solution for the South Bronx. Rather than spend millions and millions of dollars to wipe out the urban decay, New York City will spend a federal grant of three hundred thousand dollars on vinyl fronts and cover up the shattered tenements and burned-out buildings along the expressways leading from Manhattan to Westchester and Connecticut.

The false fronts will show windows with curtains, shades, and flowerpots, and nice varnished doors. According to city officials, the façades will definitely improve the look of the neighborhood.

The idea has already been dubbed by skeptics as "20th Century Bronx."

Anthony Gliedman, the Commissioner of Housing Preservation and Development, denied he was doing it as a substitute for rehabilitating the blighted area. He was quoted in *The New York Times* as saying, "We want to brighten up the face of the neighborhood while waiting for new federal programs to rebuild the neighborhood. . . . I recognize that this is superficial. We don't want anyone to think we're doing this instead of rebuilding. But that will take years and millions or hundreds of millions of dollars. And while we're waiting, we want people to know we care."

Not knowing what to make of the idea, I discussed the proposal with Humberto Cortez, a New York taxi driver, who was trying to take me crosstown on 37th Street the other day.

Mr. Cortez said he lived in the South Bronx, and while he thought it might improve the morale of people commuting from Westport and Greenwich every day, he didn't believe that it would change the lives of those who live in the area.

"Every four years all the presidential candidates visit the South Bronx with television crews, and each one announces the first thing he will do if he is elected is rebuild the neighborhood. Then, if he gets into office, he gives the money to El Salvador."

"Do you have a better solution than covering up your blight with vinyl decals?" I asked him.

"Yup. After the next election we should invite Castro to build a ten-thousand-foot airplane runway in the South Bronx."

"Are you crazy?" I shouted in the middle of a Madison Avenue gridlock. "Castro would send in soldiers disguised as workers to export Marxist revolution. The South Bronx would become a dagger pointed right at Scarsdale. We couldn't stand for that."

"That's the idea. No president could allow it. So he would send in the US Marines and the 82nd Airborne to stop the construction."

"But that could mean war."

"The South Bronx looks like a war zone now. How much more damage could the Marines do?"

"All right, so the United States invades the South Bronx. How does that help you?"

"After the fighting stops, the Americans wil have to ship the Cuban workers back to Havana, and then the Bronx will become a United States problem. The Americans will have to send in army engineers and AID officials to help us get on our feet. The President will go to Congress and ask for millions of dollars to keep the borough from falling into the communist camp. He could make the Bronx the showcase of the Western Hemisphere, and persuade everyone that the United States will really help those who turn their backs on Castro."

We got into another gridlock on Fifth Avenue. "Mr. Cortez, you make a very good case, but it's hard to believe that any president would get excited about Castro's plans for the South Bronx. The US government wrote off your borough long ago."

"They might ignore our borough politically, but they can't afford to overlook the ten-thousand-foot runway. You don't think we're going to build it to attract tourists to the South Bronx do you?"

"It's the wildest idea I've ever heard of," I said.

Mr. Cortez replied, "It isn't half as crazy as covering up a city's urban decay with a bunch of phony vinyl fronts."

When Nobody Blinked

This is my think piece about the TV film "The Day After." ABC, which produced the picture, went out of its way not to take sides as to who was responsible for trashing Lawrence, Kansas. They spent seven million dollars showing us what could happen after an area was mushroomed, but not one buck on what caused the holocaust in the first place.

I think they owed us just one scene between a few survivors discussing the why of it all.

The scene could have taken place between Jason Robards, who played the role of a doctor, and the last political science professor alive at the University of Kansas.

The men, covered from head to foot in atomic ash, are sitting on a pile of rubble that was once a nursery school.

"What the hell do you think happened?" Jason Robards asks the political science professor.

"Nobody blinked," the professor replies.

"What does that mean?"

"Well, it all goes back to the Cuban missile crisis. Remember when Dean Rusk said the Soviets and the US came eyeball to eyeball, and the Russians blinked first? Ever since then our foreign policy has been based on the premise that the Soviets would always blink before we did."

Robards says, "I guess we miscalculated."

The professor, looking over the desolation, says, "That would be a fair statement. What the people in Washington refused to take into account was that the Soviets considered the missile crisis the biggest defeat they had suffered since World War Two. They booted out Khrushchev and vowed they would never blink again."

"Do you want an orange?"

"No. For some reason I feel nauseated. In order not to blink, the Soviets started an unprecedented nuclear arms buildup. Soon, the military on both sides insisted that the other side had nuclear superiority, and so the arms race was on. The thinking in Washington and Moscow was that the more deterrents they had, the less chance there was of someone starting a war."

"Why didn't it work?" Jason says.

"It worked for a while. But then the arms talks came, and both sides engaged in playing the numbers game. We promised not to put any cruise and Pershing missiles in Europe if the Soviets reduced the SS-20s. The Soviets said we had to include British and French missiles in the talks, and we refused. When neither side would blink, we started deploying our new missiles, and the Russians walked out of Geneva."

"Why the hurry?"

"Because our credibility was at stake. Had we not gone ahead with the threat, the Soviets would have said that Reagan blinked. If they hadn't walked out, we would have said that Andropov blinked."

"'And that's when the missile race began in earnest?"

"You could say that. They surrounded us with all their nuclear warheads and we surrounded them. We got ourselves into a spot where any spark could set off Armageddon."

"Didn't both sides realize this?"

"The leaders were assured by their experts that the other side didn't have the guts to use their nukes because they knew they would also be wiped out in the process. The only way to keep the peace was to build more horrifying weapons until the other side came to its senses."

"So why are we sitting on the rubble in Lawrence, Kansas, full of gamma rays?"

"I guess we'll never know," the professor says sadly. "It might not even have been a human decision. With a response time of only six minutes to react, the whole thing could have been started by a faulty computer that wouldn't *stop* blinking."

Is Anybody There?

A recent column of mine dealt with subliminal voices. This one deals with liminal ones. We are now entering the age of recorded messages. I didn't realize how pervasive it was until I had to fly to Atlanta the other day. After I deplaned, I took a long walk and then a long escalator into the bowels of the earth, and waited for a two-car train to take me several stops to another long escalator which would bring me back up to the crust to claim my baggage.

The train pulled in and a voice said, "This is the B station. Please enter and go to the center of the train."

This was a reasonable request, but as I followed the mob trying to board, my carry-on bag got caught and I held the door so I wouldn't be dragged along the train. The voice said, and I swear I am not making this up, "Someone is holding the door and is preventing the rest of you from moving."

"I can't help it!" I shouted. "My strap is caught."

The voice sounded angrier. *"Someone is holding the door. The train cannot start."*

I finally broke the strap and squeezed onto the train. Everyone was staring at me. I tried to smile. "It wasn't my fault," I said defensively. A dozen hostile eyes were on me. The voice said, "Please do not stand near the door as we approach station A."

"I'm not standing near the door!" I shouted at the loudspeaker. "Does anyone see me standing near the door?" The other passengers looked away in disgust.

By the time I got to station A, I was in a cold sweat trying to figure out how to get off the train by not standing near the door. I made it to the platform just as the door closed behind me.

Then I went to rent a car. It was a new sedan, and when I started it up, a voice came out of the dashboard and said, "Your safety belt is not fastened." I could have sworn it was the same voice that bawled me out on the train. I quickly fastened the safety belt. The voice repeated itself: "Your safety belt is not fastened. " I undid it and fastened it again.

The voice repeated, "Your safety belt is not fastened."

After being told two more times, I called over the rental attendant. "This car keeps telling me my safety belt isn't fastened."

"Don't pay any attention to it," he said. "It's been telling our customers that for three days."

I drove to the hotel. By the time I got there I was smashing my fist against the dashboard.

I checked into one of those huge glass greenhouses with the elevators on the outside of the building. As soon as I got in the voice said, "There is no smoking on the elevator. Press the button just once. This elevator does not go to the roof garden. If you wish to go to the roof garden, take the elevators on the other side of the lobby."

"I don't want to go to the roof garden, and I'm not smoking!" I yelled. A couple took one look at me and got off.

I finally reached my room and locked the door. The first thing I did was search it for loudspeakers. If they were there they had been very carefully hidden. Then I called down for room service. A recorded voice answered, "All lines for room service are busy now. Please hold on until someone is available to take your order." I slammed down the phone.

Then I turned on the TV set. It was the same voice. "In case of fire, follow these instructions carefully. . . ." I turned off the set.

There was nothing left but to go to sleep. I asked for a wakeup call for seven A.M.

The phone woke me up: "It is seven A.M."

"Thank you," I said. "What's the weather like?"

77

The voice said, "It is seven A.M."

"Hello. This is a guest in room 1209. Is anybody there? This is a guest in room 1209. *Is anybody there?*"

The voice spoke once more: "It is seven A.M." And then there was a click and dead silence. There was nobody there.

Photo
Opportunity

This is a true story which has more significance for Americans than whether Wayne Newton or the Beach Boys should have sung on the Mall on the Fourth of July in 1983.

It concerns a man whom we shall call John Doe, who attended an antiwar demonstration near the Vietnam Memorial on that July 4th weekend. He came with his camera to photograph whatever was going on.

While looking around, he noticed quite a few photographers standing with the Park Police taking pictures of the people who were against the war.

Suddenly he had his theme for a photographic essay. He would do a series of pictures on law enforcement officers taking photos of people lawfully demonstrating on public land.

As Doe was shooting away, he was approached by a senior officer from the Park Police demanding to know what the blank he was doing. Doe explained that there had been many photo exhibits of demonstrators held in America, but very few of police officers taking pictures of them. Doe told the officer he hoped to win a prize.

The officer demanded identification from Doe, which my

friend refused to produce, citing the Supreme Court case Brown vs. Texas, that a person did not have to identify himself to the police unless the officer could articulate that he or she had committed a crime, or was about to, or that public safety was endangered.

Then the officer wanted to know if Doe was a member of the KGB. John denied it, claiming to be an ordinary American citizen who liked to take photographs of cops taking photographs. Later on, he thought to himself, had he admitted being a member of the KGB, the Park Police would have probably left him alone. It was Americans they objected to taking pictures of them.

It was more than the Park Police official could deal with. Doe was bundled into a Park Police car and taken off to the station, where it was hoped he would break down and tell the real reason why he was taking photos of innocent police photographers taking pictures of people who didn't like the war.

In true tradition, Doe was permitted to call a lawyer. He called an old friend fom his ACLU days and said, "Barry, I've got a great case. I've been taken into custody for taking pictures of Park Police undercover photographers. We can make legal history."

Barry, who was at home, said he'd come down, but his relatives were in town, and he was looking forward to celebrating the Fourth with his kids, and he wasn't about to spend the weekend in court arguing the merits of Brown vs. Texas with John Doe.

"But, Barry, if we don't fight for our rights, who will?"

"Lawyers who don't have their relatives in town."

The police officer seemed to be losing his patience, and said that if Doe did not identify himself he would be taken to St. Elizabeth's, Washington's mental hospital, for observation.

"But," protested Doe, "that's what the police do in the Soviet Union. Are you sure *you* people don't work for the KGB?"

By this time Barry the lawyer had shown up and a deal was struck. Doe would not have to identify himself, keeping the Brown vs. Texas principle intact, but he would have to promise not to take any more photos of police officers taking photos.

Unfortunately, the main legal question was never resolved. Is someone crazy for taking pictures of police taking pictures of people demonstrating, or are the Park Police crazy for thinking you shouldn't be allowed to do it? It would be nice for us camera buffs to know.

The Loan Renegotiator

I met a man the other day who has a very interesting job. He renegotiates loans for Third World countries. A loan renegotiator is not to be confused with someone who gets a nation a loan or collects one. He goes to work after a country has the loan and can't pay it back.

We shall call the man Jean Valjean, and he works for the Crédit Béarnaise. He told me, "A loan renegotiator is the most important figure in the banking world today. Without him the monetary system would go under."

"How do you renegotiate a loan?" I inquired.

"You renegotiate a loan by not paying it. The service you perform is to come up with a legitimate reason why a country cannot repay a loan to a foreign bank."

"Does it have to be a good reason?"

"Of course. Everyone knows long before the payment date that the Third World country can't repay its debt. But you still have to go through the ceremony of pretending it's a surprise to all parties."

"Could you give me an example of how you renegotiate a loan?"

"At the moment I just renegotiated a loan for the South American country of Santa Busta. Santa Busta is a Third World country that owes one billion dollars to a consortium of Western banks."

"Why did the banks loan it that kind of money?"

"Because it was willing to pay two percent more for the loans than other countries. Besides, at the time, Santa Busta was getting four dollars a pound for mining raw Velcro, its only natural resource."

"What did Santa Busta do with the billion dollars?"

"Some of it went for roads, some of it went for Mercedes Benzes, some of it for scotch whiskey, some of it went to pay for tear gas, and quite a bit of it wound up in numbered Swiss bank accounts belonging to Santa Busta politicians in power."

"Okay, so the money was well spent. Why can't they pay it back?"

"Last year the price of raw Velcro tumbled to ten cents a pound and the country went bankrupt."

"So that's when you were called in to renegotiate the loan?"

"Right. Both Santa Busta and the consortium of banks asked me to come up with a plan that could justify their not paying the loan back. I talked Santa Busta's leading families into announcing a tough austerity program, which they were more than happy to do, since most of them live in Florida. Then I went to the banks with the austerity program and asked them to renegotiate the loan by not demanding principal for seven years. The banks accepted this providing Santa Busta pay interest on the loan."

"Where could Santa Busta get the money to pay the interest?"

"I persuaded the consortium to loan Santa Busta the funds to meet the interest payments."

"Why would they do that if the country was bankrupt?"

"The consortium had to do it so they could keep the Santa Busta debt on their books as a viable loan. If Santa Busta couldn't pay the interest, the banks would have to tell their stockholders that a major loan client was in default, and then everyone would be in the soup. As far as the banks were concerned, it was just an accounting transaction. They put the interest money they loaned to Santa Busta in one computer and transferred it to another computer in the same office. Now everyone can relax until the loan comes up for renegotiation next year."

"I can now see the true value of your job. What do you get paid for this sort of thing?"

"A nice percentage of the loan, which the banks are only too happy to pay anyone for getting them off the financial hook."

Now I
Understand

Due to an illness, my wife has been out of action and I have found myself in the role of home manager. I must admit, I never paid too much attention to what a wife did to maintain a house, and assumed that it was a snap compared to solving the Iraq-Iran war.

I am now realizing that there is more to housekeeping than the TV commercials would have us believe. Here are some of the things I discovered in my new consciousness-raising position:

A laundry hamper only holds dirty clothes. It does not wash them.

There is no such thing as an empty dishwasher.

Garbage disposal units do not grind up steak bones, or forks and spoons.

Appliance repairmen all have answering services but never call them for their messages.

You cannot grow food in a refrigerator. You have to go to a supermarket and buy it. No matter what you buy for dinner, your bill always comes to $49.50.

Many varieties of food have to be cooked. This requires pots and pans. Fresh fish and meat do not come with instructions. Neither do fresh vegetables. Frozen meals taste just as good as frozen meals.

A person can overdose on hamburgers and scrambled eggs in less than five days.

Garbage has to be put out on the street once a week, or no one will take it away.

Grass has to be watered or it will turn brown.

After making up beds two days in a row, the thrill is gone.

A neighbor never congratulates you on your waxed floors.

Polyester-blend suits start to smell if you don't take them to the dry cleaner.

When a fuse blows in the house it has to be replaced or the lights won't go back on.

United Parcel rings your bell only when they have a package for the person next door who isn't home.

The telephone rings only when you're in the bathroom, or outside watering plants.

You never have enough cord when you're vacuuming a rug. But you always have too much when you're trying to put it back in the closet.

People who live in glass houses have to wash their windows all the time.

The one item you need to complete a chore is downstairs when you are upstairs, and upstairs when you are downstairs.

Dogs and cats have to be fed or they'll turn on you.

The only serviceman who will come when you call him is the piano tuner.

The best way to clean up a son's room is to close the door and pretend it is not part of the house.

Taking a headache remedy does not necessarily mean there will be less dust in the living room.

No one gives you a bonus for getting a stain out of the sofa.

Illegal alien housekeepers are better than no housekeeper at all.

It's amazing how little comfort you get out of hearing sympathetic friends tell you they know exactly what you're going through.

I discovered, admittedly late in the game, that there is no such thing as upward mobility in home management, no chance for advancement, and no opportunity for a wage increase. I now understand for the first time why wives need soap operas and *The National Enquirer* to get them through the day. It's their only link with reality. Somebody else's infidelity sure beats the hell out of getting grease off the stove with the perfect paper towel.

Questions of Finance

Dear Sir,

I am a lobbyist representing 500 of the leading polluters in the United States. I would like to contribute money to the political campaigns of several members of the House Subcommittee on Acid Snow. Should I give them money before a particular anti-pollution bill is up for a vote, or after? —Rich But Perplexed

Dear Rich But Perplexed,

The best time to donate to an incumbent's political campaign is when there is no legislation pending. In that way the pol can accept the money from a special interest group with a clear conscience, and then support your cause at a later date when you really need him (her?).

Dear Sir,

I represent a small political action committee interested in keeping out Honduran-made tent poles. We can't afford to finance every candidate running for office this year. How do we make an impact with our limited funds? —Poor But Proud

Dear PBP,

Every PAC organization faces a similar problem. Your best bet is to finance the campaigns of the chairpersons of crucial committees involved with tent poles, leaving enough money aside to donate to the present administration's committee to reelect the President. Be sure and specify to the treasurer of the political party that the money is being given not to keep communist tent poles out of Honduras but Honduran tent poles out of the United States.

Dear Friend,

I am running for the presidential nomination and am having a terrible time collecting money at this stage of the game. Do you have any suggestions? —The Best Man

Dear Best Man,

Have you ever thought of giving a $1000-a-plate dinner to honor your wife's mother? Or holding a $10,000-a-person cocktail party at the Playboy Mansion to explain where you stand on pine tar? Or sponsoring a punk rock concert at the Los Angeles Coliseum for kids who want to grow up in a better world? If you can't raise a lousy $25 million for a primary campaign, how are you going to find the hundreds of billions of dollars the country will need in the next four years to balance the budget?

Dear Sir,

I would like to give money to a candidate, but I want to make sure he knows I gave it. When is the best time to make a political contribution? —Good Citizen

Dear G.C.,

Timing is everything when it comes to giving to a candidate. The consensus seems to be that "late money talks more loudly than early money." That is to say, in a close race when the person running for office gets more desperate at the end, money becomes a lot more important to a candidate than it was at the beginning of his/her campaign. Therefore, if you hold out until the last week and then suddenly hand your man a check, he will remember you a lot more fondly than if you stuffed a thousand dollars into his pocket months ago when his campaign was in the doldrums.

Dear Mr. B,

I used to give a lot of money to a certain political party and I was invited to many social functions, including the White House. This year I had some severe business setbacks and have been unable to donate anything. I seem to have been dropped from all parties that I used to be invited to. Is there any correlation between a person's social life in Washington and how much he gives to the political party of his choice? —Tapped Out

Dear Tapped Out,

I don't know where you got this idea. Politicians never allow money to play a part in friendship. You were probably dropped from everyone's list this year because people found you boring.

PART THREE

PENTAGON GARAGE SALE

SLIGHTLY USED SALE

Pentagon
Garage Sale

The Pentagon was having a spare parts garage sale the other day, and I went over to see if I could pick up any bargains. There were spare parts spread out all over the parking lot.

I picked up a Phillips screwdriver, and a colonel came over and warned me, "If you break it, you pay for it."

"How much is it?"

The colonel looked in a book, "I'll let you have it for $760."

"Seven hundred and sixty dollars for a screwdriver?"

"We paid $990 for it. It's a heckuva bargain. This is not an ordinary screwdriver. It was made to screw bolts into F-16s."

"Let me think it over. What else have you got?"

"Here's a chief petty officer's flashlight that you can't pass up. It's yours for $230, without batteries."

"How much are the batteries?"

The colonel referred to his manual again. "We paid $140 for two. I'll throw in the batteries for $50 if you take the flashlight for $220."

"You'll be losing a lot of money on the deal."

"This is a garage sale, and we've been told to get rid of our spare parts before Congress finds out how much we've been paying for them," the colonel said.

"What are these little black squares?"

"They're silicon chips for our night fighters. The aviation company who made the fighters sold them to us for $1500 apiece. But you can have a dozen fo $999."

"You can buy these chips in any Radio Shack for $4.95," I said.

"We just found that out," he replied. "That's why we're selling them so cheap."

"What are those tires over there?"

"They're for mobile missile launchers. They're a steal. The defense contractor charged us $1200 for each tire, but we've reduced them to $600."

"How can you afford a fifty-percent markdown?"

"We're suing the contractor for overcharging us $900 a tire, and if we win we'll come out ahead."

"And if you lose?"

"It doesn't matter, because every time we fire a missile, all the tires on the launcher blow out."

"I really don't need any tires."

"If you want a good buy, you ought to take one of these M-1 tank transmissions. We paid $400,000 for each one, but we're letting them go for $50,000."

"Do they work?"

"If they worked do you think we'd be selling them for $50,000?"

"Are those army pup tents over there?"

"You better believe it. They've never been used. The list price was $6000 for each one, but because it's General Patton's birthday, we're giving them away for $4000 today. You'll never get to buy a pup tent at that price again."

"I've been to garage sales before," I said, "but this one beats them all."

The colonel said, "The way we look at it is the taxpayer paid for these things, so he should get first crack at buying them at a discount. It's our way of thanking him for supporting the military buildup."

"There are so many bargains, I'd like to buy everything in the parking lot."

"I wish you could. It would get me off the hook."

"Why?"

"I was the chief purchasing officer for the Pentagon until they found out that this walkie-talkie, which we paid $5000 for, could be bought at Sears Roebuck for $18.95."

When the Kids Return

What brings the kids back once they've left the nest? What makes them want to return home after they have declared their independence? I wish I could say it was love of parents. I even wish I could say it was the dog or cat they left behind. I discovered what finally brings offspring back to their mommies and daddies.

There isn't a child who hasn't gone out into the brave new world who eventually doesn't return to the old homestead carrying a bundle of dirty clothes.

"Hi, Pop, I'm back."

"It's Ezra. When did you return from the Amazon?"

"A week ago. I just stopped by to throw my laundry in the washing machine."

"How did the jungle look from the interior?"

"Terrific, Dad. Listen, I can't talk now. When the wash cycle is finished, would you put my stuff in the dryer?"

"Of course, son. I'm mighty glad to see you. Would you like to say hello to your mother?"

"Tell her I'll see her when I come back to get my laundry."

"I'll do that. She was a little nervous about your being in the Amazon for two years.'

"Goodbye, Dad."

"Who was that?"

"It was Ezra, Mother. He came back to do his laundry."

"Where is he?"

"He'll be back once his socks are dry."

"I hear someone downstairs."

"I'll go down and look. . . . Well, if it isn't Lucy from Birmingham. Why didn't you write you were coming?"

"I didn't know I was coming. But my washer broke a week ago and the kid's dirty clothes kept piling up on me, so I just got on an airplane to fly up and do them. Can I stay for a couple of days? I've got four loads."

"Of course you can. You're going to have to wait, though, because Ezra has his clothes in the machine now from his trip to Brazil. Wander up and say hello to your mother. She'll be delighted to see you."

"Sure, Dad, but call me as soon as Ezra's stuff is done, will you?"

"No problem. Now who could that be at the door? Why, it's Paul! I thought we said goodbye to you last month when you went off to college."

"I just came home for the weekend to do my laundry."

"Don't they have Laundromats at the school?"

"They do, but they won't let you put your tennis sneakers in the washer."

"That sounds like a weird school. Your brother Ezra is back from the Amazon, and your sister Lucy flew up from Birmingham to do four loads. So you might as well stay overnight, because I don't think that that old Whirlpool will be available until sometime tomorrow."

"Why can't I put my stuff in with Ezra's?"

"Because his has already completed the first cycle and it wouldn't be fair to stop it and start all over again. You want something to eat?"

"No, I'll go out and see the guys. Here's my stuff. Tell Lucy not to get it mixed up with hers."

"I'll keep an eye on it, son. It's good to have you home. I see a car driving up. It looks like your sister Rose, who has her own apartment across town. Why don't you go out and help her in with all those dirty sheets and pillowcases?"

"Hi, Dad. I can't stay long. I have to do these sheets before my roommate gets back. Whose stuff is that in the washer?"

"It's Ezra's. He just got back from two years in South America."

"That's a dirty trick. He knows Friday is my day to use the washer."

"Maybe he forgot. He's got jet lag. You want to put your stuff in the washer with Lucy's when I put Ezra's in the dryer?"

"What's Lucy doing using our washer when she lives in Birmingham?"

"Perhaps she's trying to find her roots."

"'Til Divorce Do Us Part"

The prenuptial contract is getting more and more prevalent as the divorce rate rises in the country. Since getting married in many cases is not one of those things you do forever, lawyers are advising their clients to make out a contract specifying who gets what when love flies out the window and recrimination knocks down the door.

I was the best man at a prenuptial legal-contract ceremony the other day. The groom to be, Horace Pipeline, was attended by the famed divorce lawyer Roy Bone, and the bride to be, the lovely Grace Willowy, was being given away by Stephanie Tuff of the firm Rock, Sock & Needham.

The bride and groom sat in the love seat in Mr. Bone's palatial office, which, for the occasion, had been decorated with magnolias and white roses.

Mr. Bone, reading from a yellow legal pad, said, "Dearly beloved, we are gathered here today to bring this man and this woman together in a happy prenuptial contract, spelling out the property claims of both parties in case, for reasons we shall not go into here, this marriage is broken asunder. Do you, Horace Pipeline, agree that, in case you do not choose to continue in wedlock, you will bestow on your lovely bride a lump sum equal to five percent of your present assets, excluding your boat, your penthouse, and your home in Southampton?"

"Wait a minute," said Miss Tuff. "Who said anything about a lump sum, and who said anything about excluding Mr. Pipeline's boat, penthouse, and home in Southampton? My client, under law, is entitled to fifty percent of all of her husband's property. But we don't want to be greedy about this. We'll settle for ten thousand dollars a month until she gets married again."

"Alimony is out of the question," Mr. Bone said. "I cannot permit my client to enter the sacred institution of matrimony unless he can get out of it by paying off a lump sum at the dissolution of the marriage. How can we be sure when and if Miss Willowy will get married again?"

"How do you feel about it, Grace?" Miss Tuff asked.

"I love Horace very much, and if he wants to provide me with a lump sum, I don't have any objection. But I want to know what numbers we're talking about before I say, 'I do.' "

Mr. Bone smiled. "You're a reasonable young lady. Would five hundred thousand satisfy you?"

Miss Tuff said, "No, it wouldn't, Roy, and you know that before we came here we researched Horace's assets down to the last nickel. Now let's be serious or call off this prenuptial legal-contract ceremony right now."

Mr. Bone scowled. "As Horace's lawyer I can't go over five hundred thousand, but if he wants to be more generous I'll leave it to him. Horace, what do you think?"

"Grace is the only woman I've ever loved," Horace said. "I can't imagine anything but death parting us. But just in case something did happen, I'm willing to give her a cool million—the same as I gave my second wife."

Miss Tuff said, "Horace's second wife was much older than Grace, and the million he settled on her was before inflation set in. We want one million five and the house in Southampton."

"It's just not possible," Mr. Bone said angrily. "These people hope to live happily ever after. My client would not have a day of happiness if he knew it would cost him a million five plus the house in Southampton to get out of the marriage."

Miss Tuff said, "How do you think my client would feel if she knew she could be tossed out in the street for a lousy million dollars?"

Grace became upset. "This talk is so sordid, it's destroying our love for each other. I'll take a million two hundred thousand and the penthouse in New York. But that's the bottom line."

Horace said, "Don't be angry, darling. You're asking for more than I planned to give you, but I want you to be happy. Give it to her, Roy, provided we have it in writing so she doesn't go to court and try to sock it to me for anything more."

"All right, Horace, it's your money. I'll have this typed up while we open a bottle of champagne and drink a toast to the happy couple. Please excuse my tears. Prenuptial marriage-contract ceremonies always make me cry."

Mission Impossible

The most important thing to do before sending men into combat is to explain to them why you want them there.

I would hate to be the briefing officer on a Marine amphibious ship explaining to the troops why they are going into Beirut.

"All right, men, let's knock it off. I am here to explain your mission for the next few months. You are being sent into Beirut on a peacekeeping mission. Any questions?"

"Yes sir. What's a peacekeeping mission?"

"It is a mission by which a neutral power stations troops in a volatile area to keep the various factions from killing each other until a government can become strong enough to defend itself. Now you people will take up positions around the Beirut airport down here on the low ground. Up here in the hills overlooking the airport are members of the Druze sect armed with heavy artillery, mortars, and snipers. Over here are the Christian Phalangist militia, also heavily armed. The Christians are also in this part of Beirut next to the airport, and Moslem forces, not to be confused with the Druze, have control of this part of Beirut here. Intelligence also indicates there are one thousand PLO troops who returned to the area since Israel pulled out of the city to this position down here. Is that clear?"

"Sir, are we supposed to keep the peace between all of them?"

"That's your mission. But you can only do this by remaining in the Beirut airport area."

"If they all have the high ground and we have the low ground, how do we keep the peace?"

"You will not be alone. We have a large naval task force off the beaches that will cover you."

"Cover us from what?"

"Artillery and mortar fire from the hills, as well as snipers in the city. We now have the authority to use air power when you become a target of one of the dissident factions."

"You mean we're sitting ducks?"

"It means you will dig in as deep as you can until President Reagan, your Commander-in-Chief, can arrange a cease-fire between the Druze, the Christian Phalangists, the present Gemayel government army, and the Syrians. Once this cease-fire is arranged and holds and a new government coalition of the various antagonists can be formed, you will be permitted to leave."

"Why are we called a peacekeeping force if we can't use our guns to keep the peace?"

"Because, since you are designated as such, the President has the authority to keep you there as long as he deems necessary. If you are sent in as a combat force, the War Powers Act has to be put into effect, and then Congress may dictate foreign policy. Technically, the US Marines have been engaged in 'hostilities,' but the White House cannot admit that without giving up the President's executive powers. Is that clear?"

"No, sir."

"Good. We will continue. As a peacekeeping force, your mission is not to take sides in a family dispute. What is going on now is that the Druze, Moslems, and Christians are settling old scores that go back hundreds of years. They have committed atrocities against each other for centuries. If Washington can get them all to sit around a table and forget the past, we can bring peace to the Middle East."

"And if Washington can't, we get our butts shot off."

"I can assure you Washington has no intention of letting you get your butts shot off. If we wanted to, we could waste Lebanon in ten minutes. Okay, you now know all you need to about your mission. Remember men, hold your fire. As a peacekeeping force you can't afford to get mad at anybody."

More Damage Control

No one seems to be able to take a joke anymore. When Secretary of the Interior James Watt said, in describing a panel appointed to study the coal-leasing situation, "We have every kind of mix you can have. I have a black, I have a woman, two Jews, and a cripple. And we have talent," he started another political firestorm.

In one sentence, Mr. Watt managed to offend a race, a sex, a religious group, and almost every afflicted person in the United States.

The last time he blew it was when he banned the Beach Boys from the Mall on the Fourth of July. Then the White House decided to laugh it off by giving Watt a big foot with a hole in it where he shot himself. It made a great photo.

The damage control people met right after Watt's new booboo to see what to give him this time.

One political expert said, "Why don't we give him a large watermelon to stick in his mouth?"

"How about letting him come out of the White House in drag and blackface, wearing a skullcap while sitting in a wheelchair?"

A White House chief said, "I'm not sure that the people he offended will see the humor in it."

"Oh, come on," said another White House aide. "If we can't laugh at ourselves in this country, we're in a lot of trouble."

"We *are* in a lot of trouble," the political aide said. "The Chief spends all his time saying his administration has done more for blacks, women, minorities, and the handicapped than any other president, and then that born-again nerd, in one stupid statement, blows it."

"We have to come up fast with something that can get us off the hook."

"Why don't we just publicly censure the guy?"

"We can't do that. We'll only offend the people who thought his remark was very funny."

"I have an idea. You know those things they have at carnivals where a guy sits on a platform and people throw balls at him, and every time they hit him he gets dumped in a tub of water? We could set one of those up on the White House lawn and invite the public to throw things at Watt. The President could throw out the first ball."

"That would be sort of fun, but don't you think it's slightly undignified for one of the President's Cabinet officers?"

"Not for Watt. He has a great sense of humor."

"I have a crazy idea. Instead of treating it like a joke, why don't we get the President to fire the Secretary?"

"What for? We have to give Watt a reason," a White House aide said.

"We'll say we need the post to appoint a member of one of the groups he offended."

"He offended a lot of people."

"Suppose we found a black Jewish woman with one leg that was shorter than the other?"

"We'll go through the mail that we have been receiving since he made his remark. I'm sure we'll find a candidate there."

"The President will have to make the final decision. In the meantime we have to put the fire out. Schedule the President to speak to a black group, a women's group, a Jewish group, and a handicapped group during the next week."

"It will be too obvious if he addresses all of them at this time."

"We'll declare October Black Jewish Handicapped Women's Month. It's about time the President recognized them for what they've done for the country."

Guilty But
Not Guilty

I am constantly fascinated when I read in the newspapers that the Justice Department or a federal agency has just arrived at an agreement with a large company or powerful individual accused of wrongdoing.

The stories read something like this: "The Double Jeopardy Automobile Company agreed with the Justice Department not to manufacture any more of their Double Y cars without brake pedals. The company paid a $50,000 fine and said that it would recall all Double Y cars now on the road that are missing the brake pedal. While paying the fine and making the recall, Double Jeopardy executives denied that there was a problem with the Double Y car, or any reason for the recall."

I consulted a lawyer friend of mine in Washington, and asked him what exactly it meant when the company was fined, agreed to recall all its cars, and still was able to maintain its innocence.

"They have to do that," he said. "Otherwise the company would open itself up to a lot of frivolous lawsuits."

"I understand that. But why would the government allow them to maintain their innocence when Double Jeopardy forgot to put a brake pedal on the car?"

"The government is more concerned with getting the cars fixed than with punishing the company for incompetence. If they bring Double Jeopardy to trial, it's going to take years to resolve the problem, and in the meantime a lot more people could get killed."

"Suppose the company knowingly was selling cars without brake pedals? Isn't that a criminal offense?"

"Possibly. But let's start at the beginning. Double Jeopardy puts out a Double Y car without brake pedals. The engineering department catches it after the millionth car is on the market. They inform their salespeople, who tell them to shut up. Finally, the government safety people get wind of it and, after testing the vehicle for two years, come to the conclusion that the Double Y could cause a danger on the highway.

"They contact Double Jeopardy and say that their data indicates the Double Y car may have a flaw in its braking system. The company responds by saying that the safety agency did not test the car under road conditions, and the only time people have accidents in a Double Y car is when they try to stop it.

"The safety agency studies the data submitted by Double Jeopardy and concludes that the only thing that can stop a Double Y car is a brick wall. In preparation for this negative reaction, Double Jeopardy has hired the best law firm in Washington—that usually means the law firm with the best connections to the present administration. The lawyer calls his friends at Justice and says he is shocked that the auto safety agency would pick on an American car firm just as the economy is starting to shape up. He offers to meet with the Justice Department lawyer to work out an equitable solution that will satisfy the company and the government. They make a date for a golf game at the Burning Tree Club."

"It sounds so civilized," I said.

"It is. Usually by the ninth hole an agreement can be hammered out. In the case of the Double Y car, the Justice man says, because of the publicity, he can't look the other way and Double Jeopardy will have to be fined and go ahead with a recall.

"The lawyer for the company says that this is all right with him, provided Double Jeopardy doesn't have to admit there is anything wrong with the car, or else the settlement could be construed as an admission of guilt.

"The Justice Department lawyer says he is sure he can get the auto safety agency to agree to the stipulation, provided Double Jeopardy promises not to do it again."

"This is where I always get confused," I said. "Double Jeopardy agrees with government there is a serious defect in the Double Y car, but doesn't have to admit it to its customers."

My lawyer friend told me, "That's because you don't understand how the government and big business work. The government's job is to protect the consumer; the company's job is to protect their sales. As long as both sides sign an agreement that they know the company botched, the law is satisfied without admitting it, and no one really gets hurt."

The New Pep Talk

Football coaches of major college teams are a different breed from those a few years ago. And so are the locker room speeches they give at half time.

"Men, we're getting creamed out there by Steroid Tech. I'm not going to give you the usual pep talk. Instead I'm going to level with you.

"Half the revenue of the University of BLT comes from football. We are now negotiating a TV contract which will be worth four million dollars a year. Our new stadium will hold eighty-five thousand fans. With parking and concessions it will bring in ten million dollars. If we go to one of the major bowl games, we'll take in another million dollars, and licensing fees for BLT sweatshirts, footballs, pom-poms, and bumper stickers will bring in a million three.

"But we're not going to do it if you guys stink out the place as you have done in the first half. A school can only demand that kind of money when it produces winners.

"As for myself, I have a lot more at stake than just a coaching job. You people know that I do TV commercials for the Guggenheim Ford dealership, Sucker's Root Beer, Tony's Pizza Parlors, Carson's Savings and Loan, and Buffet Carry-on Luggage. I represent them because I have winning football teams.

"What I haven't told you is that I am being considered for a Miller's Lite Beer commercial, the highest honor anyone in football coaching can aspire to. The beer commercial scouts are in the stands today. But they're not going to sign me if you guys let the Steroid backfield stomp all over you as you did in the first half.

"Now let's talk about my restaurant. I have five hundred thousand dollars invested in that joint. How many people do you think are going to show up after the game if we can't even score a touchdown from the ten-yard line? Miselski, do you realize the field goal you missed in the second quarter could cost me three thousand dollars in bar business tonight?

"I know Steroid is tough. Their coach does the commercials for United Airlines, and he has a no-cut contract with Preparation H. But that doesn't mean Steroid is ten feet tall. What killed us in the first half was penalties. I want you to hit hard and I want you to hit often, but if you're going to play dirty it reflects not only on your school, but on all the fine sponsors that I endorse.

"I'm going to tell you a story now which I've never told anyone before. It's about the greatest running back I ever coached, George Snorter. Snorter went on to the National Football League, where he broke every record. One day tragedy struck. Snorter was arrested for selling three hundred kilos of painkillers. He got twenty years in the Atlanta federal pen.

"I went to visit George last year. He weighed one hundred and thirty pounds, his face was pallid, and his hands were shaking. We talked about BLT football and what it meant to him. Then, as our hour was almost up, he looked at me through the wire that separated us and said, 'Coach, someday the going will get tough for a BLT football team. They're going to be pushed all over the field by the opposition. They're going to be dragging their tails and they're going to be hurting and bruised. You will run out of things to say to them to bring their spirits up. When the time comes, Coach, I want you to tell them my story, and I want you to tell them to go out there and win for the Snorter.'

"I gave George my word. And now I'm asking you to do him the only favor he ever asked of me. Wherever he is, men, I know if you can pull this game out, he'll hear about it. Don't do it for me, don't do it for BLT, don't even do it for Miller's Lite Beer. Do it for a great guy whose career was tragically cut short by the DEA.

"I don't have any more to say, because I have to do the half-time radio show for Hechinger's Hardware Store.

"NOW GET OUT ON THAT FIELD AND START PLAYING FOOTBALL THE WAY A TOP TEN TEAM IS EXPECTED TO PLAY, OR TURN IN YOUR BMWs AFTER THE GAME!"

Information Please

Ma Bell hardly had time to rest in her grave, when a well-dressed man in a dark pin-striped suit, a beautiful shirt, and a natty Harvard Business School tie came up to me and said, "Hi, I'm your brand-new AT and T man and I'm here to save you money."

"How are you going to do that?" I asked suspiciously.

"I'm going to cut your long-distance rates by an average of ten-point-five percent," he said, slapping me on the back.

"How are you going to do *that?*"

"We're asking the Federal Communications Commission to lower our rates by January first."

"Neato," I said. "And it isn't going to cost me anything?"

"No sir. Except we're asking a measly two-dollar-a-month surcharge for your home and six dollars for your office so that the local company can hook into our lines."

"Then it is going to cost me more money to get a price cut."

"Not in long-distance calls. But we will have to charge you a seventy-five-cent fee for each long-distance information call you make, which will hardly cover our expenses."

"But Ma Bell used to give us telephone information for free," I protested.

"Ma Bell is dead and gone and is now in that big switchboard in the sky. We have to charge you seventy-five cents because the local telephone company will bill us sixty-six cents to service your call."

"Suppose I don't make any long-distance calls. Will I still be socked with the two-dollar surcharge?"

"Everyone makes long-distance telephone calls. Look, if you just spend fifteen dollars a month calling someone you love, with our new low rates you'll be even."

"Ma Bell would never have let this happen."

"We're in a new ball game now," he said. "AT and T is not in the telephone business—we're in telecommunications."

"When Ma was alive, she let the long-distance calls subsidize the local phone service. Most long-distance calls were made by businesses, so they could deduct it anyway. Now you're telling me every household in America can call long-distance more cheaply as long as we pay through the nose to the local companies to do it."

"Look fellow, we all miss Ma. She was the salt of the earth. But when the Justice Department made AT and T spin off their local companies, we had to get realistic about long distance. We have to make our money now when Aunt Mary in Virginia calls Cousin Suzy in California. There's nothing in it for us if Aunt Mary calls her sister four blocks down the street. By the same token, the local companies are now on their own, and they have to charge Aunt Mary what it *really* costs her to call her sister. It's every phone company for itself."

"Suppose everyone stops making long-distance calls to protest your surcharges?" I asked.

"That's fine with us because we're also going into electronic mail, the satellite business, and we will be the biggest telephone-equipment supplier in the United States. You can even use our lines to communicate by computer."

"Whose dumb idea was it to split up AT and T and knock off Ma Bell?"

"The government's. They figured if they split us up there would be a lot more competition and the consumer would get a break."

"Apparently they were wrong."

"Why don't you call your congressman long distance and tell him how you feel about it?" he suggested.

"He's campaigning in New York. I don't know his number." The AT&T man said, "It will only cost you seventy-five cents to find out."

Crisis Center

I have this hot line to a crisis center. Every Monday morning I call up a guy and ask him, "What's the crisis of the week?" and for twenty-five dollars he tells me.

I called him recently and he said, "The 'big C' is the airline crisis. It could be a Mount Saint Helens."

"What happpened?" I asked him.

"The thing that started it all was the big boys in aviation wanted the airlines deregulated because they claimed they weren't making enough money. So the administration deregulated the friendly skies of America and opened them up to the marketplace."

"Free competition is what this country thrives on," I said.

"The only problem was that after they got deregulated, all the major airlines wanted to fly the same routes. A company that used to fly to Charlotte, North Carolina, decided to fly to London, England, instead. Every large company put on flights to Hawaii and canceled flights to middle America. Instead of going to Missoula, Montana, one airline started a daily service to Tokyo. Pretty soon you could fly to Miami every fifteen minutes, but you could only go to Buffalo once a week.

"With all the competition for the major cities, the airlines got into a price war. First they cut their fares—then they offered you a free seat for your spouse. Then they advertised that you could take all your children with you. And finally, during the recession, they let you take all the people you had met in a bar. There wasn't an empty seat on the plane, but there was only one paying passenger.

"To make things worse, the little guys started taking on the big boys and price-cut the hell out of them. The little guys were non-union, no-frill companies who offered you nothing but a seat. But for thirty-nine dollars, you could fly from New York to Los Angeles with a layover in Newfoundland."

"I guess the free market was really working."

"It was for the little guys, but the big boys were going nuts. They came up with new sales gimmicks. If you flew a certain number of miles on their airline, they would upgrade you from tourist to first class. If you flew fifteen thousand miles, they would let you sit in the copilot's seat. If you flew one hundred thousand miles, they made you president of the company. Most of the poeple now running a losing airline came up through the ranks from the 'frequent-flyer plan.'

"The situation didn't get any better when the big boys guessed wrong on what planes they would need for their companies. Some ordered planes that were too big—others ordered planes that were too small. When they had too many planes in moth-balls, they had to sell a lot of them to the little guys who were putting them out of business. Of course it wasn't their fault. One of the major airline executives was walking through his terminal at Kennedy Airport and it was jammed with people. He immediately ordered six new 747s. What he didn't realize, until later, was that all the people there were from Central America, waiting for their grandmother to get off the plane."

"That was an honest mistake," I said.

"Then, in order to protect themselves from their stockholders, the large companies invested their cash flow in other businesses, such as hotels, fast-food franchises, and natural gas. Since they were making money in these enterprises, the stockholders started demanding they spin off the airline part of their business.

"Everyone made mistakes. Eastern Airlines thought it could get healthy by having Frank Borman do their TV commercials. He was very credible but he didn't sell any tickets."

"Why didn't they scrub the advertising campaign?"

"What advertising executive is going to tell the chairman of the board of Eastern Airlines that he can no longer do the company's commercials?"

"What a mess," I said. "I guess the big boys are sorry they ever asked for deregulation of the airlines. Are they going to go back and lobby for airline regulation again?"

"That's their only chance. Most of them have decided free air competition is for the birds."

The New Guilt Trip

The computer companies are now laying a real guilt trip on parents through TV commercials. They state that you're really cheating your children out of a chance to make it when they grow up if you don't buy them a computer. The kids see these commercials, too, and it's causing a lot of trouble between the haves and the have-nots in our school system.

"Johnny, where is your report card?"

"Here."

"Why did you get a D in math?"

"It wasn't my fault. You wouldn't buy me a computer."

"We can't afford a computer right now. They cost two hundred dollars."

"Don't matter to me. The man on TV said that if you don't want to give me a head start in life, you'll have nobody to blame but yourself."

"That's a lot of television-commercial nonsense. I did math without a computer."

"Maybe that's why you can't afford to buy me one."

"We didn't have computers in those days. Besides, it hasn't been proven yet whether computers are good or bad for children. There is a school of thought that they can be harmful to the learning process and kids should depend on their own brains instead of machines. The computer can tell you what four plus four is, but you don't know how you arrived at the answer."

"They don't care in school how you arrive at it as long as it comes out right."

"Let's forget math for a moment. Why did you get an F in deportment?"

"I hit Jill Gleason with a book."

"Why did you hit her with a book?"

"Because she's got a computer, and she wouldn't tell me the answers to the math problems."

"You can't go around hitting people because they have a computer and you don't."

"You have to if they say your parents are too cheap to buy you one."

"Did Jill say that?"

"Yeah. She said you were depriving me of a chance to make something of myself and I should be taken away from you and put in a foster home."

"She couldn't have said that."

"The other kids heard her. Those who had computers laughed, and those who didn't all wanted to hit her too."

"What did the teacher say?"

"She told me to go to the principal's office, and he put my name in his computer and said that if I did it again, I'd be kicked out of school."

"What about spelling? How do you explain the D in that subject?"

"I have to do all my own spelling. If I had a computer it would check my spelling for me. When Jill Gleason hands in her paper she never has a mistake in her printout. She says she gets her homework done five times faster than I do."

"Yes, but is she learning how to spell?"

"She said that her father told her it doesn't make any difference because when she grows up computers will do all the spelling for you anyway."

"Her father apparently doesn't realize that the disciplines you learn by doing your own work in school are far more important than whether you make a mistake or not in your papers."

"That's what Michael Parks' father said. His father won't get him a computer either."

"Well, I'm not about to buy you one, so you'd better straighten out and come home with a better report card than this the next time, or you can spend your weekends in your room."

"I don't care. I'll probably end up in jail anyhow."

"Who told you that?"

"The guy on TV. He said that if parents didn't buy their kid a computer, the kid would probably wind up robbing liquor stores when he got out of school."

High-Stake Poker

I just returned from Las Vegas where I observed the World Series Poker Championships at Binion's Golden Horseshoe. They don't quit until everybody but one guy is wiped out.

I was telling a friend in the White House about it when he said, "They don't know what *real* poker is."

He took out a blue disk from a drawer and showed it to me.

"Do you know what this is?" he asked.

I said that it looked like a poker chip.

"It's an MX bargaining chip," he said. "Congress just voted to stake the President to six hundred twenty-five million dollars' worth of them so he could buy into the arms race game."

He showed me ten red chips. "These represent nuclear warheads. You bet them on top of the MX missile chips."

"How much are they worth?"

"A billion dollars each. But without them the MX missile chips aren't worth anything."

"Boy, that's big-time poker."

"The President says he has to have them if he's going to play

111

cards in Geneva with the Russians. If he doesn't have the MX chips, the Soviets will try to bluff him out of the pot."

"So the President has the MX missile chips and he puts them on the table?"

"He doesn't put them on the table. He buries them in hardened old Minutemen missile silos, and he tells the Soviets he's only willing to reduce his pile if they're willing to reduce their land-based missile chips at the same time."

"Why would we be willing to give away the MX missile chips?"

"Because in an arms race poker game they are not as valuable as they look. The Soviets could probably knock them out with a pair of aces. That's why the President needs them as chips. He's willing to throw them into the pot because he wants to keep all the other land, sea, and air chips we have in our arsenal."

"If the President says he needs the MX missiles as throwaway chips in Geneva, what's to prevent the Soviets from coming up with missile chips of their own that they don't mind losing?"

"Nothing. They probably will come up with a chip they don't really care about to match the MX."

"Why are we staking the President to billions of dollars in MX chips if they don't really have any value?"

"To show that we're serious about playing poker in Geneva. If we didn't have the MX missile chips, the Soviets would believe the President doesn't have enough guts to stick out the nuclear war games."

"When do we get down to serious poker with the Russians?"

"Not for a very long time, because the President says that the Soviets are playing with a stacked deck, and they cheat on every hand. He's not going to bet his stack until he's sure we can beat them at their own game."

"Suppose the President puts all his MX chips on the table and the Russians call him with their chips. Does that mean they will agree on a limit for future pots?"

"Not necessarily. The President may go back to Congress and

ask them for another stack of arms chips because he'll say that the Soviets have a lot of cards up their sleeves, and he can't win if he has to play with one hand tied behind his back."

"What I don't understand is why are we playing poker in Geneva if one side keeps accusing the other of cheating?"

"Because it's the only game in town."

Last of the Heroes

Who says there aren't heroes left in America anymore. Not long ago, in a surprise ceremony, the CIA awarded CIA Director William J. Casey the Distinguished Intelligence Medal, the agency's highest award. Casey was cited for "outstanding leadership" and for restoring the credibility of the CIA and bringing "imagination to our operation."

In the past, a decoration of this magnitude was usually reserved until the Director retired or resigned from the job. But apparently the people who work for Mr. Casey couldn't wait. I am not privy to how these awards are made, but I know they're not easy to get.

There must be an awards committee out at Langley that goes over every one of the citation nominations to make sure that the person is deserving of the honor.

"Gentlemen, our first nominee is James Blickstein, who, in a clandestine operation, dropped behind enemy lines in Afghanistan and delivered needed radio equipment to the rebels. He then walked barefoot five hundred miles across Russian-held territory back to Pakistan. Does he get a medal?"

"He's paid to do that. Why should he get an award? If we give out the Distinguished Intelligence Medal to every Tom, Dick, and Harry involved in a clandestine operation, it will deflate its value."

"Okay, let's forget Blickstein. The second nominee is Hiram Cope, who managed to go over the wall of the Soviet's submarine base at Murmansk and steal all the USSR's naval codes. He then swam in a frog suit to Norway."

"Big deal. I'll admit it wasn't a bad operation, but is it worth a medal?"

"All in favor say aye—all against, nay. The nays have it. Scratch Cope."

"We now come to Nicaragua and Honduras. Our man down there, T. L., managed to get around all the restrictions the congressional Committee on Intelligence laid down for covert operations, and got his people to bomb Nicaraguan soil."

"He should get a medal."

"But do we want to give him the highest one?"

"I don't think we do, because we have to make him the fall guy in case Congress starts raising a ruckus. Let's give him the CIA's Good Conduct Award. We can always give him the biggie just before we fire him."

"We're all agreed then on T. L. Now I have a CIA person that I am proud to nominate. I propose that we give the Distinguished Intelligence Medal to none other than our revered Director, William J. Casey."

"I have no quarrel with that. The man has certainly gone beyond the call of duty."

"You won't hear a nay from me. He's the bravest of the brave."

"The smartest of the smart."

"His outstanding leadership has made this organization what it is today."

"If it wasn't for his imagination I just don't know where we'd all be."

"I take it then that there is no opposition to awarding the Director our highest decoration."

"I've still got five years to go before retirement. You won't hear any objection from me."

"Good. Then I'll write up the citation and we'll get Deputy Director John McMahon to present it to him in a full-fledged formal ceremony, with the CIA Undercover Band."

"It's the least we can do for the old man."

"No one in the CIA deserves it more."

"How did you ever think of it, Willoughby?"

"When you're in the intelligence business you *have* to think of everything."

Twenty Questions

"Hi, Colonel, where are you going with your parachute?"

"I can't tell you, son. It's a military secret."

"I'm from the press. Can I come along?"

"No way, son."

"Why not, sir? I'm paid to cover wars."

"I'd be too worried about your safety. We have a mission to accomplish, and we don't want you to get hurt."

"With all due respect, sir, that sounds like a load of bull-feathers. How are the American people going to know what's really happening if you exclude the media from the operation?"

"We'll brief you at the White House, with great maps and wonderful pictures."

"That isn't the same as being on the scene. Are you trying to tell me that from now on we have only the government's word as to what happens when American troops are sent into a foreign land?"

"Why not? Do you think the government would lie to the people?"

"No, they wouldn't lie. But they do tend to see things from a different point of view. In a free and open society the American people demand to be informed as to what their government is doing."

"You may think so, but the latest polls show that the American people would rather believe what their government tells them than what the media reports. The trouble with you guys is that you're always bringing them bad news, while the government prefers to give them good news. As far as the Pentagon is concerned, you people covered your last war in Vietnam."

"Well, if you won't let me come along with you, can you give me a little hint of where you're going?"

"We're going in to overthrow a repressive government that took power through force and wiped out all the opposition."

"You're not going into Chile, are you?"

"You're not even warm. The present leaders of this particular country are no more than thugs with curfews and death squads and they have no respect for human rights."

"I got it. You're going into El Salvador."

"We are in El Salvador. The government we're going to overthrow is a totalitarian regime that rules with an iron fist, has martial law, and doesn't think twice about assassinating its critics."

"Wait a minute. You're not going to attack the Philippines?"

"You're in the wrong ocean. It's a communist government steeped in Marxist philosophy, with contempt for all democratic reforms."

"Poland?"

"We have no intention of being bogged down in Poland, or anyplace behind the iron curtain."

"There are so many countries in the world that fit your description, it's hard to come up with just one. Let's see, we've eliminated all totalitarian governments we support because they're not communist, and we've eliminated all the major communist countries because militarily it's not feasible. I'm stumped. You have to give me another hint."

"Ask me if it's bigger than a breadbox."

"I forgot that one. Is it bigger than a breadbox?"

"No, it isn't bigger than a breadbox."

"It's not bigger than a breadbox and it's a threat to the United States?"

"It isn't a threat to the United States in itself, but it's a way of sending a message to Cuba and the Soviet Union not to mess around with us because we mean business."

"You mean it's not bigger than a breadbox and the press can't even accompany the American troops going in?"

"Now you're getting warm. Give up?"

"What choice do I have? Where are you going with your parachute?"

"I can't tell you. But if you go over to the Pentagon tomorrow they'll give you all the details, and to show that we have nothing personal against the media, the coffee and doughnuts will be on the house."

A No-Foreign-Policy Foreign Policy

Every time something serious happens, my relatives from around the country call me to find out what is going on. They do this on the false assumption that someone who lives in Washington must know more than they do.

Cousin Ziggy, who is a nervous Nelly when it comes to the Caribbean, called and said, "Why did we land in Grenada?"

"Because of leftist Marxist thugs who overthrew the other leftist Marxist thugs running the government."

"But why would we care if one Marxist government overthrew another one?"

"Because the guys who took over made the Marxist thugs who used to be in power look like altar boys."

"Can I ask you a serious question?"

"Shoot."

"Does the Reagan administration have a foreign policy?"

"Of course it has a foreign policy. You can't be a superpower without having a foreign policy."

"What is it, then?" Cousin Ziggy asked.

"Our foreign policy is not to have one."

"What does that mean?"

"If the other side knows that we have no foreign policy, then the Kremlin thugs have no idea what we'll do next. Up until recently when a president spelled out a foreign policy, the Soviets immediately worked out a policy to counteract it. But now they're as confused as the American people are about our objectives, and they're climbing the Kremlin walls."

"Under the No-Foreign-Policy Foreign Policy of the US, are we getting closer to going to war with the USSR?" Ziggy asked.

"No, but they are getting much closer to going to war with us."

"What's the difference?"

"The Soviets will not sit down with us unless they know we are willing to fight."

"Are the Soviets willing to fight if they know we are?"

"That's the sixty-four-thousand-megaton question. Until that moment comes, we must do everything to make them understand that we will use every weapon in our arsenal, up to and including the big H, before we'll bow to blackmail."

"And that's our foreign policy?" Ziggy said.

"That's our broad policy. We are also in the business of destabilizing governments favorable to Moscow's thugs, and supporting governments that Moscow is trying to destabilize.

"We'll give the job to a third party which will be financed and trained by the CIA. The Soviets use the KGB to find and train their third parties. If destabilization doesn't work through third parties, then we are prepared to use American brute force, just as the Soviets do when one of their covert operations fails."

"Whatever happened to diplomacy where nations talked things out first before flexing their muscles?"

"Our foreign policy is to use diplomacy only as a last resort, when all else fails. The President can't endanger the lives of two hundred and twenty million Americans, not to mention everyone else on the globe, by using diplomacy, when the only thing the other side understands is armed might."

"It doesn't sound like a foreign policy that can last for a very long time. At some point one side will test the other to see if it's bluffing or not."

"Reagan doesn't bluff," I said. "That was the true message of Grenada."

"And the Soviet leaders?"

"They don't bluff either. That was the true message of Afghanistan."

"So what do we have to look forward to?"

"More of the same, with clearing skies and light parachuting on Thursday."

The Hunger Test

Assuming that Ed Meese is right, and some people in soup lines are there only because the food is free, and assuming that President Reagan was correct when he told *The New York Daily News* it's only logical that if there were people who cheated on welfare, there would also be those who cheat on cadging meals, the question arises, do you feed the hungry and stonewall the ones who can afford to pay for their food?

Unfortunately up until recently there has been no way of checking up on those standing in front of soup kitchens to certify if they truly need the food or could pay for it.

But Professor Heinrich Applebaum, head of the Mother Hubbard Institute of Nutrition, has just developed a foolproof hunger test.

The tests would be monitored by a government Hunger Strike Force. As each person lined up in front of a church, the Salvation Army, or volunteer food kitchen, he or she would be asked to respond to the following questions on a printed form:

Name, Social Security number, present address (if you have one; if you don't, address where you slept the previous night).

List three references (not including members of immediate family) certifying your good character and willingness to pay for a meal if you could afford one.

Please answer the following questions:

1. Circle the last time you had a decent meal: (a) 24 hours ago, (b) 48 hours ago, (c) one week ago. (Note: If you have had a decent meal within less than 24 hours, please leave the line as you will not be permitted to enter the soup kitchen.)
2. Choose one of the following to describe your hunger pangs: (a) rumbling in the stomach, (b) dizziness, (c) depression, (d) nausea, (e) anger.
3. Do you have any coins in your pocket at the present time?
4. List all members of your family who have been to a soup kitchen in the last 12 months.
5. If you are under 13 years old, did you come here of your own free will or were you forced to by a parent or guardian?
6. Are you a chronic freeloader?

The following is a math quiz. You have ten minutes to complete it.

I. If an American dairy farmer is paid $35,000 a year not to produce milk, how many dairy farmers will it take for the government to pay $1 billion in agricultural subsidies?
II. If an agri-business receives $200 million a year for not planting wheat, corn, or soybeans, how much money can it shelter in taxes under present IRS rules?
III. If the government cuts out 5 million children from its free lunch program at a cost of fifty cents per child, how much money would it save by cutting off 7 million children?

This is the essay part of the test. In 200 words describe why you feel you should get a free meal. Please include anecdotes of people you have stood in line with who shouldn't have been there because they could afford to pay for one. These anecdotes will be forwarded to the White House for future presidential speeches on the hunger problem in America.

Once the test is completed, it would be handed to a member of the Hunger Strike Force who would feed it into a computer and decide whether the person waiting for a plate of spaghetti and two-day-old bread would be permitted to enter the free food facility.

Those who perjured themselves or failed to give complete answers would be turned over to the Justice Department for prosecution under the Truth in Hunger Act.

Applebaum claims the test will have chilling effect on hunger cheaters, and he hopes to have it distributed to every volunteer food kitchen before they serve Christmas dinner.

In the meantime, if you know of any family that is planning to cadge a free Christmas dinner this year, and can afford to buy their own, please call your nearest FBI office immediately. You will help the Reagan administration in the war on hunger cheaters, a war we all have to win.

Anything But the Truth

There is only one worse sin than to lie in the Reagan White House, and that is to tell the truth.

Dr. Martin Feldstein, the chairman of the President's Council of Economic Advisers, discovered this not long ago.

Dr. Feldstein's job is to advise the President on the future of the economy, regardless of political race, ideological creed, and bookkeeping color.

What is driving Mr. Reagan's political advisers up the wall is that Dr. Feldstein has not been painting the same rosy future of the economy that the President intends to use in his reelection campaign.

Recently the Harvard professor was called on the carpet once again by the President's inner circle.

They made him put his right hand on the Federal Budget.

"Do you swear to tell the economic truth, the whole economic truth, and nothing but the economic truth, so help you God?"

Dr. Feldstein said, "I do."

"You see," said Reagan's right-hand man, "I told you he wasn't a team player."

"Why do you have to tell the truth during an election year?" another right-hand presidential aide asked him.

"Because if I don't I'll look like an idiot," Dr. Feldstein said. "We're going to have to face up to a two-hundred-billion-dollar deficit in 1985 that could destroy any hope of a recovery. The only way to deal with it is to raise taxes and cut back on military spending."

"Dr. Feldstein," a third right-hand aide said, "you're not only not a team player, you're a Benedict Arnold."

"Look," said Dr. Feldstein. "Here are the figures. I'm not making any of this up."

"Don't back up your argument with figures," the first right-hand man said. "That's the coward's way out. Do you realize that you are making the deficit a political issue?"

"But the President made it a political issue in 1980, and that's one of the reasons he won," Dr. Feldstein protested.

"That was before it became 'his' budget deficit. Your job is to give us economic reasons to show why a two-hundred-billion-dollar deficit is good for the economy."

"How can I do that?" Dr. Feldstein said. "If the government has to go out on the public market and borrow money to pay its debts, it will send interest rates sky-high, and the private sector won't be able to afford to borrow money to keep the recovery going. Doesn't anybody here want to deal with reality?"

"We're only willing to deal with one kind of reality," a right-hand man said. "And that's getting the President reelected. Now you either shut up about budget deficits or get off the team."

"I don't want to get off the team," Dr. Feldstein said. "I believe that I'm serving the President by telling him the truth about the economic future of the country. If he gets reelected and doesn't realize what lies ahead for him, he'll become the laughingstock of the nation."

"All right, doctor," said the hardest right-hand aide. "You haven't got the message, so we're going to have to play rough."

"I'm not going to listen to any more of this claptrap," Dr. Feldstein said, and walked out.

"Ask Larry Speakes to come in," someone said.

The President's press secretary came in with his notepad.

"Larry," said the chief aide, "Dr. Feldstein refuses to be a team player. At your next press briefing we want you to go out and ridicule him in front of the entire White House press corps."

"Oh boy," said Larry. "This is going to be fun. Can I mispronounce his name every time I say it?"

"Give the wimp the full treatment," the aide said. "You can use every joke about him in your book. We're going to get rid of Dr. Gloom one way or another."

Disarmament

"What are you getting your grandson for Christmas?" I asked Borodin.

"I got my grandson a GI Joe doll," he said.

"I got my grandson a GI Joe doll and a missile-firing jeep," I said.

He seemed taken aback. "I'm thinking of getting David a

Cobra helicopter, with rockets that can fire from both the front and the rear."

"I saw them at Toys-R-Us," I said. "The rockets just bounce off the radio-controlled tank I bought Ben at Woodie's."

"That's not what they told me at FAO Schwarz," he said.

That night I went home and started going through a Sears Roebuck catalog. My wife wanted to know what I was doing. "Borodin is going to buy a Cobra helicopter for his grandson that could knock Ben's tank out of action. I have to come up with a deterrent to blow it out of the sky. Here is an antiaircraft mobile carrier with ground-to-air missiles that could do the job."

I called up Borodin. "If you buy the Cobra, I'm going to give my grandson an air-to-ground missile weapon."

"You do that and I'll go to Montgomery Ward's and order a radar station which will make your missiles worthless."

"I'll call you back," I told him.

My wife said, "Have you gone crazy? How much money are you going to spend on Ben this Christmas?"

"As much as it takes to keep superiority over Borodin's grandchild. The only thing Borodin understands is power."

"What I think is that you better both meet and stop this ridiculous toy race," my wife said.

"There is no sense meeting until Borodin realizes I mean business. I think I'll buy a few missile-firing submarines and a nuclear aircraft carrier from People's drugstore to use as chips in our talks."

"You don't even know if Ben wants a GI Joe doll. What he asked for was a bicycle," she protested.

"That's just because he doesn't know what Borodin's grandson is getting for his Christmas. I'm willing to meet and talk but don't expect any miracles."

I arranged a lunch at the Swiss Chalet for the talks.

"Before I begin," I told Borodin, "I should warn you I ordered Ben a chemistry set so that he can make his own nerve gas. I'm willing to cancel the order if you give up the radar station."

"I'm not giving up the radar station unless you give up the radio-controlled tank."

"How do I know you won't go out and buy GI Joe an entire MX system?" I asked.

"You have my word for it."

"That's a big joke, Borodin. Your word stinks when it comes to Christmas."

"If that's the way you want it," Borodin replied, "there's no use our discussing this any further."

That night my wife asked me how the talks had gone.

"Borodin walked out on them. Give me the toy catalog from Radio Shack."

"But both your grandsons have enough weapons to destroy their GI Joes ten times."

"There's no such thing as enough weapons in a toy war," I said. "This looks interesting. It's a space platform that shoots rockets from the air."

"It costs sixty-nine dollars," she said.

"It's a bargain if it sends the right message to Borodin."

Veto

"Quick," I said to Hogsgood at the State Department. "I'm in a hurry. What's our position on human rights?"

"We're for them, but against certifying them."

"Which means?"

"The President vetoed a bill which linked El Salvador military aid to human rights and land reform."

"Why?"

"Do you want the policy line or the truth?"

"Both."

"The policy line is the military aid–certification link plays into the hands of the leftists and undermines the President's authority to conduct foreign affairs. The truth is there hasn't been any progress in human rights and land reform since the new government was elected."

"Where do we stand on right-wing death squads in El Salvador?"

"What right-wing death squads? The policy line is the right-wing death squads are really left-wing death squads, trying to give the right wing a bad name."

"You believe it?"

"The President believes it and that's good enough for us."

"Then the people in El Salvador have nothing to fear from right-wing death squads?"

"The policy line is that we don't condone death squads from the extreme left or the extreme right. The major priority is to bring stability to the area by strengthening El Salvador's army."

"The army is supposed to be running the death squads."

"That's media propaganda. The elected officials are pledged to democracy and political freedom. But they can't do anything about it until the leftists are wiped out."

"What about land reform?"

"We're for it."

"But you're not in any position to certify that there is any in El Salvador?"

"Our policy is military aid to El Salvador should not be contingent upon land reform. Why give the peasants land if the leftists are going to take it away from them?"

"That's the policy. What's the truth?"

"We can't get the present government in El Salvador to budge on land reform, so what good is it to certify that they have?"

"Congress linked military aid to human rights progress and

land reform in their bill which the President vetoed when they were out of session. What happens when they come back in January and pass another bill asking for the same thing?"

"Our policy is to stonewall them until we can wipe out the Marxist rebels."

"Suppose the President has to request more money for military aid for El Salvador?"

"Then we'll certify that there has been progress made in human rights and land reform."

"How?"

"Our ambassador down there will provide us with the evidence."

"Suppose he can't?"

"Then we'll replace him with one who can."

"Will Congress buy the evidence?"

"They will if we can prove the Soviets are behind the human rights and land reform policies in El Salvador."

"How can you prove that?"

"By saying it. It's our word against the Kremlin."

"Is it safe to say we're powerless to do anything to pressure the right in El Salvador to ease up on the people?"

"Our policy is that we have tremendous power to bring about the needed reforms and we are prepared to use it if they don't see how counterproductive their methods are."

"And the truth?"

"I can't tell you the truth. It's against State Department policy."

PART FOUR

THE LATCHKEY HUSBAND

The Latchkey
Husband

Much has been written about the latchkey kids—children who are left to fend for themselves because they have a single working parent, usually a mother.

But there is another social phenomenon which has sprung up in the last few years as more women enter the work force—the latchkey husband.

I wasn't aware of his existence until I ran into Bronfman at the water cooler the other day. Around his neck he wore a string, which held a key.

"What's that?" I asked.

"The key to my apartment. My wife's a lawyer and she works until seven or eight every evening, so she gave me this key to get in when I come home."

"Why are you wearing it around your neck?"

"So I won't lose it. She doesn't like to leave it under the mat because she's afraid someone will find it and break into the flat."

"You mean every night when you go home, there's no one at the door to greet you?"

"You get used to it," he said. "My wife always leaves cookies and milk in the ice box for me, and a note telling me I can watch television until she gets there."

131

"Aren't you afraid to be in the apartment all alone?"

"Nah. I don't mind it at all. But my wife has made me promise not to open the door to strangers. Also, she's given me permission to bring a male friend home providing we don't mess up the house."

"You must feel neglected."

"Why should I? My wife has to work, and she always tries to make it up to me on the weekends by taking me to a movie or the park if it's a nice day. There are a lot of latchkey husbands in our neighborhood, so it's not as if I'm the only one who walks into an empty apartment. Besides, if I get scared or have a problem there's always Mrs. Pennyweather."

"Mrs. Pennyweather?"

"She's the lady in apartment 4-C down the hall. She lives alone and has taken pity on me because I wear this key around my neck."

"That's nice of her. How old is she?"

"About thirty-five. She's blond, with a very nice figure and beautiful legs."

"How did you meet her?"

"Well, one day I lost my key and I was standing in the hall crying, and she came out of the elevator and invited me to wait in her apartment until my wife came home."

"Did she give you cookies and milk?"

"No, she gave me a couple of dry martinis until I stopped crying. Then we watched 'People's Court' together on her couch. She told me I could stop by anytime I wanted to, and now I'm not afraid to come home after work anymore."

"Mrs. Pennyweather sounds like a wonderful person."

"She is. There aren't many thirty-five-year-old women who would take care of somebody's husband while his wife was working. Once my wife had to go out of town, and Mrs. Pennyweather fixed me a candlelight dinner with cherries jubilee and let me sleep on her couch in the living room."

"Does your wife know you have such a good friend in the apartment house?"

"No, Mrs. Pennyweather made me promise to keep it a big secret just between the two of us. She doesn't want my wife to feel any more guilty than she does now."

"It's great to know there are still people out there who care what happens to latchkey husbands."

"Mrs. Pennyweather told me she gets as much pleasure out of it as I do, because I represent to her the husband she never had."

The Family Christmas

Christmas is a trying time for many people. Originally a family holiday, it now divides people as much as it brings them together, especially as the children grow older.

I discovered this when I talked to Fritzie Newmeyer.

"I guess we'll see Danny for the holidays," I said.

She pursed her lips. "Danny isn't coming home for Christmas. He's going to his girlfriend's family in La Crosse, Wisconsin."

"I'm sorry to hear that. You must be disappointed."

"Why should I be disappointed? He's a big boy and if he thinks it's more important to spend Christmas with some girl he's only known for six months, in a houseful of strangers instead of with his mother and father, who are shelling out fifteen thousand dollars a year to send him to college, that's his business."

"I'm glad to see you're not taking it personally," I said. "I guess Danny's in love."

"Maybe he is or maybe he isn't. It could be he thinks he'll have a better time in La Crosse than he will in his own home with the people who raised him. After all, what have we got to offer him but a bed and three good meals a day?"

"Well even if Danny isn't coming home, your daughter Sarah and her children will be here."

"I don't think so. Sarah's husband Allan wants to spend the holidays with his parents in Fort Lauderdale. They've already sent them the airline tickets. I told her it didn't matter to us, and we could always mail the grandchildren's presents to them. She seemed apologetic about it, but I said not to make a big deal of it. She doesn't owe us anything now that she has her own family. After all, Florida sounds like such a nice place for Christmas compared to Bethesda. We could always see the grandchildren in the spring and it would save me the trouble of shopping for a big dinner and decorating a large Christmas tree, which the whole family used to love to do."

"You're a good soldier, Fritzie," I told her. "Most mothers would be upset if two of their four children weren't coming home for the holidays."

"Larry isn't coming home either."

"He isn't?"

"He's going skiing in Vail with a group of people from his office. He told me it would be the only opportunity he had and asked me if I minded. Of course I told him I didn't mind. How can you compare skiing in Vail with a bunch of people from the office with a boring two days talking about Christmases past and dredging up childhood memories that everyone has heard a hundred times?"

"Well, at least he called to ask your permission."

Fritzie said, "I called him."

"So that just leaves Mary Lou. Surely she'll be home for Christmas," I said.

"She's living here. She doesn't do anything but lie around the house and complain since she lost her job. To be honest I wouldn't mind if she went somewhere also."

"It's funny," I said. "On television all the commercials show three generations of families together opening presents and drinking eggnogs. I guess in real life it isn't that simple."

134

"They don't make children like you see on television anymore," Fritzie said.

"Home may be where the heart is, but it isn't where the skiing is," I added. "I guess they'll all call on Christmas Day, though."

"Probably, unless all circuits are busy," Fritzie said.

"I better be getting along," I said, "to check out what's going on at our place."

"Are your kids coming home?"

"We don't know yet. They said that if we didn't hear from them by Christmas Eve, we should assume they were."

The Potomac
Tape Bug

The news that Charles Z. Wick, the Director of the United States Information Agency, was taping the telephone conversations of everyone from United States senators (Mark Hatfield) to movie stars (Kirk Douglas) to his most intimate friends (Walter Annenberg), without their knowledge, left everyone in Washington with an uncomfortable feeling.

It's all right to read another person's mail (we do it all the time), but it is still considered bad manners to turn on a Dictaphone when your phone rings.

After Watergate, it is also considered very, very dumb.

"What the hell got into Wick?" I asked one of my pals at the USIA.

"He caught the Potomac Tape Bug," the friend explained. "I've seen it happen time and time again. A guy comes to Washington to do a job, and slowly paranoia begins to set in. He's afraid that something he says on the telephone may be misinterpreted, so he decides to tape the conversations. That way he can refer to the transcripts in case someone takes anything he said out of context. At the beginning, he only pushes the Record button when he's talking to the press."

"Is that fair?"

"The government will never object to you recording conversations with the press," my friend said. "Especially when you have to assume that the press is recording its conversation with you. But when you start down that secret taping road it's hard to stop. The Dictaphone is there, and pretty soon you automatically turn it on when you're talking to a subordinate on business. It is very helpful when you're making out his or her fitness report."

"So far the official is keeping his secret taping within the bureaucratic ballpark," I said.

"Now this is where the guy goes off the track. He figures that if he can tape his subordinates without their knowledge, there is no reason why he can't tape his equals in other departments of the government without telling them. Pretty soon he has a stack of taped conversations with White House staff, Cabinet members, senators and leading citizens in the country."

"They could have historical value," I said.

"That's what the official talks himself into believing every time he turns the machine on. No longer is he taping to refresh his memory, but he decides he's doing it for future generations of Americans who want to know how he arrived at so many momentous decisions."

"I can understand a person wanting to secretly tape his official calls. But why would he record his conversations with friends?"

"Because by now he has become a compulsive taper. He has to tape whether he wants to or not. If the Dictaphone stops whirring he can't talk on the phone."

"Couldn't he tell his friends that he was recording the telephone call?"

"If he did he wouldn't have friends for very long. How would you like to tell Walter Annenberg he was being taped?"

"I wouldn't have the heart," I said.

"The worst thing about having the Potomac Tape Bug is that even if you stop, no one will believe you. Once the secret is out that you have been taping people's conversations without their knowledge, no one will call you again. It will be pretty hard for someone like Wick to run the world's largest propaganda machine when everyone in and out of the country will now put him on Hold."

"Didn't anyone ever tell him about Nixon?"

"We tried to, but all he said was, 'Let Poland be Poland.' "

A Girl's Best Friend

Well, it appears that diamonds are no longer a girl's best friend.

The resignation of Deputy Secretary of Defense Paul Thayer, caused by SEC allegations that he provided insider information to friends when he served on corporate boards in private life, has repercussions far beyond the business world.

The SEC has charged that Mr. Thayer, while not profiting personally from the tips, helped several friends become rich, one a beautiful Texas divorcée with whom he had a "very close personal relationship."

If the charges are true, or even if they aren't, it's going to change the financial arrangements between men of substance and the "other woman."

"Hello, Sweetie Pie. I had a terrible day. Give your Big Daddy a nice warm kiss and a nice cold, dry martini."

"It's been so long, Big Daddy, I thought I'd die."

"I had a board meeting in San Francisco, and then I had to fly to New York and meet my investment bankers. But I brought you a little surprise from Tiffany's. It's a diamond necklace."

"I don't want to know from diamonds. What's the latest poop on the Archer takeover of Magnum Electronics?"

"Now, Honey Bun. You know I can't talk about what goes on in the Archer boardroom."

"Then make your own dry martini."

"If you promise not to tell anyone, we're going to announce our takeover intentions tomorrow afternoon."

"So what do I do, Big Daddy?"

"Archer's will probably go down and Magnum's is certain to go up. Sit down on the couch and rub my neck."

"What happened in New York?"

"Nothing happened in New York."

"I thought you told me Snow White Petroleum was going to acquire Stonebridge Communications, which had just merged with Fungus Chemicals."

"The deal fell through because Snow White has secretly made a deal with Calypso Avionics."

"But I bought forty thousand shares of Stonebridge at fifty-seven on your say-so. It's now at forty-five. Why didn't you let me know?"

"I heard about it when I was in the hotel room with my wife. How could I call you?"

"So your wife is still more important to you than my stock portfolio?"

"I didn't say that, Barbie Doll. I'll make it up to you. I just came from a board meeting of Turtle Express. They're going to report a fifty-percent earnings profit for their first quarter. The stock should go up four points after the announcement."

"Oh, Big Daddy, what a wonderful tip! Let me take your tie and shoes off."

"That's more like it, my Sugar Candy. Do you love me?"

"Of course I love you. What gives with Rupert Murdoch?"

"What do you mean what gives with Rupert Murdoch?"

"Do you have inside information on whether he'll get control of Warner's or not?"

"I don't know, baby, and I don't want to talk about Rupert Murdoch now. I've got a lot of loving to catch up on. Then you can cook me a nice big steak dinner."

"Are you sure you aren't holding anything back on me, Big Daddy?"

"What would I hold back?"

"Should I still stay long in soybean futures?"

"Damn it, I'll tell you when to sell your soybeans! Now, are we going to have any fun or aren't we?"

"Of course we're going to have fun, Big Daddy. But first I have to slip into something more comfortable so I can call my broker."

The Hit List
Mafia

American politics is now in the hands of a lot of tough people.

I didn't realize how tough until I walked into Arnie Bridle's office. Arnie runs the Political Action Committee for a Strong, Healthy and Prosperous United States, a multimillion-dollar front supported by certain special interest groups.

Arnie was seated behind his desk, smoking a big cigar. Two hoods were sitting over on the couch. He told me to sit down.

"What can I do for you?"

"I hear you have a contract out on Congressman Finger."

"Who told you that?" he wanted to know.

"It's in all the papers. You're out to get him because he voted against lowering the minimum wage to one dollar an hour."

"We warned Finger if he voted against the bill his political life wasn't worth a nickel. Going to the newspapers won't save him."

The phone rang and Arnie picked it up. "Yeah? . . . I don't believe it. He said that at a political rally? . . . The guy is committing suicide . . . I'll get back to you." Arnie hung up and said to one of the hoods on the couch, "Senator Plankton just came out for hazardous-waste control."

"What do you want us to do, boss?" one of them asked.

Arnie took $400,000 out of his drawer. "Go into his state and bury him. Rough him up on TV, buy up every billboard you can find, hire as many demonstrators as you need, flood the radio talk shows with calls. We've got to make an example of Plankton and put the fear of God into everyone running for office this year."

"The guy is as good as dead," the hood said, putting the money into a valise.

"I don't want any fingerprints leading back to here," Arnie warned.

"You can count on us, boss."

The two hoods left the office.

"How many political contracts have you put out on politicians this year?" I asked Arnie.

"Enough to see that the wrong guys don't get back into office."

"You're in a cold-blooded business," I said.

"Everyone we have a contract out on knew what he would be facing if he double-crossed us."

Another hood came into the office. "Arnie, we just got a tip that the Anti-Lifers PAC has just put out a contract on Congressman Dreadnought in Arizona."

"So they want to go to mattresses, do they? How much have we put into Dreadnought's campaign?" Arnie asked.

"Two hundred thousand."

"Tell Sammy we're sending in another two hundred thou, and if he needs more to call. We can't lose Dreadnought in the next Congress. Who are they going to try to knock him off with?"

"Some woman schoolteacher from Tucson."

"Hit her," Arnie said.

"You mean you have a hit list for women politicians too?" I asked.

"There is no gender gap when it comes to political executions," Arnie said. "Look, this is a tough business. For every contract we've put out on a politician this year, there is a PAC that's put out a contract on one of ours. When it comes to the American political process, it's kill or be killed."

"And money is the ammunition?"

"That's the name of the game. The first thing you do when you put out a hit on a politician is break his legs financially. If he still won't listen to reason, then you let him dig his own grave."

"There's got to be a better way of electing our officials than putting out hit lists on their opponents," I protested.

"Nobody's come up with one yet," Arnie said.

The same hood came back into the office. "Senator Partridge's campaign manager is outside. He wants to know what he can do to lift the contract on his man."

"Tell him it's too late. The moment Partridge voted for mandatory seat belts he was a dead man."

The Poverty Line

The most dangerous place to be in America these days is anywhere near the poverty line. As the President's Task Force on Hunger reported, cuts in food assistance have not hurt the "truly needy," who are still being taken care of. But they have reduced benefits for many people "just above the poverty line."

Mabel Newbaum, a mother of five in South Succotash, is an example of someone who is having a tough time because she can't stay *below* the poverty line.

"The way things are going now, the nearer you get to the poverty line, the more trouble you're in," she said.

"In what respect?" I asked.

"Well, if you're way below the line, the government has to take care of you. And if you're way above it, you don't need help from anyone. But it's when you get close to the line that you're walking a tightrope. The main problem is no one is quite sure where the poverty line is. Every time you think you've found it, the government changes the guidelines."

"Would hunger be a test?"

"Not necessarily. Your family could be hungry, but if you own a TV set, they could still put you above the line."

"Where are you right now?" I asked Mabel.

"Last week I was eligible for food benefits for my family. But this week they added the benefits I was getting to my income, and decided that I was above the poverty line by this much," she said, holding her two fingers a sixteenth of an inch apart.

"Are you trying to tell me that without the food benefits you might have remained below the poverty line?"

"That's what the lady down at the welfare office said. She told me that as long as I didn't take my benefits I could qualify for them. But the minute I took them I went above the poverty line, and was no longer entitled to them."

"It's a kind of Catch-22 situation."

"It's a Crock-22 situation. I told the lady my kids were still hungry even though the government decided that we weren't poor. She said that she didn't make the rules. David Stockman had to draw the line somewhere."

"Why don't you quit your job? Wouldn't that put you safely below the poverty line?"

"I've thought about that, but I can't make it with five kids on government handouts. I also can't make it on my salary. What I

142

need is both. If the government would stop moving the poverty line up and down every day, I'd know where I stood."

Mabel continued, "Even President Reagan can't agree on who is poor and who isn't. I saw him discussing the homeless on TV and he said that the fact a person sleeps on a grate doesn't necessarily make him homeless, because many people in America like to sleep on grates."

"I think you're being too harsh on this administration, Mabel. After all, they have to cut the size of the budget. They can either do it by announcing that they're going to ignore the poor people—or by insisting that there are far less of them than anyone would like to believe. The latter method is much more palatable to the American people. That's why the poverty line is so important to the budget cutters. The fewer people they include below it, the fewer benefits they have to make available to them. That's just good Reaganomics."

"Yeah, but how does that put food on my table?" Mabel wanted to know.

"I wouldn't look at it from that angle," I said. "Aren't you proud that your government no longer considers you a poor person and a drag on society?"

"I suppose so," Mabel said. "But just because they arbitrarily put me above the poverty line doesn't mean I can pay my bills."

"Look on the bright side of things, Mabel. If they turn off your heat, you'll probably drop below the poverty line again, and then you'll be entitled to government assistance."

"Are you sure?"

"Well, they're certainly not going to ask your family to sleep on a grate—unless, of course, you want to."

You Can't
Win Them All

The complete collapse of the Lebanese army came as a surprise to most Americans, who kept being reassured by the Reagan government that it was in shape to take on the "peacekeeping role" assigned to it by President Amin Gemayel.

US military advisers in charge of training the Lebanese soldiers kept sending back optimistic reports that Gemayel's army was prepared to handle any situation.

What went wrong?

I asked a high-level official in the Pentagon if he had any ideas.

"The Lebanese army was well equipped, morale was high, and the average Lebanese soldier could be counted on to hold his own against any fighting man in the world," the official said.

"Then why did the army fall apart?"

"We didn't count on the fact that the Christian soldiers would not take orders from their Moslem officers, and the Moslem soldiers would not take orders from their Christian officers."

"Why not?"

"Because we found out recently that the Christians and the Moslems hate each other."

"Didn't we know that when we gave the army all that equipment?"

"Of course not. How could we know something like that?"

"It's been public knowledge for over a thousand years."

"It was our opinion that the religious differences would play no part once everyone wore the same uniform. We felt a soldier's loyalty toward his comrades in arms would overcome any antipathy one sect in Lebanon felt for the other. This proved true when everyone slept in the same barracks. Unfortunately it didn't when the army took to the field."

"Didn't you have any inkling that the army would fall apart when the soldiers were asked to fire on their own people?"

"No, we didn't. The first hint we had that things weren't going as we planned was when half the troops went over to the other side with their weapons. When we complained about this, the Christian officers gave orders to shoot the Moslem soldiers, and the Moslem officers to shoot the Christian soldiers. That's when we realized that we had a morale problem on our hands."

"Was the President informed about this?"

"I imagine he was. But our advisers were instructed not to worry about it, because the US Navy would fire on Syrian-supported rebel positions to protect the Lebanese army soldiers from killing each other."

"Apparently the strategy didn't work."

"There was a mix-up in signals. The White House said we were only firing at the Moslems to protect the peacekeeping force of US Marines, and the Secretary of the Navy said we were shelling the Druze to support Gemayel's troops. Before this could be straightened out, the Druze started their own offensive against Christian positions, and this was the signal for the Moslem soldiers to stop fighting."

"So now the Moslems have half our arms and the Christians have the other half. What did we accomplish by training the Lebanese army?"

"It gave the President an excuse to move the Marines out of Lebanon, something he's been wanting to do for some time."

"That's a big plus. But wouldn't you say that this was a blow to President Reagan's Mideast policy?"

"He doesn't seem to think so. After all, there is a lot more at stake in the Middle East than what happens in a tiny country like Lebanon. Once the Christians and Moslems settle their feud amongst themselves we can get back on the track again."

145

"What will happen to the US advisers that were training the Lebanese army?"

"They'll be sent to El Salvador to beef up the government's army there. We've had good reports the Salvadoran soldier can hold his own against any fighting man in the world."

Arm-Wrestling the Prez

My Uncle Phil called me from Fort Lauderdale.

"You know anyone at the White House?" he asked me.

"Well, yes and no. I know people there, but we've never munched any jelly beans together, if you get what I mean. Why do you ask?"

"I want to arm-wrestle the President."

"Are you crazy, Uncle Phil? You can't arm-wrestle the President of the United States."

"I not only can, I can take him—two out of three."

"Hold it. What are you talking about?"

"Didn't you see the picture in the paper? They showed this heavy guy named Dan Lurie, who edits a magazine called _Muscular Training_. He was in the Oval Office of the White House and they said he got there to present Reagan with a plaque as 'The best physically fit president of all time.' So, according to the papers, Lurie, who is sixty-one years old, challenges Ronnie to an arm-wrestling match and the President wins hands down."

"It seems to me I did see the picture, Uncle Phil. But what has that got to do with you wanting to arm-wrestle the President?"

"I'm seventy-five, and I'm sure I can beat him. I studied Reagan's grip in the photograph. His fingers were too widespread."

"Uncle Phil, I believe I ought to explain to you how the White House operates. They get thousands of requests from people who want to give the President plaques. When the one from *Muscular Training* magazine came in, they were going to dump the letter in the wastebasket when a Reagan political manager said, 'Wait. If the President gets an award for being the best physically fit president of all time, this will take care of the age gap once and for all.' "

Uncle Phil didn't seem to be listening. "I haven't lost a match since I moved to Florida. You know Sam Braunberger in apartment 2-C in my condo?"

"I don't believe we've met."

"He's a kid—seventy years old—and built like a brick wall. He has arms like the smokestacks at Three Mile Island. Last week I had him screaming and gasping for air on the gin rummy table in twelve seconds."

"Uncle Phil, you have to listen to what I'm saying. So they let Lurie into the White House to give the President a plaque. The White House photographer is there for the picture. Then someone jokingly says, 'Do something physical,' and Lurie, who is no dummy, says, 'How about arm-wrestling?' The Secret Service starts moving in on Lurie when the political manager says, 'Wait. It's a great idea, and the best photo opportunity we've had in a month.' One of the President's aides says, 'Stop. Suppose the President loses?' And the political manager says, 'Then we'll shred the picture.' "

Uncle Phil started taking in something of what I was saying. "So you don't think that the Oval Office arm-wrestling match was on the up and up?"

"I can't say that because I wasn't there," I told him. "Maybe the President won fair and square—after all, he does chop wood and clear brush on his ranch—but then again, maybe Lurie didn't push as hard as he could have. But look at it from his point of view. If Lurie wins the match, no one is going to know him and his magazine. If he loses it, he'll be on the front page of every newspaper in the free world."

"I never heard of a guy throwing an arm-wrestling match in my life."

"You never saw an arm-wrestling match where four Secret Service guys were standing around one of the participants."

"You're trying to tell me you can't arrange a match for me with the President?"

"The people running the White House have proved their point. I don't think the President will be arm-wrestling anybody else in the near future."

"So what do I tell the people in the condo?"

"Tell them it wouldn't have been worth your trip to Washington because even if, by some wild chance, the President agreed to arm-wrestle with you, and you won, no one would ever know."

Operation-of-the-Month

The latest news from the medical world is that hospitals are having more difficulty attracting patients. Occupancy rates are down and many institutions are now resorting to advertising and hiring marketing personnel to get people to use their beds.

The competition is getting fierce, and no one can predict what kinds of perks a hospital will offer to get a patient to make use of one of its rooms.

I visited a marketing consultant who works for one of the major hospitals in the Washington area.

He was very excited about a new idea he had just come up with.

"What do you think of an Operation-of-the-Month Club?" he asked.

"It sounds good," I told him. "What do you get if you join?"

He showed me a full-page layout he had designed. Bannered on the top: SAVE ONE THOUSAND DOLLARS ON EVERY OPERATION. *Join the Operation-of-the-Month Club.* Then there were photographs of different parts of the body and large type: WHEN YOU JOIN YOU ARE ENTITLED TO ANY ONE OF THESE OPERATIONS FREE. Then in smaller type: *All you have to do is have four operations a year, and you will be entitled to another AT NO COST TO YOU.*

"Wow," I said, "that's really a buy. How does it work?"

"Every month we will have a distinguished panel of surgeons choose the Operation-of-the-Month," he said. "Let's say the main selection for April would be an appendectomy. You would get a notice in the mail that it is being offered. If you don't return the card within ten days, we'll send an ambulance to your house and whisk you off to the hospital and perform the operation for one-half of what it would cost if you just went in and asked for one."

"Suppose I don't want an appendectomy?"

"Then you will have the choice of thirty alternate selections, anything from a tonsillectomy to implanting a pacemaker, at the same low prices. And remember, you only have to choose four a year and you get a free one as a bonus."

"What an ingenious marketing plan! I know as a member of the Book-of-the-Month Club, I always forget to send the card back and I'm stuck with the main selection. I'll bet the same thing happens with the Operation-of-the-Month Club. Will major medical pay for my membership?"

"I'm working on that now," he told me. "The savings from our operations as a club member should be very attractive to all the medical plans."

"How do the doctors feel about it?"

"Most of them are very excited, because they'll get a large advance. For example, if an artificial hip is chosen Operation-of-the-Month, the hip specialists stand to make a fortune, particularly if the surgery becomes a best seller."

My friend showed me the mockup of the *Operation-of-the-Month News Bulletin.*

"When you become a member you will receive fifteen issues of this beautiful colored, illustrated magazine outlining the various operations the hospital performs and biographical information on the surgeons who perform them. We'll also have reviews by medical critics of the various surgeons' techniques."

"Here's one on Dr. Paramedic, reviewing his skill at removing gallstones."

My friend read it to me. "Doctor Paramedic has performed two thousand gallstone operations in his time. Once he gets a scalpel in his hand, he can't put it down. Fast paced, and riveting, a Paramedic gallstone operation is a must for someone who is looking for an exciting operation, with no pain. *The New York Times* says, 'When it comes to gallstones, Paramedic is in a class by himself.' "

"You've got this all thought out," I said admiringly. "If the Operation-of-the-Month Club catches on, hospitals will never have to worry about filling their beds again."

He seemed pleased with my reaction. "I'll tell you what. If you sign up as the first member, I'll arrange a hernia operation for you for nothing."

"But I don't need a hernia operation," I told him.

"Then choose one of the alternates. It's all the same to us."

To Sleep—
to Dream

I went over to the Justice Department the other day at about eleven o'clock, walked into the antitrust division, and found everyone sleeping.

I woke up one of the attorneys.

"Sir," I said, "I'm sorry to disturb you, but I have some important news for you. Standard Oil of California is buying the Gulf Oil Company."

"You woke me up to tell me that?"

"I thought it could be important. SOCAL and Gulf are among the largest firms in the oil business, and the merging of the two is certainly a violation of the antitrust laws."

The attorney at the next desk said, "Hey, Harry, will you guys hold it down? I'm trying to catch a few winks."

Harry said, "This guy says SOCAL is going to buy Gulf, Frank."

"So what? It's a free country." Frank yawned.

"Yes," I said, "but if you let two oil Goliaths merge you'll be stifling competition."

"What concern is that of ours?" Frank wanted to know.

"I just thought the antitrust department of Justice should be alerted. Isn't it your job to see that there is competition in the marketplace?"

"You mean you want us to *sue* SOCAL to prevent them from buying Gulf?" Frank asked. "What kind of antitrust lawyers do you think we are?"

"If we stuck our nose into every two-bit takeover case in this country we'd clog the courts with work," Harry said.

I protested, "This is not a two-bit takeover case. It's going to cost SOCAL thirteen billion, and it won't produce one cup of new fuel for the country. You can't let oil companies eat each other up without a fight."

Frank said, "We didn't do anything about Texaco taking over Getty. Why should we interfere if someone is taking over Gulf?"

"Takeovers are good for business," Harry said. "They drive up the company's stock and a lot of lawyers get rich overnight."

"But what about the public?" I said. "How do we benefit from competition when two companies in the same business make a sweetheart deal with each other?"

Frank took a Twinkie out of his drawer and started nibbling on it. "If we thought the merging of two of the largest oil companies in the world would hurt the public, we'd be in court right now. But a marriage of this kind should benefit everybody. It could put a damper on these ruthless gas-price wars that are cutting into everyone's profits."

Harry said, "And it will be a warning to the independent stations to stop giving away free car washes when you buy a full tank of gas."

"What about the banks?" I asked. "SOCAL wants a fourteen-billion-dollar credit to buy Gulf. That's fourteen billion the banks can't loan to other types of companies that might create jobs and invest in new equipment."

"That's not our concern," said Harry. "Our job is to see that the antitrust laws are not violated. There is nothing in the Gulf takeover that will hurt competition in the marketplace."

"What have you people done in the last four years to stimulate competition in the marketplace?"

"We broke up the phone company," said Frank proudly. "And there isn't a person in the country who isn't better off for it. If you don't believe me, just wait until you get your bill next month."

No Exit

A person's vote used to be the most sacred thing in his life, and the one thing he was permitted to do in privacy. Not anymore.

When Joe Procter walked out of the voting booth on election day, he was surrounded by six people with clipboards.

"What's your religion?" one person shouted.

"How old are you?" another demanded.

"How much money do you make?" someone else wanted to know.

"Hey, what's going on?" Procter said.

"We're conducting an exit poll," one of the clipboard people replied. "We want to know who you voted for."

"I don't think that that's any of your business," Procter said.

"What do you mean it isn't any of our business? We have to know so we can report it on television."

"I don't want my vote shown on television," Proctor said.

"We'll report you for interfering with the electoral process," someone said. "It's your duty as an American to tell us how you voted."

"And also to reveal if you're married or single, and whether you're a conservative or a liberal."

"And why you voted for one candidate as opposed to the other."

"Says who?" Procter demanded.

"The public has a right to know. How can we tell who won the primary if you won't answer our questions?"

"Why don't you wait until the ballots are counted?" Procter asked.

"We can't do that or the other networks will scoop us. Americans don't have time to sit around until the ballots are tabulated."

"Well, they're going to have to wait if they want to know how I voted," Procter said.

"Okay," said a clipboard holder. "If you won't tell us who you voted for, will you tell us who you voted against?"

"Not on your life."

"Does that mean you voted against Mondale?"

"I've got to go home for lunch."

"Don't be hardheaded. We're not going to use your name. If you didn't vote for Hart just tell us why."

"I'm going to call a cop."

"Does that mean you voted for Glenn because you think he's stronger for law and order?"

"Hold it. There are two things in my life that I can do in privacy—and one of them is to vote secretly for the candidate of my choice."

"What's the other?"

"Go to the bathroom, which is what I've got to do right now."

One of the pollsters shouted, "If you don't answer our questions, you're threatening the sanctity of exit polls."

"If you're not talking, that means you voted for Jackson," another person said.

"Why don't you all buzz off?"

"You can hang tough if you want to, but Tom Brokaw is going to hear about this."

"If you won't play the game, don't ever ask Dan Rather for a favor."

"You could cost Jennings and Brinkley their jobs."

"Is that all you have to say?" Procter asked.

"No, there is one more thing. Don't ever meet Sam Donaldson in a dark alley."

Political
Advertising

The group from Argyle, Argyle and Sox Advertising Agency was ushered into Senator Dimblebutton's office. They were there to get the account for Senator Dimblebutton's political race.

"Senator," said the vice president of AA&S, "we've worked on a campaign that is going to knock your eyes out."

The AA&S creative VP said, "We're going to give you something that your opponent doesn't have."

Two flunkies set up an easel and put a large white sign covered by a cloth on it.

"Get ready for this, Senator," a VP said.

The cloth was removed. There was one large word: MOMENTUM.

The advertising men all looked at the Senator for his reaction.

"That's it?" the Senator asked.

"What do you mean, that's it? This is going to get you reelected for the next six years. Our research people have been working on this campaign for six months. The one thing they discovered that every voter in your state wanted was momentum. No candidate who has ever run for public office ever lost a race if he had it, and no candidate has ever won if he lost it."

"How do I get momentum?" the Senator wanted to know.

"That's our job. We'll run commercials, plaster billboards, and place newspaper ads, and every one of them will say that you have the Big Mo."

"But where's the beef?"

"Show him the videotape of a proposed TV commercial, Jerry."

Jerry inserted a videotape into the machine.

A runner wearing a big "M" on his sweatshirt came on the screen, jogging along a freeway. He said, "My name is Senator Dimblebutton and I'm running for a third term. If I am reelected I will give this state something it has never had before—momentum." The jogger started to speed up and passed a car with a driver who looked exactly like Dimblebutton's opponent, and as the TV commercial ended, Dimblebutton was fifty yards ahead of the car.

"It says it all in thirty seconds," the VP said.

"Don't you want me to do any TV commercials stating where I stand on unemployment, the Soviet threat, and how the big interests are taking over the country?"

"You'd be wasting your money. The only thing the voter is interested in is a candidate's momentum. If a candidate has it everybody wants to be on his or her side because America likes winners."

"I see your point," the Senator said. "But aren't we putting all our eggs in one basket with a momentum campaign? Couldn't we have some backup commercials emphasizing my charisma?"

"Charisma is old hat. Look what it did to John Glenn. This is new, this is fresh, and if you don't mind my saying so, with your voting record, momentum is the only thing you've got going for you."

"It's not just the advertising campaign that will put you over," the VP said. "The media are crazy about a candidate who has momentum. Look at Gary Hart. Before he ran in Iowa and New Hampshire, no one knew he was in the race. But after those victories, the press could talk about nothing but Hart's M Spot. How did the political pundits explain it? Very simply. They said Hart had momentum and Mondale lost it."

"Okay, you persuaded me," the Senator said. "How much will it cost me?"

"Ten million dollars, including the jogging suit."

"That's a lot of money."

"Senator, that's the beauty of momentum. Once the lobbyists think you have it, the campaign money starts dropping from the sky like acid rain."

Exit Polling in Russia

Have you ever wondered how the Soviet elections would go if American political methods were applied?

"This is Dan Ratevich reporting to you from the Soviet Broadcasting System with a special edition on the elections. With only point-oh-one precincts counted, SBS has declared Mikhail Gorbachev the winner in a surprising landslide election.

"With us in our studio now is Vladimir Gallupsky, one of the Soviet Union's leading political pollsters. Vladimir, explain to us exactly what happened."

"For one thing it was a very large turnout, which is always a good sign for the Communist Party. Gorbachev's popularity crossed all age groups, from the young hooligans to the old-time Stalinists. Labor strongly supported him and so did the army. But I believe that the deciding factor was the unexpected big turnout of the KGB at the polls."

"To vote?"

"No, they just turned up there. They stood next to the ballot boxes to *watch* the people vote. As soon as the undecideds saw them they weren't undecided anymore."

"So you believe that Gorbachev owes his victory to the KGB?"

157

"Dan, no Soviet leader has ever been elected without the support of the KGB."

"Thank you, Vladimir. Now let's go to an exit polling station and talk to Alexander Novisty, who is standing by in Kiev with a voter who has just cast his ballot for Gorbachev."

"Dan, I'm here with Comrade Mikhail Dobrinsky, a steelworker from the Lenin Foundry. Comrade, what was it about Gorbachev that made you decide to vote for him?"

"He's young, and he has new ideas. I was sick and tired of hearing the same promises from the same old Soviet politicians every election year. I decided to vote for someone who could get the country moving again."

"Thank you, Comrade. Dan, I will now talk to someone who didn't vote for Gorbachev. He's in the police van over here, and although our cameras can't see him, I'll put the microphone up to the grille. Comrade, can you tell us why you didn't vote for Gorbachev?"

"How did I know they were going to do exit polling?"

"If you didn't vote for Gorbachev, who did you vote for?"

"I left my ballot blank. I put it in the box, stepped outside to light a cigarette, and the next thing I knew I was inside the police van."

"How many people are in the van with you?"

"Three dissidents, four enemies of the state, and two counter-revolutionaries who keep yelling, 'Where's the beef?' "

"Alexander, this is Dan. I have to interrupt. We're going to switch live to Gorbachev's headquarters in the ballroom of Hotel Moskva where Roger Muddnikov is standing by. Roger, there seems to be a lot of celebrating going on."

"It's a madhouse, Dan. The Gorbachev supporters have been screaming and shouting ever since you declared their candidate a winner. I hope to speak to the new Secretary of the Party when he comes down, which should be any minute. He must be arriving now because the orchestra is playing the theme song from *Rocky*. Here he is. Comrade Gorbachev, would you say that this has been the biggest night of your life?"

"It's been a long hard battle from the first primaries in the cold steppes of Siberia in February to our squeak-through by the Caspian Sea in November. The turning point for me was the debates."

"We didn't see any debates."

"They all took place in the Kremlin. You don't think we'd show them on television, do you?"

"Comrade Gorbachev, forgive me for asking the tough questions, but that's the Soviet media's job. Why do people believe that so many Soviet politicians are phonies?"

"What is your name?"

"All right, if you won't answer that one, how about doing your imitation of Yuri Andropov?"

"Comrades, this is Dan Ratevich. Because of technical difficulties we seem to have lost Roger Muddnikov. We'll return to him as soon as possible—but then again, who knows?"

Let's Have Lunch

The trouble with foreigners in this country is that they take everything Americans say literally. I have a French friend named Michel Bernheim. I met him the other day on the street, and after the usual chitchat about Paris I said, "Give me a call sometime."

The next day he was on the line.

"Bonjour," he said. "It's Michel. You said to give you a call."

"I did?"

"Oui, don't you remember? I spoke to you yesterday on Pennsylvania Avenue."

"I didn't mean for you to give me a call right away. I was just finding a nice way to say goodbye to you."

"Then you don't want to talk on the telephone?"

"I can't think of anything to say, frankly."

"But you asked me to call you."

"You're right, Michel. Look, I'm terribly busy right now. Let's have lunch sometime."

"I would like that. When?"

"I'm not sure. Why don't you give me a holler?"

Two days later I heard someone calling my name from the sidewalk. I opened the window in my office and Michel was down below.

"What in the devil are you shouting about?" I yelled down to him.

"You said to give you a holler when I wanted to have lunch. How about today?"

"I'm busy today."

"Well, when _can_ you have lunch?"

"I'm not sure. I'm tied up for the next three weeks."

"Why did you tell me to give you a holler when I wanted to have lunch if you were so tied up?"

"Michel, you've been around long enough to know when an American says, 'Let's have lunch sometime,' he doesn't necessarily mean it. It's a pleasantry. The French say, 'Au revoir,' the Germans say, 'Auf Wiedersehen,' the Spanish say, 'Hasta Mañana,' and Americans say, 'Let's have lunch,' which in our country means, 'Don't call me, I'll call you.' "

Michel said, "I didn't mean to bother you."

"You didn't bother me. I'll tell you what. Let's check in with each other and have a drink one of these days."

"That would be great," Michel said.

I was sweating out a column the next day when the door opened and Michel stuck his head in.

"Now what?"

"I'm just checking in to see if you wanted a drink."

"Can't you see I'm busy?"

"I can see that now, but I couldn't before I checked in with you."

"Michel, you're driving me nuts. You can't take everything we Americans say as gospel. The only reason I said, 'Let's have a drink sometime,' is because I wanted you to stop hollering under my window about us having lunch together."

"All you have to do is tell me you won't want to see me," Michel said in a hurt voice, "instead of asking me to meet with you all the time and then breaking the date."

I felt bad. "You're right. I feel terrible about the way I've treated you. Our problem is that we're so used to saying goodbye to each other with a promise we'll get together soon, that no one in this country expects the other person to keep it. We wouldn't be able to get anything done if we had lunch with everyone we accidentally met on the street."

"I understand," Michel said. "But if you change your mind, you have my card and you can call me."

"I don't have your card, Michel. That's another thing you don't understand. When Americans exchange business cards with each other, they usually throw them away when they get home."

Death of a Salesman

THE DEVELOPING COUNTRIES ARE SLOWING THEIR RUSH TO RE-ARM, SPELLING LEANER TIMES FOR ARMS MERCHANTS —headline in *The New York Times*.

Willy Loman arrived home from his trip around the world and dropped his two large sample cases in the hall.

His wife Linda rushed out to meet him. "How did it go?" she asked, although she could tell the answer by the look on his face.

"I didn't get a nibble," Willy said. "It used to be that I could walk into the capital of any Third World country with a pressed suit and a shine on my shoes, and come back with a couple of billion dollars in orders. But now I'm lucky if a minister of defense will even look at my line. I think I've lost my touch."

Linda took his coat. "It isn't your fault, Willy. I heard on the radio this morning that Third World countries can't get the loans to buy arms like they used to in the go-go days of the seventies."

Willy said, "My arches are killing me. I almost closed a deal with King Hussein for sixteen hundred Stinger antiaircraft missiles. It would have made the whole trip worthwhile."

Linda asked, "What happened?"

"The King got sore at Reagan, attacked the US, and said he'd probably buy the stuff from the Soviets. Hell, ten years ago he was on his knees *begging* me for anitaircraft missiles."

"You gave it your best, Willy."

"My best isn't what it used to be. Damn French are underselling us in Iraq, the British are telling their Commonwealth countries that our F-16s are kites, and the West Germans are giving all sorts of credits on their Leopard tanks to the South Americans."

"What about Brazil? You always used to be able to sell Brazil tons of guns."

"Brazil's broke. Besides, they started their own arms business and now they're exporters."

"You never came back without an order from Argentina," his wife said.

"They got a new government in Argentina. The military junta that was thrown out had stockpiled enough arms for eight Falkland wars. It used to be when I went there everyone in the defense ministry would say, 'Willy Loman is here.' And I'd walk by all the other arms salesmen right into the commanding general's office with a big smile on my face, and he'd say, 'Get out your order book, Willy. Have I got a shopping list for you.' Now the general's in jail, and this time when I showed up, they all laughed at me. No one pays attention to me anymore."

Linda said, "Oh, come on, Willy. Everyone likes you. Didn't

you tell me the King of Saudi Arabia took you to dinner after you sold him the AWACS?"

"That was two years ago. This time I tried to get in the palace and some third cousin stopped me at the gate and said that because of the oil glut, the King wasn't in the market for any stuff anymore. I tried to show him a Northrop F-20 in my sample case and he slammed the gate in my face. If I can't make a sale in Saudi Arabia, where can I make a sale?"

"What about India? They always gave you an order."

"They used to, but now they're buying from the Russians. I don't know, maybe I should buy a new suit. I just don't seem to have it anymore. There was a time when I could sell a squadron of torpedo boats to the Filipinos, and they didn't even ask about the price. Now to make a sale they want a ten-percent kickback for their orphans' foundation, thirty percent deposited in some damn numbered soup kitchen in Switzerland, and ten percent for their brother-in-law's church mission in Luzon. I can't go back to the home office with an order like that."

"Willy, you're tired. Tomorrow I know you'll get something. I hear the war's heating up in El Salvador. And Libya could invade the Sudan, and they'll always want arms in Lebanon. And don't forget Taiwan and China, Willy. The Third World is always going to need arms salesmen, and you're still the best in the business."

Biff, Willy's son came in. "How did you do, Dad?"

"Great. I did just great. The King of Morocco told me last night, 'Willy, if I ever get a loan from the US again, I'm going to buy every cruise missile in your sample case.' "

The Forty-Million-Dollar Man

All I know about sports is what I read in the newspaper. Not long ago headlines bannered the signing of a Brigham Young quarterback, Steve Young, for forty million dollars by the Los Angeles Express, a USFL franchised football team.

Details of the contract varied in different sports pages as to how the money would be paid. The one story I read said the payout would be over a period of forty-three years. The article did not indicate whether Mr. Young would have to play for forty-three years or not. But I can't believe that any professional football owner shelling out forty million bucks would not expect a quarterback to play out the full life of his contract.

Since Young is now twenty-five years old, I can see him playing up to his reputation for the first fifteen years.

But then things could start getting a little tough, when he approaches the forty mark.

The first sign that he isn't the quarterback he used to be might come in a key game in 1999 against the Chicago Blitz. Young is intercepted for the fourth time and his coach is steaming mad.

"What happened?" screams the coach.

"I don't know. My shoulder seems to hurt. I could use a few weeks off."

"We can't give a forty-million-dollar quarterback a few weeks off. You're costing us so much money we can't afford a backup quarterback. Now you go out there when we get the ball again and get us three touchdowns!"

Ten years later Young, at fifty, his knees having been operated on fourteen times, hobbles onto the field. He is sacked nine times. A new coach is frothing at the mouth.

"Why didn't you scramble on that last play?" the coach cries.

"I tried to but I just don't seem to have the moves I used to," Young says.

"Don't give me that. You're the highest-paid quarterback in football. We wouldn't have signed you if we thought you couldn't scramble."

"My knees are killing me."

"We'll give you another operation when the season is over. But right now you better play football or we'll trade you to the Alaska Eskimos. The owner didn't pay forty million bucks to see his quarterback fall all over the ground."

Ten years later, at sixty, Young, with two artificial knees, two artificial hips, and one artificial shoulder, is still calling signals for the Los Angeles Express. He calls for a screen pass in the huddle, and then tries to hand off the ball to his fullback, whose assignment is to block a tight end. The ball drops to the ground, Tampa recovers, and goes in for the score.

This is too much for the owner of the Los Angeles Express, who rushes down from his box and starts chewing out Young.

"What are you doing to me?" the owner demands.

"I'm sorry, sir. It's just that it's getting harder and harder for me to remember the plays."

"That's what you're being paid for. Do you think that I shelled out forty million for a quarterback who doesn't even study his play book?"

"I study it, but I forget. Sir, is there any chance of getting out of my contract?"

"A contract's a contract. You've still got eight years to go. I've got a lot of money invested in you, Young, and I'm not going to let you go now, just when you're hitting your prime."

Eight years later, it's Young's last game.

He has had two cataract operations, a pacemaker implant, a

kidney transplant, and is taken in and out of the game in a wheelchair.

Two linemen have been assigned to hold him up when he gets the ball. On the first play, the entire defensive line of the Georgia Gorillas breaks through and smashes Young to the ground.

When he doesn't get up after five minutes, the Express sends out the paramedics, who wheel him off the field on a stretcher. As they work over him, the reporters say to the owner, "Was he worth forty million?"

"In retrospect probably not. But you never know about these things until you play the guy for a while."

Like Old Times

A wonderful thing happened to me a while back. I turned on the set and got to see Richard Nixon on television again. After it was over, I said to my wife, "He looks great. Doesn't he look great?"

"He looks just like the old Nixon," she agreed. "He hasn't changed one bit, except possibly he's more mellow."

"He does seem to have mellowed," I said. "But every once in a while, when he was talking about the people who gave him the shaft, you got the feeling that the old Nixon spark was still there."

My wife took my hand in hers. "You miss him, don't you?"

"Of course I miss him. Who wouldn't miss Nixon? He was the greatest president we ever had. If it wasn't for him, you wouldn't be sitting here tonight in your ermine-lined bathrobe, and I wouldn't be wearing Sulka silk pajamas and Gucci slippers."

"Watergate was good to us," my wife sighed.

"It was the best," I said. "Just seeing Nixon on the air brings back so many memories."

"Do you think he's sorry?" she asked.

"Sure he's sorry. Didn't you hear him say he was sorry he didn't burn the tapes?"

"I mean sorry about Watergate."

"I think he is. He said it was a dumb thing to do in the first place, and then he said it was a dumb thing to try to cover up, and then he said he was sorry the CIA didn't keep the FBI out of the inquiry, and you got the feeling he's very sorry about the people who talked when they should have kept their mouths shut. But he doesn't seem to hold any malice toward those who drove a stake into his heart. Then again Nixon was never a hater."

"I had the feeling he still holds a grudge against the media for driving him from office."

"I didn't get that," I said. "Nixon has been a pragmatic man all his life. If there is one thing he believes, it is that your enemies are always out to get you, so you have got to get them first. But as far as carrying grudges, it's just not in the man's nature."

"Will you ever forget the night he told us on television, 'I am not a crook'?"

"He was the first president in our history to say it. He reassured the country in its darkest hour."

"I wonder why he'd go on television at this time?"

"I suppose he wanted to set the record straight. There were so many illegal things they discussed during the cover-up, that Nixon wanted the public to know how much of it he personally rejected. What I liked about him tonight was that he said he didn't reject them because they were wrong, but because they wouldn't work."

"You can't be more candid than that," my wife said.

"No one ever accused Nixon of lacking candor. But he has nothing to lose now by personally taking the blame and saying that the advice he got from his lawyers was what really did him in."

"I believe him," my wife said. "Why didn't he have better lawyers?"

"They were all on the other side, trying to get the goods on him."

"I think it was very moving when he told about his last night in the White House and how he and Henry Kissinger got down on their knees and prayed together."

"It would have been much more fascinating if we knew what Henry was praying for."

He Had a Dream

The new trend in commercial real estate is to construct tall buildings as close to airports as possible. Washington's National Airport is a perfect example of this imaginative way of using what were once vast wastelands of air space.

Just across the Potomac River, in the small town of Rosslyn, is a silver tower reaching up to the sky; a beacon of welcome to all pilots attempting to land and take off from one of the busiest terminals in the country. A twin building is now going up next to it, so that soon there will be two towers instead of one to greet passengers arriving in Washington.

The father of airport skyscrapers is Alf Klagstrom, a developer who started out with fifty dollars and a dream.

I sat with Alf in his Cloud Suite on the 30th floor of the Klagstrom Tower, and he told me how he came up with the idea for his unique real estate development plan.

"I was selling mobile homes door to door in the early sixties," he said, "and did a lot of flying. I noticed that most major airports were out in the sticks, surrounded by farmland and ugly one-story buildings. There was no decent architecture within miles of the terminals, and no one seemed to care that all this good land was going to waste. 'Why,' I said, 'can't I develop a city close to air terminals so that businesspeople would not have to buck the traffic to catch their flights?'

"There was no godly reason for airports to be so isolated from the passengers they served. So I took an option on all the land at the end of the National Airport runway and hired an architect to develop a plan to make use of the air space.

"I told him I wanted something that would not only be utilitarian, but also beautiful to the eye, so that people flying in and out of National would be awestruck by what they saw."

"It's amazing you were the first to think of it," I said. "Very few people would have the imagination to build a skyscraper in the flight path of a commercial airport."

Alf said modestly, "I'm sure other people thought of it before I did, but no one had the persistence to follow through. Everyone was against me at the start. The banks laughed at me and said no one would want to rent space in a building at the end of a runway. When I told them all the footage had already been spoken for before I even broke ground, they were flabbergasted.

"Then I had to deal with the bureaucratic airport officials who complained that the skyscrapers could present a safety hazard to their flights. I told them people once said the same thing about the Empire State Building when it was proposed. I also argued that the skyscrapers would make pilots more alert when they were landing at National. To calm their fears I offered to put a red light on the top of all the buildings at my own expense."

"That was a very decent thing to do," I said. "Did you have any trouble with the Arlington County officials in getting a permit?"

"They were the only people on my side from the start. They saw the enormous tax revenues that commercial buildings would bring to the county, not to mention the jobs it would provide for people in the community.

"Compared to the federal government officials, who tried to stop me at every turn, the supervisors gave me encouragement during some of my darkest hours. Their faith in me has been rewarded. Arlington, which was formerly a bedroom community, now has one of the most beautiful skylines in the country."

"It must be a great feeling to see what you have accomplished in such a short period of time."

Alf said, "It's only the beginning. I've heard from counties all over the United States who want me to build skyscrapers next to their airports. I can see the day when every runway will be surrounded by glass and concrete towers, and high-rise hotels and apartment houses, creating an environment that will enrich the life of every American."

As we were talking, a DC-8 flew by Alf's window, its wing almost touching a large azalea plant out on the balcony. Alf waved at the passengers, who could clearly be seen through the windows. He said, "I'm making money on the deal, but the real thrill for me is to see the delighted expressions on the travelers' faces every time they fly by my building."

PART FIVE

SUPER BOWL VS. INAUGURATION

Super Bowl vs.
Inauguration

If anyone is wondering why the inauguration of the President of the United States was postponed from Sunday, January 20th, to Monday the 21st, all they have to do is go back to their history books and read about the creation of the Constitution of the United States.

Fifty-five of the founding fathers met in Philadelphia in the summer of 1787 to write the greatest document in the history of mankind. It wasn't easy, because every paragraph was fought over to protect the interests of the individual states.

One of the biggest stumbling blocks was when to swear in the President of the country. The suggested date for his inauguration was January 20th, and there didn't seem to be any argument about it until John Adams of Massachusetts stood up and said, "Suppose the January 20th falls on a Sunday, the same day as the Super Bowl is to be played? Do we still hold the President's inauguration on that day?"

The founding father from Rhode Island said, "I say verily the inauguration of the President of the United States must have precedence over the Super Bowl."

A founding father from Pennsylvania, who also owned a piece

of the Philadelphia Eagles, jumped up and cried, "The American people will never stand for it! They didn't fight a bloody revolution to see the Super Bowl be moved from Sunday to Monday. I say verily the Super Bowl be played on its traditional Sunday and the President have his inauguration at a less auspicious time."

Another founding father from Pennsylvania said, "Speaking for the Pittsburgh Steelers, I fully concur."

The founding father from New Jersey, who never dreamed the New York Giants and the New York Jets would one day move to his state, took the floor. "How can the United States become the most powerful nation in the world when it would put off the inauguration of its leader to pander to sports tastes of its countrymen?"

This enraged the representative from Georgia, who had received PAC money from the Atlanta Falcons. "Nobody in my state cares when they inaugurate a president, but everyone knows you only play a Super Bowl on Sunday. I cannot go back home and ask my people to ratify this Constitution if the day of the Super Bowl has to be postponed in the name of political expediency."

The founding father from North Carolina hooted. "What difference does it make to you? The Atlanta Falcons will never get to the Super Bowl anyway."

The house broke into booing and laughter.

George Washington, who was presiding and had no idea that someday an NFL team would be named after him, said, "I think we should table this matter for the moment until we can speak to football commissioner Pete Rozelle, to see if his feet are in cement on the January 20th date."

John Adams rose and said, "I can speak for Commissioner Rozelle, as I represented the New England Patriots at the last league meeting. He said he would be breaking faith with the millions of people in the thirteen states if the game was not held on a Sunday two weeks after the playoffs."

The founding father from Delaware roared, "The President

comes first—first in peace, first in war, and first in the hearts of his countrymen."

Alexander Hamilton, who had season tickets to all the New York Giant games, said, "The delegate can easily say that since Delaware could never support an NFL franchise if every person in the state came to every game."

The constitutional convention was in shambles and about to disintegrate when James Madison offered his famous compromise. "Gentlemen, in deference to the states that do not have NFL franchises, I propose we do not put it in writing that the Super Bowl have precedence over the inauguration of the President. But let us include in the minutes that it was the will of this body that if the 20th of January falls on a Sunday we wanted the Super Bowl to be played first."

The motion was adopted and the Constitution was saved. That is why President Ronald Reagan, a strict constitutionalist, was sworn in privately on Sunday, but his inauguration, according to the wishes of the founding fathers, was held on Monday.

Covert, Overt and Out

An old-timer from Langley, now living in a safe house in McLean, said of Nicaragua, "I've never seen a CIA covert operation more overt in my life."

"I was thinking the same thing myself," I said. "I thought you guys were supposed to have deep cover when you went into the jungles of Central America."

"That used to be the case. But present US foreign policy demands that we let the whole world know we're operating covertly to save El Salvador and bring down Nicaragua. President Reagan wants to make sure friend and foe are aware that the United States is actively involved."

"Why doesn't he just declare an overt war and let it go at that?"

"He needs Congress to declare an overt war. He's not going to ask for one during an election year. So the President is conducting a covert war, with all the fanfare of an overt one. The only problem is that when you conduct a covert war you have a lot of restrictions placed on you in order for it not to become overt. The mining of Nicaraguan harbors is a good example of that. The President said it was covert—the rest of the world considered it overt."

"And Congress cut off the CIA's funding for its war in Central America."

"It was a big mistake on the President's part, because up until then the House and Senate supported the CIA's covert operations in the hemisphere. You see, the object of fighting a secret war is that when something goes wrong, the government can say it knew nothing about it. But in the case of the mining, everyone in the administration defended it, and there was no way of dumping it on a wild rogue elephant at the CIA.

"The administration's strategy was, the more publicity the covert mining operation received, the stronger message we would be sending to the Sandinista government that we really meant business. Unfortunately, Congress got the same message."

"Does this mean that the CIA's covert war in Central America is over?"

"Of course not. But it will have to be done much more covertly. Funds for it will have to be channeled from money buried in the education budget, CIA agents will have to be given cover in the Honduran-American Coffee Bean Exchange, and President Reagan will have to shut up about how well his administration's covert operations are going in the Western Hemisphere."

"That's going to be hard for the President to do," I said.

"He has no choice. He needs congressional support for his

policy in El Salvador to train the army to fight the Nicaraguan-trained Salvadoran rebels."

"You mean the Nicaraguans are fighting a covert war against El Salvador at the same time we're fighting a covert war against Nicaragua?"

"Yes. The only difference is that Nicaragua is denying it, which I must say is to their credit."

"Why is that?"

"If you deny you're fighting a covert war, then everyone can pretend your country is not involved. But if you make a legal case for it like President Reagan did, and it goes sour, you're up a Central American creek without a paddle."

"What should the President have done when the mining story leaked out?"

"He should have been publicly horrified. Then he should have appointed a presidential commission headed by Henry Kissinger to see how such future incidents could be avoided. Finally, he should have told Bill Casey if the CIA was going to act in such a despicable manner, he didn't want to be his friend anymore."

"But the country needs a CIA," I protested.

"There's nothing wrong with having a CIA," the old-timer said. "But there is something wrong when it suddenly becomes the most overt agency in the government."

Argentina Bailout

As you may have read in the newspapers, Argentina was bailed out of a serious debt situation not so very long ago. It was advanced money by friends so that it could pay interest on its enormous debt.

While this was not big news, the fact that Mexico and Brazil came to the rescue caused a few raised eyebrows because they owe more money than Argentina does. How does a country that is broke itself borrow money to bail out another country that is also bankrupt?

It's all done with mirrors.

The Finance Minister of Brazil goes to a consortium of American and European banks and says, "We want to borrow fifty million dollars."

"But," protests the consortium, "you are into us for billions already. How can we loan you any more money?"

"This money isn't for us. It's to give to Argentina so that it can pay interest on its debt."

"Why would you want to give money to Argentina when you can't pay back what you owe us?"

"Because Argentina is our friend, and Latin Americans always help each other."

"That isn't a very good excuse for giving you fifty million dollars."

"All right, then, I'll give you another reason why you should do it. If you don't loan us the money to give to Argentina, she will be in default on all her loans and then the American and European banks will be stuck for the money."

"We're prepared to take the loss," the consortium says.

"Wait, there's more. If Argentina goes into default, then Brazil won't feel obliged to repay her loans. Are you prepared for that?"

"You're blackmailing us for fifty million."

"It's more than fifty. The Finance Minister from Mexico is outside, and he's going to ask you for a hundred million to loan to Argentina."

"But Mexico's broke too."

"Who isn't? If you people want to stay in the international banking business, you're going to have to continue loaning money to countries who want to bail out the one whose interest is due at that moment. Look, I'm not asking you to give me fifty million in a satchel. The money doesn't have to leave your banks. It will be purely a paper transaction. You take the fifty million that you're loaning Brazil, and you just credit it to Argentina's interest and you have it again to loan to somebody else."

"Does the United States government know what you're doing?"

"They put us up to it. They were afraid that if they bailed out Argentina by themselves it would set a precedent. So they got Mexico, Brazil, Venezuela, and Colombia to go along with the deal. Everyone looks good. The US doesn't have to resolve the problem unilaterally, and if we can loan money to another country it shows that we're not the deadbeats everyone thinks we are. And the consortium can carry Argentina for another six months on their books as a good customer."

"Suppose we give you the money? What happens when the interest payments on Brazil's loans are due?"

The Finance Minister of Brazil smiles. "Then it will be Argentina's turn to borrow the money from you to loan to us."

Sex and First Names

As if there weren't enough sex discrimination in the business world, a study by Rensselaer Polytechnic Institute says that women with sexy names have less chance of being selected for managerial jobs than those with nonsexy first names.

The study, conducted by Deborah Linville, a former graduate

student in industrial/organizational psychology, is titled "Prejudice Toward Women Applicants Based on Their First Names," and claims that men more often than women hold the traditional sex-role stereotype view about managers.

That stereotype: Managers should possess masculine characteristics, such as motivation and decisiveness, and that first names create expectations about people.

Ms. Linville asked seniors and graduate students at RPI, a popular training ground for Fortune 500 company managers, to rate the "perceived sexiness" of 250 female names on a scale from 1 (nonsexy) to 7 (sexy).

She did not define the word sexy, but left that up to the students.

They considered some first names sexier than others. For example, among the highest-rated sexy names were Dawn (4.8), Jennifer (4.8), Cheryl (4.9), and Michelle (4.8). The least sexy were Ethel, who only got a 1.0, Mildred (1.5), and Esther (1.8).

She then asked another group of students to play "boss" and rate job applicants with these seven names. The nonsexy applicants were chosen for employment and promotion over the sexy ones by a much larger margin of men than women, which made Ms. Linville conclude that men, when choosing women for jobs, are prejudiced by the perceived sexiness of their first name.

In case anyone is interested, here are some of the other first names that RPI men saw as "sexy": Alicia, Adrienne, Andrea, Candace, Christine, Gail, Heather, Holly, Jacqueline, Julia, Kathy, Maria, Marilyn, Melanie, Renee, Susan, Tamara, and Tina. Christine got a 5.08, the highest. There were no 7s.

If Ms. Linville's conclusions are correct, these women will have a tough time making it in a man's world.

Here are a few of the names that were seen as nonsexy: Alma, Cornelia, Doris, Edna, Elvira, Florence, Magdalena, Myrtle, Rosalind, Silvana, and Zelda.

These women will have no problems rising to the top of the corporate ladder.

So what are we to make of all this? There is nothing much one can do at this stage of the game unless a woman wants to change her first name. But if the prejudice continues in the business world, new parents may think twice when it comes to naming their daughters. If they give them "sexy" names, they may never see them rise to a vice presidency. If they give them nonsexy ones, their daughters could become very successful professionally, but might scare away nervous prospective suitors.

Of course, parents can compromise by giving a girl one of the first names that wound up in the middle of the Linville survey. Those polled disagreed as to whether the following first names were sexy or not: Anne, Audrey, Barbara, Betsy, Betty, Carolyn, Catherine, Charlotte, Elaine, Ellen, Faith, Hope, Jean, Jill, Joanne, Joyce, Laura, Linda, Marcia, Marian, Mary, Patricia, Priscilla, Ruth, Shirley, Virginia, Wendy, and Yolanda.

These first names may never make it to the top, but at least they won't starve to death.

Space forbids me from printing how all 250 first names were rated, and one should say that this is not the only criterion for promotion used in selecting women for responsible jobs. But Ms. Linville's study should be invaluable as evidence in a job discrimination suit. If an Ethel gets promoted over a Christine, although Christine has been in the organization much longer, I think Christine has got one heck of a case.

On the other hand, if Candace gets to marry the boss and Mildred winds up as only the controller of the firm, Mildred has nothing to blame but her first name.

Who Will Run the Country?

According to former Secretary of State Al Haig, he had tremendous problems in his job, not with the President, but with the palace guard in the White House that surrounded Mr. Reagan and protected him from "outsiders" such as Cabinet officers and the like.

I don't know why General Haig was surprised by this. When he worked in the White House for President Nixon, he did exactly the same thing.

The truth of the matter is that the United States is not run by the President, but by a closely knit staff, all unelected and none having to answer to anyone but the man who sits in the Oval Office.

Where does the President recruit his "team"? Usually from his campaign staff.

I was talking to one of the presidential candidate's baggage handlers the other day. He was perspiring and puffing as he kept putting luggage on a cart.

"You work awfully hard," I said. "'What do you hope to get out of it?"

"If I don't get a hernia, I'd like to be the White House National Security Adviser."

"That's a big job," I said.

"Well, you don't think that I'm doing this for my health, do you? Actually I'd like to be put in charge of all domestic affairs for the President, but that slot has already been spoken for by

Harry Silver, the candidate's advance man in Bethesda, Maryland."

"I would think that with your experience in handling luggage, you would want to be Secretary of Transportation."

"The power's in the White House," he said, loading a loudspeaker system on the cart. "Besides, Mary's been promised Transportation."

"Who's Mary?"

"She keeps track of the candidate's travel expenses. No one gets a voucher without first clearing it with Mary."

"If you don't get National Security Adviser, what about becoming the President's legal adviser?"

"The candidate wants someone in that office with more law experience. If elected, he's indicated that he'd give it to a paralegal who is in charge of seeing that the press always has fresh coffee on the bus."

"Appointment Secretary is a key position in the White House. Everyone has to come to you before they see the President."

He said, "I wouldn't mind it, but Allen Taylor has it lined up."

"Who's Allen Taylor?"

"He's in charge of stuffing envelopes in our Dallas headquarters. They say he's the best worker in the mail room."

"What about White House Director of Communications?"

"Ramey Harper, who works the mimeograph machine on the candidate's plane will probably get that. He understands the press a lot more than I do."

"And Chief of the President's staff is out of the question?" I said.

"I had a shot at it, but I lost the candidate's wife's luggage in Louisville, Kentucky, and she's been mad at me ever since. So I imagine that the candidate will give me something where I won't have to deal with her directly."

He finished loading the cart and started to count the bags to make sure everything was on before he pushed it toward the plane.

"Suppose you don't get the job you want in the White House? You will have put all this time in for nothing."

"Maybe, maybe not. Nobody on the candidate's staff has spoken up yet for Director of the CIA."

The Price Is Right

There is some question as to whether NBC paid for an exclusive interview on the "Today Show" with Colonel Qaddafi after the Libyan Embassy shootout in London. CBS claims they were originally offered Qaddafi for five thousand dollars and turned it down. But CBS did pay a half million dollars for a three-part interview with former President Nixon.

It is obvious that the price of exclusive interviews with world figures will soon be an important part of the "news" business.

Every world leader worth his salt will eventually hire show biz agents to haggle over fees for appearing on American TV.

"Hello, Gerry, this is Sam at the William Darkness Agency. Are you sitting down? How would you like the Ayatollah Khomeini, on his rug, for five minutes tomorrow night?"

"How much are you asking for him?"

"One hundred thousand dollars."

"You're crazy, Sam. We got Qaddafi for five thousand."

"Qaddafi is a bush-league terrorist. Khomeini hasn't been seen on American television for a long time. He's willing to dump on the United States and the Soviet Union, and declare a Holy War on China. If you don't want to deal I'll call ABC."

"Do I have your word that he won't appear on any of the other networks for six months?"

"You have to be kidding. If you want an exclusive it will cost you two hundred thousand. Look, we're talking about one of the most hated men in the Western World. You want ratings, you have to pay through the nose."

"Okay, we'll take him. Who else have you got for next week's morning show?"

"How about Madame Marcos? She knocked them dead on '60 Minutes.' "

"Will she talk about the Aquino assassination?"

"She'll talk about anything if the price is right. Cable TV offered me seventy-five thousand and I turned them down. Madame Marcos is one of a kind, and I'm not going to sell her for scale."

"For that kind of money we're going to ask the tough questions."

"She's used to tough questions."

"Okay, we'll book her."

"Gerry, are you sitting down? How about Klaus Barbie? I can let you have him for fifty thousand. You'll be the first network to interview the Butcher of Lyons. You could put him against 'Love Boat.' "

"He's not that well known in the States."

"Okay, forget Barbie. Would you go for a package deal of Assad of Syria, Arafat of the PLO, and Fidel Castro?"

"What will it cost us?"

"Seven hundred and fifty thousand. The other networks have expressed extreme interest, and the only reason I'm mentioning it to you is that they won't guarantee the show for prime time, which is the only way my three guys will go on."

"Let me get back to you on that. What have you got in your American stable?"

"I can give you Louis Farrakhan, but he's real hot now and it'll cost you."

"Will he promise to stay off the other news shows if we sign him?"

"If the price is right, he belongs to you people until the elections."

The End of the Sexual Revolution

The Sexual Revolution, according to *Time* magazine, is over. It started in the sixties and apparently was fought to a standstill. Finally, according to the magazine, both sides got tired and have now given up.

I remember the beginning of the Sexual Revolution as if it were yesterday. Three friends came over to my house and told me quietly, "The revolution begins at midnight. Are you with us or against us?"

"I'm with you. But for heaven's sake, what took you so long?"

"We had to wait for the post–World War Two babies to grow up. Now we're ready to overthrow the bourgeois mores of the forties and fifties."

I went upstairs to the bedroom and put on my old Marine uniform, which had been hanging in my closet since Japan surrendered to the United States.

"What are you doing?" my wife wanted to know.

"If you don't let it out of this room I'll tell you," I said. "The Sexual Revolution is going to start tonight and I'm signing up."

"But you're too old," she said. "Sexual revolutions are for young people."

"You're never too old for a sexual revolution," I said gently. "I just couldn't face myself in the morning if I knew there were so many kids out there fighting for it and I was sitting safely at home. Besides, they need a cadre of experienced GIs from the big war to show them how to do it right."

"What about our children?"

"I'm doing it for them," I told her. "I want them to grow up in a world where they can be free of the dogmas and restraints that our generation was saddled with. I want them to have opportunities that were beyond our wildest dreams. Someday, when the battle is won, I hope they'll be proud of the role I played in shaking off the sexual taboos and restrictions of the past."

"But suppose you don't come back?"

"Then hang this gold-framed picture of Hugh Hefner in the window."

My friends took me down to the recruiting station. "What do you want, Pop?" a bearded fellow in a sweatshirt and blue jeans asked me.

"I want to join the Sexual Revolution."

He laughed. "You couldn't even pass the physical."

"That's how much you know. I'm in better condition now than I was in 1945. Test me."

"We don't have time for that. We have too many recruits already."

"Look, drop me behind the front lines—Vassar, Radcliffe, Sweet Briar. Experience counts a lot more than age."

"We're sorry, Pop. The Sexual Revolution doesn't trust anyone over thirty."

"All right, so don't send me to the front lines. But let me serve in some capacity. Maybe I could be a forward observer?"

"The only position we have for guys your age is in a 'M*A*S*H' unit in the rear, to take care of the sick and the wounded."

"You mean I won't see any action?"

"No, but the wounded and sick need love too."

So I was assigned to the 450th 'M*A*S*H' unit at Berkeley, where some of the heaviest fighting of the Sexual Revolution took place in the late sixties. The kids were brought in on stretchers, most of them in shock, and wasted by fatigue. A sexual revolution sounds very glamorous when it begins, but when you see what it does to the bodies and minds of young people, you quickly get disillusioned. After a few years I decided I couldn't take it anymore and asked for a psychiatric discharge. They gave it to me with a Good Conduct Medal.

I'm glad *Time* magazine has declared the Revolution over. We should have pulled out the troops long ago, because it was one war that no one could ever have won.

The Beauty
of Star Wars

The beauty of the Star Wars defense system is that everyone can discuss it with authority, because no one, including the people in charge, have any idea of what it is.

I realized this when I attended one of those Washington cocktail parties where the power elite gather to exchange gossip and information that only decision-makers are privy to.

"Is it true," I asked a source, who has one of the largest offices in the Pentagon, "that Star Wars will become a bargaining chip in the Soviet-American arms talks?"

"Nuts," he said defiantly. "If we ever decide what it is, we will never give it up."

"Isn't it easier to give something up in arms talks that we *don't* have, than something that we *do?*"

"Not if they have it and we don't."

"Do the Soviets have a Star Wars defense?"

"They must have or they wouldn't want us to give up ours."

"Maybe they don't have it, but hope we'll go ahead with it anyway," I suggested. "Did it ever occur to you that the reason the Soviets are making such a big thing of it is because they want us to spend all our money to develop it, so we won't have any left to make the weapons they *don't* want us to build?"

"Of course it's occurred to us," he said. "But our answer to them is there's no price you can put on national security. Once we figure it out, all our other weapons will be obsolete."

"How can you say that when you have no idea what it is?" I asked.

"We may not have any idea what it is, but we do know what we want it to do—and that is blow up every Soviet missile before it hits its target."

"That's a tall order. Will Star Wars be able to do that?"

"We may never know, but neither will they. Once we install it in the sky, no one will have the slightest idea if it can do the job. But it will keep the other side guessing. And that's the best deterrent there is."

A man who has one of the largest offices in the White House joined our group. "The President wants Star Wars because he believes once we develop it we will no longer have to depend on mutual terror to avoid nuclear war."

"But the President says he doesn't know what Star Wars is either," I pointed out.

"He's not a scientist and doesn't claim to be one. But he believes in it more than anything he has ever advocated. Besides, since he's proposed it, he has to go ahead with it, or he would be sending another wrong message to the Soviets."

An assistant secretary, who has one of the largest offices in the State Department, said, "Even if Star Wars doesn't pan out the way we envision, it will still be worth the cost just to show our NATO allies that we have no intention of leaving them in the lurch. If nothing else, it will strengthen the West's commitment to repelling the Soviet military threat."

"Then our allies are for it?"

"They are as long as it doesn't cost them any money."

A labor secretary said, "When you're talking about Star Wars, you're talking about the hundreds of thousands of jobs it will provide for the next twenty years. It's not just a dream, but a shot in the arm for every defense contractor in the nation."

"I take it then," I said, "that everyone in the government is sold on it?"

"They better be if they want to keep their jobs in this administration."

"But how much will it *really* cost?"

The Pentagon man tittered. "When it comes to funding Star Wars, the sky's the limit."

Going for the Gold

The United States has a very serious problem. It doesn't want the Russians in El Salvador, but it does want them in Los Angeles.

The Soviets, according to President Reagan, are running all over Central America, but they don't want to send one weight lifter to the Olympics.

The State Department is now working day and night to reverse this situation.

"What do you plan to do about the problem?" I asked one of the American diplomats working on the impasse.

"We're in touch with Moscow and our message to them is that we have no objection to them testing us in Los Angeles, but we take a serious view of them competing with us in Central America."

"The Russians say the reason they won't come to L.A. is that it's too dangerous for their athletes."

"We're trying to tell them that they've read our signals all wrong. They're in physical danger in Nicaragua and Cuba, but they have nothing to fear if they show up in California."

"I'm not too clear on why Ronald Reagan is unnerved about the Soviets being in El Salvador, but is not afraid of them in Los Angeles."

"The reason is quite simple. Los Angeles is farther away from Washington than El Salvador is from Houston. The President is very hurt that the Soviets have decided to boycott the Olympics because they feel they won't get enough protection here. Russian lives are sacred to Mr. Reagan when they are in the United States. At the same time we have informed the Soviet leaders that they are not going to win any gold medals if they keep swimming in our hemisphere."

"I guess both messages coming at the same time must have Moscow very confused."

"I don't think so. We want the Soviets to compete in the Olympics. We'll give them all the visas they request to come to Los Angeles. But we're not going to give them permission to send one more hammer thrower into Central America."

"Maybe the Soviets are retaliating because we refused to go to their Olympics in 1980."

"We had a very good reason for not going to Moscow at that time. They invaded Afghanistan and we wanted to send a strong message that we wouldn't stand for this outlaw behavior. Just because we wouldn't go to their Olympics is no reason for them not to come to ours."

"I understand that the other reason the Russians decided not to come to L.A. was because of the smog. Have you been able to assure them that there would not be any smog in Los Angeles if they agreed to compete?"

"There's always smog in Los Angeles. The Soviets damn well know that. We consider this excuse a red herring. If you want the truth, we suspect that one of the reasons they are not coming is because they will have to be tested for steroids. Everyone knows their athletes are full of it."

"Do you think the Soviets are using steroids in Central America?"

"We have a strong suspicion that they are. But it's the arms they are shipping to the rebels and not the steroids that we're concerned about," he said.

"I know this is a crazy idea, but if the Soviets are in Central America and we're there also, why don't we just move the Olympic Games from Los Angeles to El Salvador?"

"That's the most stupid thing I've ever heard. Suppose the Russians come to El Salvador for the Olympics and then refuse to leave after the games are over? What do we do then?"

"What guarantee did we have that they wouldn't stay in L.A. after the Olympics were over there?"

"None. And frankly, we think that that's the main reason the Soviets decided not to come."

Chariots of Mongolia

It was a body blow to the West when the Soviets pulled out of the Olympics, but it was nothing compared to what happened when the news reached Mongolia.

While the Soviet athletes had to accept their government's decision whether they liked it or not, it wasn't easy to persuade Outer Mongolia's only long-distance runner that he wasn't going to Los Angeles.

Genghis Khan was jogging out in the Gobi Desert when his track coach, Yurt Temugin, rode out on his camel twenty miles to break the tidings.

"How am I doing?" Genghis asked, hardly puffing.

"You're doing fine. But we just got word from Ulan Bator that Mongolia is withdrawing from the 1984 Olympics."

Khan was flabbergasted. "You're putting me on."

"I'm not, Genghis. We received orders from the KGB to tell you to stop running. The Russians are pulling out, and they told us we have to support their boycott or else."

"You mean I've been pounding barefoot on this hot sand for four years for nothing?"

"What can I tell you, Genghis? The Kremlin says they're doing it for your own good. They were afraid that if you went to Los Angeles your life would be in danger."

Khan said, "Who would want to hurt a Mongolian in California?"

"Genghis, it isn't for us to question the decisions of Moscow. But if the Russians don't field their team, we can't send ours."

"Why not? We don't have any quarrel with the United States."

"If we showed up and they didn't, it would be a signal to the West that the socialist nations are in ferment."

"Good. Let's go."

"It's not that simple. They won't fly us out of the country."

"Maybe I could run to the Caspian Sea and pick up a foreign freighter? It would be good practice for me."

"I'm sorry, Genghis, but you're going to have to live with the idea that you won't be competing this time."

Tears formed in Kahn's eyes. "This means I won't see Lana Turner. You promised me that if I trained real hard I could meet her in California. My dream for four years was that she would be in the stands cheering for me when I crossed the finish line."

The coach dismounted from his camel and put his arm around Khan. "I know exactly how you feel. I was hoping to meet Claudette Colbert. I loved her last movie, *It Happened One Night*, which just showed in Mandal Gob. But there is nothing we can do about it. The Politburo is getting even for what the United States did to us four years ago in Moscow."

"If they weren't going to Los Angeles, why didn't they tell us in 1980, so that I wouldn't have calluses all over my feet?"

"I can't answer that question, Genghis. You know the Kremlin never tells Mongolia anything."

Khan put his head in his hands. "I could have been a contender. I could even have won a gold medal. I could have seen Disneyland. I might have even been invited by Joan Crawford for a weekend in Malibu."

"You must never mention these capitalist thoughts when you get back to Ulan Bator."

"Why do I have to go to Ulan Bator?"

"The Soviet Minister of Athletics wants you to hold a press conference for Soviet television telling the Russian people how happy you are that their Soviet leaders have chosen not to participate in the games in Los Angeles. He wants you to profess solidarity with all the working peoples of the world who will not compete against the capitalist lackeys while they threaten world peace in every part of the globe. If you say what they tell you to, they will give you a special Olympic gold medal they've minted for every athlete who doesn't compete in Los Angeles."

"It's not the same as seeing Lana Turner," Khan said.

"But it will still be better than training for the next Olympics in a Ulan Goom Gulag for four years."

Right Number, Wrong Car

What is the most important thing a person needs to succeed in business?

According to the advertisements I see, it's a cellular telephone.

The cellular phone will give you the edge over your competitors because you can keep in contact with your office and your clients *at all times.* You can confer with your staff while you are on the highway, dictate to your secretary while you're in a traffic jam, and call anyone in the world while you're waiting to be tanked up with gas.

The cellular phone differs from your ordinary car telephone in that you don't need a radio operator. You can dial direct just as you would on your home phone, and people *can dial you* while you are in your car. Pretty soon the entire country will be ready for cellular phoning. So what's wrong with it?

Every advertisement I've seen for this communications marvel shows the person holding the phone in one hand and the steering wheel in the other.

To my knowledge no instructions are issued with the phone on how to dial a friend and avoid an accident at the same time.

I'm not saying that this *will* happen whenever you make a call, but there are occasions when phoning and driving don't go together.

One is when your mother calls you in the car.

"Harold, where are you?"

"Fifth and Elm, in Bethesda. Why are you calling me now?"

"I was worried about you. I hadn't heard from you in three days."

"I'm sorry, Ma, but ever since I got my cellular phone I've had more business than I can handle. It's given me a tremendous advantage over my opposition."

"So how do you take the orders down?"

"I write them down, Ma, on my clipboard, which is attached to the telephone."

"Tell me, son, if you have one hand holding the phone, and one hand writing down the orders, who's driving the car?"

"I'm driving the car with my elbow."

"You think that is a good idea?"

"I haven't had an accident yet. Listen, I don't want to talk too long because I'm waiting to hear from a guy on *his* cellular phone. He said he'd call me back about the time I got to Rockville."

"Then you think it's progress with all the crazies on the road to be driving with one hand or an elbow on the steering wheel?"

"Ma, you don't realize how the cellular phone is going to change people's lives. Before, we used to sit in our cars listening to the radio or thinking all sorts of thoughts. Now we don't have to waste that valuable time. Every minute is precious when you're closing a deal."

"You still didn't answer my question. How do you keep from running into a lamppost when you're driving with one hand and dialing with the other?"

"Only a mother would ask a question like that. You know I'm a good driver."

"It isn't you I'm worrying about. It's the person who owns one of those phones who can't drive with *two* hands that could be a menace. Maybe Ralph Nader should look into it and start asking some questions."

"Don't get Ralph Nader into this. If he had his way we businessmen would still be making our calls from pay booths. Look, I have to hang up. I just saw Sam Kaplan on his cellular phone and he's after the same account I am. I've got to call the office and find out what's going on."

"All right, son. But please do your mother a favor."

"Anything, Ma."

"Dial carefully."

Help Wanted

A Pentagon auditor charged in a document made available recently that the armed forces pay outrageous prices for weapons because the officers in charge of procurement are hoping that when they finish their careers, they can get a job with the defense contractor they are dealing with.

Those who play along with the defense industry are rewarded with cushy positions when they leave the service, and those who gave the contractors a hard time need not apply for a job when they retire. The average retirement age for a middle-ranked officer is forty-three, so whether they like it or not, military officers in charge of procurement have a bigger stake in their futures than in saving their government money.

This is how the scenario is played out.

"Colonel Druthers, we have a slight overrun on the armored dogsleds you contracted our company to build for you."

"But you said you could produce them for five hundred thousand dollars. Now you're telling me they're going to cost a million seven hundred thousand apiece."

"We overestimated the strength of the dogs and underestimated the weight of the armor they had to pull. So we had to add an engine in the back to push the sleds along."

"But that's outrageous."

"It certainly is, and believe me, the chairman is furious about it. He's fired the manager of the dogsled program."

"Who is taking his place?"

"We're looking for somebody now who will bring it in somewhere near the price I just told you. We'd like a person familiar with the weapon carrier, preferably a retired military officer who knows procurement and is willing to work his heart out for a hundred and fifty thousand a year, plus bonuses and stock options. Of course the person would have to live in California, but we'll pay all his moving and living expenses for the first year."

"I've been working on the military side of this program for three years. I pushed it through singlehandedly and I'll never make general when I tell your budget people about the overrun."

"What happens when you don't get your star?"

"Then I'll have to retire and find a job."

"Maybe we could help you."

"The law says I can't work on any military program I've been involved with while I was in the service."

"We have many other military weapons programs you could handle. Our chairman is always looking for good soldiers."

"That's very kind of you, but I've checked your figures on the dogsled project and they're way out of line."

"In what way?"

"You charged us for a million-dollar chalet in Aspen."

"We had to test the dogsled somewhere."

"And twelve million dollars for a private Gulfstream Three airplane."

"How are our research people going to get to Aspen? By the way, when we're not using it on the dogsled project the plane is available for our other program managers and their families."

"I'm going to have to show these expenditures to my superiors before I okay them."

"Colonel, you don't look like a whistle-blower to me. If there is one type of person our chairman won't hire, it's a whistle-blower. He's told me time and time again, 'I'd rather have ten retired military officers who can't read a balance sheet than one rotten apple who knows how to run a cost-effective program.'"

"I gather then that if I don't go along with your figures, I don't get a job."

"I didn't say that. But the last colonel who complained about cost abuses in one of our weapons programs is now selling shoes at Macy's."

"Are you sure you can bring these dogsled armored vehicles in at a million seven?"

"You have my word for it, Mr. Vice President."

"Vice President?"

"Didn't I tell you? The title comes with the job."

No Golden Arches

I have a friend who is a hospital administrator. When I saw him the other day he was very depressed.

"I've just been to my hospital's board meeting," he said. "They okayed a five-million-dollar nuclear scanner but refused to let me pay forty-five thousand for a new chef."

"Why is that?"

"They said that food has nothing to do with medicine, and the hospital was losing too much money on the kitchen as it was."

"You would think that decent meals would have as much effect on people getting well as anything else in a hospital."

"I tried to make that case, and they all looked at me as if I were crazy. They said sick people don't really care what they're served. Since there was so much pressure on the board to hold costs down, the only place they could cut them was in the food."

"Can't you get the medical staff of your hospital to help you get some decent meals for your patients?"

"The doctors are afraid to speak up when it comes to the food because they believe that if we spend more money feeding our patients it will stop the hospital from buying new equipment. They've told me, off the record, that they try never to make their rounds while the patients are eating off their plastic trays, because it makes them sick to their stomachs."

"Why do you believe hospital food has traditionally been so bad?"

"Very little research has been done on the subject. If a patient doesn't eat, the doctor usually prescribes more tests to find out what is wrong. Instead of sending more blood down to the lab, they would probably find the answer if they sent the meal down and had it analyzed. I'm sure they would be shocked when the results came back."

"But there must be some learned men in the medical profession who are aware that the food going into their patients could be delaying their recovery."

"They're reluctant to speak up because all their colleagues would laugh at them. I know one physician who did a study with sick white rats. He fed half of them a typical hospital meal consisting of a piece of gray boiled fish, a half-cooked portion of noodles, and Jell-O in a paper cup. The other half were fed broiled shrimp, chicken and matzo balls, and a French crème caramel on china plates. The rats that had the boiled fish refused to eat their meals and got sicker, and the ones who ate the chicken and matzo balls became well in no time. With scientific evidence to prove his case, the doctor delivered a paper before the American Medical Association, proposing medical institutions put as much money into their food as they do into their equipment."

"What happened?"

"Blue Cross brought him up on charges of malpractice for trying to bankrupt the American hospital system."

"I can see where that would discourage all future research in nutrition."

"One of the biggest problems in trying to improve the quality of hospital food is that medical students have no choice but to eat hospital food when they are in training and they lose their taste buds before they complete their residency. Therefore, many of them are oblivious to how bad it really is. I've seen patients in my hospital who have taken their plastic trays and thrown them on the floor in rage. Instead of a doctor trying to find out why he did it, he prescribes tranquilizers to calm the person down."

"Do you think if hospitals served better food, the patients would get well faster and be out of the hospital much quicker?"

"It's hard to say because no hospital has ever been rich enough to afford it."

When a Bank Bounces

It was the legendary Willie Sutton who, when asked why he robbed banks, said, "That's where the money is."

Willie's reason may no longer be valid. Some time ago a well-dressed robber walked into the Heritage Bank in Anaheim, California, and handed a note to a woman supervisor which read, "Give me all your money or I'll start shooting."

The supervisor indignantly informed the robber that Heritage had no money and had gone bankrupt recently. The man walked out in disgust.

What the newspaper story could not report was what happened when the robber got in his getaway car and drove off.

"So how much did you get?" his partner asked.

"Nothing," was the reply. "They have no money."

"What do you mean they have no money? All banks have money. The Heritage Bank is the largest one in Orange County."

"What are you yelling at me for? They're insolvent. The depositors have been paid off and the Feds are now liquidating the place."

"Why didn't you know that when you decided to pull the heist in the first place?"

"I cased the joint for three days. The reason I picked it was there weren't any guards around. I thought they were just being careless. It turned out there was nothing to guard. I should have been suspicious when nobody bothered to lock the doors at night."

"But how can a bank go bust?"

"I guess they made a lot of bad loans and couldn't collect them. It's going on all over the country. If it's a big bank like Chicago Continental, the Feds get nervous and put more money in so there won't be a run on it. But in this case they decided to let it go out of business. Don't drive so fast. Nobody is chasing us."

"Why should they chase us? We came away dry."

"Don't get sore at me. It isn't my fault the bank screwed up. I wasn't the only one in there that didn't know they were out of money. Three people were trying to get loans, and one lady wanted to know what happened to an electric blanket they promised her when she opened her account."

"Banks should put signs up when they run out of funds. We could have been killed or gotten twenty years for trying to stick up a place that went under because of bad management."

"You just went through a red light."

"I always go through red lights after a bank robbery."

"But we didn't rob the bank. Technically we have nothing to fear. If they didn't have money it's their fault, not ours. I wouldn't be surprised if they failed to report it. The lady I gave the note to wasn't even frightened. She was just mad that I hadn't read the papers."

"You didn't by chance ask her what bank in the neighborhood might have some money in it, did you?"

"She was so rude to me, I just walked out. If she was typical of all the Heritage Bank employees, it's no wonder they went belly up."

"So what do we do now?"

"I don't know. I guess we're going to have to read the newspapers more closely and find out which banks are still in business and which ones are in liquidation."

"Do you still have the note you gave her?"

"Yeah. She handed it back to me and told me not to come in again. I assured her she had nothing to worry about on that score. I also told her I was going to pass the word to all my friends about robbing Heritage branches."

"What are you doing now?"

"I'm rewriting the note. I'm going to say, 'If by chance you have any money in the bank, give it to me or I will start shooting. Otherwise, disregard this message.' "

Nonfiction Reporting

There was a bit of a scandal at *The New Yorker* magazine. It appears that one of their writers, Alastair Reid, admitted to a *Wall Street Journal* reporter that he had created composite characters, rearranged scenes, and fabricated dialogue for nonfiction pieces he had written over the past twenty-five years.

This suprised many people in the journalistic world because *The New Yorker* has the foremost reputation for meticulously checking facts, even those in poems and short stories.

Mr. Reid justified his method of writing nonfiction by saying that when he played with facts, he was creating a reality that was more accurate than what actually took place. Bill Shawn, his editor, defended Mr. Reid.

While not wishing to judge *The New Yorker* one way or the other, I thought that the reader might be interested in knowing how the facts in my columns, and the standards applied, are checked before they get into print.

My highly paid staff consists of my assistant, Cathy Crary, and an eight-person fact-checking team that works on the floor just below me.

When I write a column it is immediately sent down to the fact-checking office to make sure everything I have said is true.

On many occasions I have written about private meetings between President Reagan and various members of the White House staff, quoting complete conversations that took place in the Oval Office.

Whenever one of the checkers calls me on this I say, "If you don't believe me, why don't you call the White House?"

When the checker does call the President's press secretary, he is invariably told, "I have no comment on that," which is just as good as a confirmation as far as Washington is concerned.

The least of my problems concerns the CIA, which will never confirm or deny a story no matter how wild it is. Therefore, while I insist that every fact in a CIA column is true, and since the agency won't say otherwise, the fact checkers have no choice but to permit the piece to stand as it is.

The Pentagon, on the other hand, will deny everything I write. Once I had a fight with one of the fact checkers because I said that the military was buying $7.50 hammers for $495. A red flag immediately went up, and the checker came charging upstairs yelling, "Who are you trying to kid? Nobody is going to pay $495 for a $7.50 hammer!" I calmly dialed A. Ernest Fitzgerald at the Pentagon, who not only confirmed it, but gave me a list of other tools that cost the taxpayer millions of dollars more than they were worth. Since then I've never had a problem with my fact checkers over any story I've written about waste in the military.

Not long ago I wrote a column about talking to God, who angrily refuted President Reagan's contention that God has been driven out of the public schools. One of the more skeptical checkers said he doubted that I had spoken to God. I told him the next time he went to church to ask Him. The checker came back on the Monday morning and apologized. He said, "I read the column to God and He admitted he did talk to you, and was only disappointed you didn't use the full text of His remarks in the article."

The only reason I am pointing out how rigorous we are in making sure that all the facts in my column are correct is not to gloat over *The New Yorker* embarrassment, but to assure the reader that everything he or she reads in my columns is checked and double-checked before it is disseminated to the public.

If I ever had to resort to fabricating dialogue or playing loose with the truth, I would never be able to look at myself in the mirror again.

Nathan the Innocent

Nathan the Innocent was a good citizen who knew nothing about the American Political System. All he wanted to do was get someone to stop a chemical plant from dumping toxic wastes in his cow pasture. He wrote to the EPA, his congressman, his senator, and the President of the United States.

EPA replied that they would look into the matter someday.

His congressman wrote that if he was reelected he would stop the dumping.

His senator said he would forward his letter to the EPA.

And the President thanked Nathan for supporting his policy in Central America.

"Why don't you go to Washington yourself, Nathan?" his wife pleaded. "Then they will listen to you."

Nathan the Innocent bought a ticket on People's Express and flew to Washington. He put on a suit and tie and went to the Environmental Protection Agency. The receptionist told him everyone was in an important meeting and suggested he come back in three months.

Nathan then went to see his congressman and was turned over to a summer intern who didn't know what toxic waste was because he was majoring in Chinese Literature.

The next visit was to his Senator. The receptionist said the Senator was out of town but gave him ten campaign bumper stickers which she suggested he distribute to his friends.

Finally, Nathan went to the White House. He asked to see the President to discuss his cow pasture. Since he wasn't violent, they took Nathan in an unmarked car to St. Elizabeth's Hospital for observation.

He was placed in a locked room with a Washington lobbyist who was suffering from deep depression. It seemed a bill he had worked on to make the MX launching pad into tax shelters had failed to pass.

Nathan told his story to the lobbyist, who said, "You are really an innocent. You can't come to Washington and just speak to anyone here. What you need is Access."

"What is Access?"

"Access is the grease that opens doors in Washington."

"How do I get this Access?" Nathan wanted to know.

"You make political contributions to the people who can help you. You can donate directly to your congressman, your senator, or the President, and indirectly by joining 'clubs' that have been set up to get around how much you can give the candidates. The more you donate, the more Access you will have."

"Doesn't that get expensive?" Nathan asked.

"Good government doesn't come cheap."

A few days later the psychiatrists decided that although Nathan was neurotic about toxic wastes, he wasn't a danger to the community.

He went back to his motel and wrote out checks to his congressman, senator, the President, and clubs such as Citizens for a Better America, The Fund for Honest Elections, Americans for the Little Guy, and the President's Golden Circle.

In two days he found all doors were open to him and everyone listened sympathetically to his problems and said they would get on it right away. He was even invited to the White House to watch the President issue a new EPA postage stamp.

Nathan the Innocent came home in triumph and told his wife, "The chemical company will never be allowed to dump toxic wastes in the cow pasture again."

"Good," said his wife.

"The bad news is I had to sell the farm to stop them."

"Why?" she asked.

"It was the only way I could raise the money to get any Access."

Archie Bunker's
Shock

Archie Bunker was sitting in his home in Astoria, Long Island, when he saw the news on television that Mondale had chosen

Geraldine Ferraro as his running mate. He let out a scream and Edith came rushing in from the kitchen.

"What is it, Archie?" Edith asked.

"That meathead Mondale has put our Congresswoman Geraldine Ferraro on his ticket as VP!"

"Isn't that nice," Edith said.

"You would say that. She's one of your people."

"I'm not Italian, Archie."

"I don't mean Eyetalian. I got nothing against Eyetalians. I mean one of *your* people—a woman."

"It's about time," Edith said.

"What does a dame know about running the United States of America?"

"What does a man know about it?"

"The vice presidency of the United States has always been reserved for a male. The founding fathers of the Constitution wanted it that way."

"There is nothing in the Constitution that says a woman can't be vice president."

"That's because at the time it was written no one in his right mind could imagine a meathead presidential candidate choosing one. But I'll bet you if you took a poll of the great men who signed the Declaration of Independence, they would have said, 'No women vice presidents or we give the country back to England.' "

Edith replied, "Mrs. Ferraro is a very smart lady. I rang doorbells for her when she was campaigning for congresswoman."

"You pushed one doorbell too many, and now look what we've got. A mother of three who could be a heartbeat away from the presidency."

Edith was losing her temper. "We represent more than half the vote, and we belong in the seat of power."

"That's the way your people always think. I knew we was in serious trouble when them women liberators was allowed to march in the street without the cops shooting tear gas at them."

"I wish you'd stop referring to women as 'my' people," Edith said.

"All right. I'll call them by their right name—dingbats."

"Archie, you have no right to call a woman vice-presidential candidate a dingbat."

"Why not? It's a free country, isn't it? Well, I'll say one thing. Since Mrs. Ferraro represents Astoria and Jackson Heights, she at least knows something about the Third World."

"That's not very funny, Archie. You should be proud that someone from our own district is running for vice president of the United States. Whether she wins or loses she's broken the mold once and for all."

Gloria, Archie's daughter, came rushing in. "Mommy, did you hear the news? Mondale chose a woman right here in Queens."

Archie said, "Another dingbat. They're all coming out of the woodwork."

"What's the matter with Daddy?" Gloria said to Edith.

"He's upset because Mondale chose one of our people as his running mate."

"One of our people?" Gloria said. "Are we related to Mrs. Ferraro?"

"No, your father is referring to our sex."

"I can't believe it, Daddy. You're living in the stone age."

"Edith is taking my remarks out of context. I got nothing against a woman running a country as long as she stays in England."

For Sale

There is now a big real estate boom in parking places in Washington. As more "No Parking Anytime" signs go up in the streets, people are desperate to have a parking spot they can call their own.

To find out about the boom I went to see a real estate agent who specializes in selling parking spaces. He had color photographs of various garages on his wall.

"I'm interested in buying a parking space," I told him.

"You've come at a good time. We have several outstanding ones that have just come on the market. May I inquire what kind of automobile you own?"

"A 1984 Volvo."

"Then you will want a quality parking spot in the upper range brackets. Here is one that was only used by the original owner. The garage is just five minutes from the Washington Monument, and your place would be on the first tier, right near the entrance."

"How big is it?" I asked.

"It's quite large, eleven by twenty-two feet. It is marked by lovely gold stripes and decorated with a handpainted 'Reserved' sign on the wall. Your Volvo will be very happy there."

"How much does it cost?"

"Since the owner is anxious to sell because he is moving to San Francisco, we can let you have it for twenty-three thousand dollars, not including maintenance charges."

"What are the maintenance charges for?"

210

"Heating, a twenty-four hour garage attendant, and keeping your space swept clean. Of course, you'll have to be passed on by a board of the other parking space owners, but I'm sure you won't have a problem, considering the make of your car and the year."

"Do you have anything less expensive in the garage?"

"I do have one on the fourth level down. It's a charming old parking space but does need some work."

"What kind of work?"

"The concrete is cracked and the white lines are fading, and during a heavy thunderstorm water seems to gather down there. But if your Volvo has been rustproofed I don't see any problem."

"How much is that one?"

"We can let you have it for seventeen thousand, which is a steal."

"It seems like a lot of money for a broken-down parking space."

"There are several advantages to being down on the fourth tier. Your Volvo won't hear the planes from National Airport overhead, and as you drive down and around you have a lovely scenic view of all the other cars parked in the garage. I have four parties interested in it now."

"Can I get a mortgage on it?"

"You'll have no problem at all. The banks consider parking places in Washington much better collateral than apartments and condominiums."

"Suppose I only want to spend ten thousand dollars for a spot. Do you have anything downtown for that?"

"We have a nine-by-sixteen-foot spot in a dark alley that has just come on the market. The front of your car would look out on a meatpacking plant and the rear would face an empty warehouse. I don't know if your Volvo would feel very safe there or not. Frankly, I would buy something with a roof over it."

"But it seems like so much money."

"You mustn't look at it as a financial burden. After all, owning your own parking place is the latest American fantasy."

211

PART SIX

"RIGHT-TO-BOMB" MOVEMENT

"Right-to-Bomb" Movement

I dropped in on a Right-to-Bomb antiabortion meeting the other night.

The speaker was holding several sticks of dynamite as he addressed his small but fervent audience.

He said, "Now, the purpose in blowing up abortion clinics is to show the country we're serious about saving unborn lives."

There was loud applause.

"Everyone talks about antiabortion, but nobody does anything about it. The Right-to-Bomb movement believes that marching and silent vigils are a waste of time, and the only way people will listen is if we make a loud explosion."

The audience laughed.

"Bombing abortion clinics is just another way of saying that we revere human life. We want to make our blasts so loud that every congressman and Supreme Court justice will hear them and know the Right-to-Bomb people mean business.

Loud applause.

"Blowing up bricks and mortar is nothing compared to killing millions of babies," the speaker said. "But if we don't prove the end justifies the means, we have no right to call ourselves pro-lifers."

The speaker continued, "The most important thing in blowing up an abortion clinic is making sure that your bomb works. Every time you set off a dud, you give aid and comfort to the criminals. Now are there any questions so far?"

A teenager got up. "I never made a bomb before. How do you do it?"

"After the formal meeting we will break up in study groups and our instructors will show you. It's quite simple once you get the hang of it."

A man raised his hand. "Suppose an innocent person gets killed when the bomb goes off?"

The audience booed the question.

The speaker smiled. "Naturally we hope no one gets hurt, but we have to expect some casualties when we're doing the Lord's work."

"Amen," we all said.

The next question from the floor was, "When we build our bombs, where do we place them?"

"Before you leave tonight we will give you a list of the abortion clinics in the neighborhood, and you can choose the one most convenient to your home."

"Suppose two of us want to blow up the same clinic?"

"All the better. Two bombs are better than one."

More laughter.

"If we get caught, will the Right-to-Bomb movement provide legal services?"

"We certainly will. Our lawyers are on twenty-four hour standby and ready to plead each and every one of you not guilty, no matter what the charge might be. But our goal is to get a law passed legalizing all abortion-clinic bombings. If we can't get it through Congress, we'll work for a constitutional amendment."

The audience got on its feet and broke into song: "All we are saying is, give bombs a chance."

The speaker raised his hand to quiet the crowd and said, "Let us pray for life."

We all bowed our heads.

After the prayer the groups went to their assigned bomb instructors to learn about explosives, fuses, and timing devices.

As I left to get my coat a man said to me, "What did you think of the meeting?"

All I could reply was, "Dynamite."

Nobody Has to Be Poor

If there are a lot of poor people in America, it's their own fault. Every time I open my mail someone wants to GIVE me money. The letters are addressed to me personally. Some enclose checks, and others certificates, bonds, and coupons.

Let me give you an idea of what my mail was like yesterday. I received one letter from an insurance company that was willing to pay me $1000 a month for the rest of my life if I came down with ANY kind of illness. I didn't even have to take a medical examination. "Yes, Mr. Buchwald," the writer said, "all you have to do is get sick and you will receive $1000 a month no matter what your state of health is at the present time."

The next letter was from First National Bank of Wilmington, Delaware. Thomas Campenni, the president of the bank, was offering to deposit in my account $50,000 as a line of credit, with no collateral up front, which I could use at my own discretion. To show me he meant business, he was even offering me an immediate cash advance of $2500 and a personalized checkbook which I could use against my account.

You can imagine how surprised I was to get this letter. For one thing, I've never lived in Delaware, and to my knowledge have never met Tom. But somehow he took a liking to me and decided he would trust me for fifty big ones, without my having to set foot in his bank in Wilmington.

I was about to send for the money when I glanced at the next envelope. It was a biggie. On the front was a great cellophane window which said, and I'm not making this up, ART BUCH-WALD SHALL BE PAID ONE MILLION DOLLARS IN CASH—GUARANTEED IN EQUAL ANNUAL INSTALL-MENTS OF $50,000.00 AND PAYMENTS MAY ACTUALLY DOUBLE TO TWO MILLION DOLLARS. There was a nice sketch of Ed McMahon on the envelope so I ripped it open.

Well, it was just as simple as it sounded. I had been assigned nine exclusive PERSONAL prize numbers and if I sent in the Gold Label I was eligible to participate in the American Publishers Sweepstakes. I would be guaranteed the money if one of my numbers had already been drawn. In a personal letter, Ed said that he would give me the check for the one million himself. I didn't have to subscribe to any of the magazines that Ed was pitching, but he indicated that I'd be a fool if I didn't.

Now unlike Thomas Campenni, I do know Ed McMahon, and he's a very frugal guy. Ed doesn't throw that kind of money around unless he means it. So I immediately sent in my prize-winning numbers to him and I guess it will just be a matter of time until Ed will send for me to give me my first down payment.

The other mail was peanuts compared to McMahon's letter. One brokerage firm sent me what looked like a US Treasury Bond which would go in my portfolio as soon as I opened an account with them. Hertz mailed me a platinum card which guaranteed a brand-new car would be waiting by the ramp when I got off my private plane at any airport in the United States. American Express enclosed a Gold Credit Card and informed me they had upped my credit to $25,000. A computer company wanted to send me $2500 worth of software as a gift if I bought one of their micros, and a publisher wanted to know how many books he could send me FREE if I joined his First Edition Club.

As I said, this was a typical sampling of my mail for one day. It wasn't a bad haul, but nothing out of the ordinary. On some days companies want to send me gold bullion from their vaults; other days I get digital watches from Indian reservations; and last week I got two free airline tickets from a real estate development company in Orlando, Florida.

There are thousands of firms and individuals who keep offering me something for nothing, and only a fool would not take advantage of their generosity.

So show me a person in this country who is always crying poor, and I'll show you someone who doesn't open his mail.

The Great Media Mystery

Sherlock Holmes tapped down the tobacco in his pipe and prepared to light it with a match. He was studying press clippings from Dallas.

Dr. Watson, who was playing "Trivial Pursuit" by himself, said, "Holmes, something seems to be bothering you."

Holmes replied, "You watched the Republican National Convention, didn't you, Watson?"

"I certainly did. Ripsnorting good show it was too. There was not a dull moment as far as I was concerned."

"Quite, Watson. But wasn't there something missing?"

"Missing? I can't think of what it could be. If anything, it had too much of everything."

"Too much of everything, and yet an important ingredient was lacking. Wait a minute, Watson. I think I may have it. Would you hand me that book on the shelf, *History of the Past Republican Conventions Since 1956."*

Holmes excitedly went through the pages. "That's it! It was right in front of our noses and we didn't see it."

"What did we miss, Holmes?"

"For the first time in modern history the Republicans did not attack the media. Not one speaker raged at the networks or Eastern establishment press. Everyone passed up a surefire opportunity to get a standing ovation by refusing to complain that the reporters were not giving their side a fair shake."

"By Jove, you're right, Holmes," said Dr. Watson. "It was a love feast. Usually the Republicans shake their fists at the convention network booths, and beat up on *The Washington Post* and *The New York Times.* What do you suppose turned them around?"

Holmes lit his pipe. "It's elementary, my dear Watson. Rather than attack the media this time, the Republicans decided to manipulate them. Whatever they wanted, the GOP gave it to them. They served up everybody for interviews from Jerry Falwell to Joan Rivers.

"All animosity toward network anchormen was absent. Vice President Bush called Rather 'Dan,' Nancy Reagan called Donaldson 'Sam,' Barry Goldwater called Brokaw 'Tom,' Jesse Helms called Brinkley 'David,' and Phyllis Schlafly called Lesley Stahl 'Honey.'

"Every Republican star was on a first-name basis with the interviewer. By playing the good guys, the Republicans wound up co-opting anyone who wore a press badge in Dallas."

"Amazing, Holmes. How did they get away with it?"

"There was no story in Dallas, my dear Watson. The networks were desperate to fill two hours of time every night, and the Republicans were more than happy to oblige them with such diverse right-wingers as Bunker Hunt and Jack Kemp. In the past the far right refused to talk to the press. This time they not only sought them out, but invited them to their thousand-dollar-a-plate parties."

"Why the change of attitude, Holmes?"

"It was quite simple, Watson. While the media and the GOP Convention had no choice but to suck their thumbs, the pack of journalists who passed up Dallas were going after Geraldine Ferraro and her husband, John Zaccaro. The Republicans didn't want to antagonize the press while they were so intent on nailing a Democratic vice-presidential coonskin hat to the wall. The GOP wrote the script in Dallas last week, but the real drama was being played in Queens, New York."

"So that's why the Republicans passed up an opportunity to make the media the scapegoats of their convention. What clue tipped you off to their strategy?"

"I became suspicious when all the media dogs were barking every time you saw Ferraro and Zaccaro on the TV screen. But not one of them barked in Dallas."

"Why didn't they bark in Dallas?"

"Between the heat, the tequila, and the speeches, they all went to sleep and gave the Republicans an opportunity to commit the perfect crime."

Cooking Numbers

I received a call from a friend in the Office of Management and Budget who said he had been asked to cook up a new batch of deficits for the elections.

"Nobody's here so it's okay for you to come over."

I found him in the OMB's test kitchen where they try out every new recipe before packaging it for the public.

"Here," he said. "Put these on to protect your eyes."

"What are they?" I asked.

"Rose-colored glasses. Everyone in the administration is required to wear them when cooking up government numbers."

"What's in the pot?" I asked him.

"Our new figures for the campaign. It looks like we're only going to have a hundred-seventy-four-billion-dollar budget deficit instead of the two hundred billion that we originally predicted."

"It smells fishy," I said.

"That's just because I put in tremendous portions of gross national product and added large tax revenues which we hadn't counted on this year. It tastes delicious."

He gave me a spoon and I tried it.

"It's not bad. But after all, you've only cooked this for the Reagan people. Will you be able to bring it in at a hundred seventy-four billion when you have to feed the whole country?"

"No question about it. For one thing we took out all the fat in government spending. With the economy really cooking along, interest rates ought to drop. The only thing that could spoil the recipe is if Congress keeps adding more ingredients than we need. If we can stick with what we've got, we can reduce the deficits to a measly hundred thirty-nine billion by 1989."

"Have you added any new income taxes to the recipe for the next year?"

"Not at the moment. The President can't digest anything that has new income taxes in it. The last time we served him a deficit stew with taxes in it, he spat it out and fired the chef."

"So you really think you can cook up a dish of deficits for a hundred seventy-four billion without adding any new taxes?"

"We can for the election, but we're keeping our options open for 1985. We might have to throw in a federal sales tax or a value added tax, but we're not going to announce it until after November."

"I still don't know how you created this so fast," I said.

"When you're cooking numbers you have to go on certain assumptions. For example, I figure that by adding optimism, the real growth in the pot will increase by four percent each year until 1989. Inflation will simmer at around four percent, and that means the government's borrowing rate will be reduced to five-point-one percent. That should make your mouth water."

"Mondale says those are unrealistic assumptions."

"What else would he say? He wants to be President. If he makes it, which we all doubt, he'll cook the figures just the way we have."

"He says you have a secret recipe for deficits that you're not telling the American people about, and what you're cooking up now is some voodoo stew that even Reagan's economic advisers can't stomach."

"It's not worthy of comment," the OMB man said. He then sprinkled one hundred large folders into the pot. .

"What did you just add?" I asked.

"Defense contracts. That's what gives the deficit its rich taste."

Church and State

The issue of the separation of church and state has reared its head once again. It may not be good for the state, but it's not bad for television preachers.

My favorite, the Right Reverend Rolls-Royce, devoted his entire hour to this subject the other morning. He said:

"I'm going to speak to you today about God, sin, and the American election. The secular humanists would have you believe that religion must not play a part in government—that we should not mix religion when it comes to reelecting the greatest President on this good green globe.

"Well, my friends, the Bible has something to say about this. What does the Bible say about state and religion? You can find out by sending fifty dollars for this velvet-bound, illustrated edition, which we have printed at cost to guide you in making what could be the greatest decision of your life. For those of you who can't afford this beautiful gold-trimmed book, we are offering a paperback edition for fifteen dollars so that no one can say he or she was not informed on the issues.

"Do religion and government mix? Well, I'm going to tell you a story. A man came to me last month and said he didn't think he was better off today than he was four years ago. He had lost his job, his benefits were running out, and he could hardly feed his family on the food stamps he was receiving. He told me because of his precarious situation he was confused and he didn't know whom to vote for in the elections.

"I told him when he goes into the voting booth, he must not think of his own petty problems. He must decide which party's platform supports God and which party's platform supports Satan. I gave him copies of both parties' platforms. Do you know what this man did after reading them? He gave me his last five dollars for a Reagan bumper sticker.

"The aggressive humanists would have us believe that the fathers of the Constitution deliberately set out to keep state and religion separate. Well, I'm holding a copy of the Constitution in my hand, the most beautiful political document ever devised by man. This document can be yours free, if you send ten dollars for postage costs and handling. It is printed on parchment with the First Amendment in bold red type. Whenever a humanist cites the Supreme Court on keeping religion out of the government, you can show him this document to prove the Supreme Court justices are wrong.

"My friends, too many of us take it for granted how blessed we are to live in a country under God. We're afraid to show our true feelings. But we have to shout to the world that we're the greatest so it can be heard all the way to the Kremlin. You may be asking how you can do this. You can do it by displaying this American flag. For just one hundred dollars, you can hang one of these flags in your window. I have personally blessed each of them, so you're not just buying an American flag, but one that was touched by God's hand.

"Don't just sit there and let the secular humanists turn this country into a communist state. Go to your phones now and call this toll-free number. If God didn't want you to have this flag, he wouldn't have let me accept your American Express, MasterCard or Visa cards.

"I want to conclude this broadcast by telling you about the wonderful prayer breakfast I attended in Dallas, where I heard the inspirational words of our great President. After the breakfast I went up to our Commander-in-Chief on earth to bless him. I would like to share that moving moment with you. My wife Lulubelle took an Instamatic photograph of the President shaking my hand. If you will send just twenty dollars, we will mail you a framed copy of that picture, which you can hang in your living room to show your friends. It is something you will cherish for the rest of your life. This is a collector's item, and the only picture in existence of Ronald Reagan and myself. The offer is limited to the first fifty thousand people who send in their checks. After that we will burn the negative and no one will be able to reproduce this miracle photograph again."

Losing Isn't
Everything

George Will, the columnist, and I used to be friends. When it came to politics we didn't always agree, but it never interfered in our social relationship. What broke up our friendship was baseball—the Chicago Cubs to be exact. George is a Chicago Cubs fan, a member of that very, very small band of brothers and sisters who, year after year, took pride in rooting for a team that had been in the cellar so many times the Preservation Society on Monuments had declared it a National Fall-Out Shelter.

George's charm was that he believed in the Cubs, who hadn't won a pennant since 1945. Every spring he would tell anyone who listened how the Cubs would rise from the ashes and regain their rightful place in baseball. To our credit, those of us who understood baseball never put George down. We always humored him and said, "Sure, George. This is the Cubs' year."

Whenever the Cubs won a game during the postwar years, George considered it a religious experience. One time the team was only sixty-three games out of first place during the middle of the season, and George had it figured out that if every other team in the National League lost every one of its games, the Cubs could win the pennant. As a believer in lost causes, George was in a class by himself.

Whether Will's faith in the Chicago Cubs affected his judgment concerning the political subjects he wrote about was something we never questioned. We just assumed that Will was able to separate his emotional attachment to the Cubs from his trenchant commentary. Except for his quirk about baseball, George made as much sense as any other conservative commentator in this town.

But something happened to Will. For reasons that no one can explain, the lowly Cubs started winning.

As they began climbing up in their division, George became more morose and nervous. He was short-tempered and bitter. He refused to discuss baseball and pretended he wasn't interested in the pennant race.

When he wasn't around, we discussed his sudden change in personality.

One of the pundits had a theory. "I don't think George is able to deal with success. He's so used to the Cubs losing that he can't live with the possibility that they may go all the way. After forty years of being a loser, he can't accept the fact that he might become a winner."

"It's even more than that," a Yankee supporter said. "Cub fans took pride in supporting a team that rarely won a game. They enjoyed playing the role of the underdog. If the Cubs go to the World Series, there will be nothing unique about them. The fans also resent the fact that after so many years of being shunned and laughed at, everyone is now jumping on the Cub bandwagon. Their privacy has been invaded. They lived in a fantasy world for so long that it's no fun when their fantasy has come true."

I decided to have a talk with Will. "George," I said, "all your friends are talking about you. You're not the same person you were before the baseball season started. We believe the Cub winning streak has gotten to you."

"Maybe it has and maybe it hasn't."

"You can't be mad at everybody just because the Cubs aren't losing. You've got to come to terms with the fact that they are winners. It was Vince Lombardi who said 'Losing isn't everything—it's the only thing.' "

"Lombardi never was a Cub fan," Will replied.

"That's neither here nor there. You should be happy your team is on top. You stayed in the cellar with them all these years. You now have every right to enjoy their success. We don't begrudge them winning, why should you?"

"I don't think it's anybody's business."

"But your attitude is affecting your work."

"How so?"

"Just the other day you wrote that Reagan would probably win the election. No one in his right mind would make a prediction like that unless he had truly lost his marbles."

God and School Prayers

I don't talk to God as often as I should because I know how busy He is these days. But every four years, during the presidential campaign, I do check in to make sure what the candidates are saying about Him is true.

After hearing President Reagan say for the umpteenth time that God has been expelled from America's classrooms, I asked Him, "Are You banned from America's schools?"

"Not that I know of," God replied.

"President Reagan said that kids can't pray in school."

"I don't know about that, but I hear schoolchildren's prayers all day long. Of course I hear more from those who haven't done their homework, or have been caught committing some infraction that will send them to the principal's office. And there is a lot of praying when report cards are sent home, and when college test scores come in. I can't understand why President Reagan said I've been banned from the classroom."

"I think he was referring to the Supreme Court decision which forbade organized prayer in public schools at the beginning of the day. Did that decision bother You?"

"On the contrary. I don't believe in people praying if they don't mean it. Fortunately in America people can pray any time and anywhere they want to."

"Well, why would President Reagan say that You were banned from public schools if You weren't?"

"I have no idea," God said. "People are always dropping My name in order to get votes during an election year. Frankly, I wish the President would have checked with Me first, before he misspoke."

"Do you believe it's a good idea to have separation of Church and State?"

"I believe it's an excellent one. Your country has survived for over two hundred years without getting Me mixed up in your government, and when you look around you seem to have more freedom of worship than any other place on the face of the earth. There are certain countries, which I'd rather not mention, where the leaders use My name to commit some of the most heinous crimes known to mankind."

"How would You feel about forced voluntary prayer in the schools in the morning, so if kids didn't want to pray they wouldn't have to?"

"It would bother Me. All My children are very fragile, and it would cause tremendous friction between those who prayed and those who didn't. I would prefer that schoolchildren pray when the spirit moves them, and not when a teacher tells them to. What your President should know is that God is everywhere, and when he states that I am no longer in the public schools, he doesn't know what in the devil he's talking about."

"Then You didn't tell him You wanted prayers officially back in the schools?"

"I certainly did not," God told me. "But I did talk to him about the asbestos problem."

"The asbestos problem?"

"It's very serious. A great many schools have asbestos peeling off the ceilings and walls, and it's getting into the schoolchildren's lungs, and they can die from it. I suggested that the President institute a crash program to see that the little children were protected from this terrible disease. But to My knowledge he hasn't mentioned it yet. If I were the President of the United States, I'd be much more concerned about the health of America's children than with what time of day they could pray."

"Well, thanks for Your time," I said. "I didn't want to bother You, but I was afraid that if I was against mandatory prayer in public schools You would think I didn't believe in You anymore. Could I put this conversation on the record?"

"Be my guest. There is too much talk by politicians about what I want and don't want and, as God, it really ticks Me off."

Washington News

Michael Jackson was in Washington not long ago for his concert, but it was really no big deal unless you turned on a television set or picked up a newspaper.

This is how all the local TV news programs seemed to play it.

"Good evening, ladies and gentlemen. Here is the news. Michael Jackson has just returned to his hotel room after a visit to a record store in Northwest Washington. For a live report we take you to Brent Studebaker at the Regent Hotel where the singer is staying.

"Brent, do you have any information as to what Michael is doing right now?"

"Grady, our latest information is that Michael is in his suite taking a nap before his concert tonight. We're going to get you a shot of the window of Jackson's suite on the fifth floor. There it is, Grady."

"Good work, Brent. We'll get back to you later in the program. And now for other news. Five thousand people were drowned in a tidal wave in Atlantic City, New Jersey, this morning. But before we give you further details on that story, Brent Studebaker has a bulletin from the Regent Hotel."

"Grady, I've received information from an impeccable source that Jackson has awakened from his nap and is taking a shower."

"Thanks, Brent, stay with it, and let us know what he does when he comes out of the shower. In other news, Fidel Castro arrived in Miami today and asked for political asylum. The dictator escaped from Havana after cadets from the military academy took over the government. We have a special report from Miami—no, delay that, we're going back to Brent Studebaker at the Regent Hotel. How does the situation look now?"

"Grady, it's quite calm here at the moment. Thousands of people have gathered in front of the hotel to get a glimpse of anyone from the Jackson family. Here is a T-shirt I just bought from a vendor and a Michael Jackson button."

"Thanks, Brent. Now this just in from Capitol Hill. A crazed gunman has taken over the floor of the US Senate and is holding all one hundred senators hostage until they meet his demands that they pass a bill outlawing seat belts on commercial airplanes. If we have time we'll try to get more information on the story. In the meantime, let's go back to Brent Studebaker, who informs us that Michael Jackson is eating dinner."

"Grady, I've been in touch with room service, and Jackson ordered a grilled cheese sandwich, a glass of milk, and apple pie à la mode. He gave the waiter a five-dollar tip."

"Did he sign the check himself, Brent?"

"We're trying to find that out now."

"And knowing you, Brent, I'm sure you will. Now this from

the United Nations in New York. Taft Huebner is standing live with Andrei Gromyko, who has just announced that the Soviets will come back to the Geneva arms talks under certain conditions. Come in, Taft."

"Mr. Gromyko, what exactly do you expect to tell the President when you see him?"

"I plan to tell him that—"

"Taft, Mr. Gromyko, forgive me for interrupting, but we have just received word that Michael Jackson is now leaving the hotel to go to RFK Stadium. We'll try to get back to you if we can. . . . Brent, is it true that Michael is about to depart?"

"Here he comes now. Michael Jackson is in the second limousine exiting from the garage and should be at the stadium in fifteen minutes."

"I can't see too well here, but did Jackson actually wave to the crowd?"

"Yes, Grady. He waved with his sequined glove. I think our camera crew was the only one who had it."

"Thanks, Brent. Once again you have done a fantastic job. We'd like to advise our listeners that President Reagan's press conference, in which he plans to announce a shaking up of his Cabinet, will not be seen tonight so that we can bring you Michael Jackson's arrival live from RFK Stadium."

"The Rest of Me Updated"

"Mr. President, I'm updating your biography for the final weeks of our campaign, and I just have a few questions to ask you, if you don't mind."

"Go right ahead."

"Okay. After you grew up, you were quoted as saying your father was never a financial success, and while you didn't live on the other side of the tracks, you were in hearing distance of the train whistle. Can you explain that?"

"I would say it was all President Jimmy Carter's fault. You know his irresponsible fiscal policies brought on the 1929 stock market crash and the depression."

"Yes, sir. But you were a boy *before* the stock market crash and the depression."

"That's correct, but Carter got us into World War One, and when the boys came home there was inflation and high interest rates that led to the crash and the depression."

"Let's go on. You decided to go to Eureka College in Illinois. Why Eureka?"

"I really wanted to attend the University of Illinois. But there was this admissions officer who turned me down."

"Can you remember his name?"

"Wait a minute, it will come to me. Now I've got it. His name was Carter—J. Carter."

"So you went to Eureka, played on the football team, and majored in dramatics."

"I would have made all-American except for one guy on the committee who voted against me."

"Do you recall who it was?"

"I don't remember his name, but I think he was a peanut farmer from Georgia. He never voted for any player above the Mason-Dixon line."

"You were a very good actor in school, and your biggest desire was to go into the theater. Why didn't you?"

"It was pretty hard to break into the business then because all the theaters in the Midwest were controlled by the Carter Brothers. I became a radio sports announcer instead. I was good at it but I really wanted to become a movie star. So I went to Hollywood. I applied at one studio for a job, but a casting director, a guy named Carter, told me I had no talent. Fortunately, Warner

Brothers saw it another way and hired me for two hundred dollars a week."

"Where you made mostly 'B' movies?"

"That wasn't my fault. Jack Warner had a flunky working for him named Jimmy C., and he never put me in the real big ones. I don't begrudge him, because if I had made it as a great star, I would have never become President of the United States."

"Now let's go on to the war years. You spent all of it in the air force in Hollywood making films."

"I tried desperately to get assigned overseas. But I had a chicken commanding officer, a General Carter, and he wouldn't transfer me. I never forgave him for that."

"Moving along. After you were discharged you were made the head of the Screen Actors Guild, and became disenchanted because the communists were trying to take it over."

"That's correct. I'll never forget one union leader who got control of the electricians, the musicians, the grips, and the painters, and turned them all into Reds. You want his identity?"

"Don't tell me. I think I can guess. Were you prevented from getting good roles because of your anticommunist stand?"

"Well, Carter didn't make it any easier on me."

"I have all the stuff on you working for GE and then going into politics and finally becoming Governor of California. One last question—"

"Mr. President, excuse me for interrupting, but we have just received word from Beirut that our embassy was blown up by a suicide truck loaded with dynamite."

"Darn. I knew something like this would happen when my predecessor dismantled the CIA."

"Are we talking about the same person?"

"Who else? But in my statement to the press, let's not use any names."

Efrem Weinreb & Son

I went to my favorite haberdashery in Boston, Efrem Weinreb &
Son, and was surprised to see a new sign over the store—ROGER
WEINREB & FATHER.

When I walked in I found Efrem back in the stockroom rear-
ranging boxes.

"I see you changed the name of the store."

"I didn't change it. My son Roger did," he replied. "He's now
president of the company."

"Roger?" I said. "But I just went to his graduation at the Harvard Business School in 1980. I remember how proud you were
when he got his MBA. You told him you were going to make him
a full partner, but I had no idea you were going to appoint him
president."

"Frankly, neither did I. Roger started out in the mailroom, and
then worked himself up to underwear and socks. After two
weeks he became restless so I made him vice president of mer-
chandising. Before I knew it, he put in a whole new computer
system, renovated all three floors, added a ladies' line, and found
a way of earning thirteen-percent interest over the weekend on
our cash flow by paying our suppliers through a bank in Hong
Kong. Roger said the one thing he learned at Harvard was you
either expand or die."

"How old is Roger?" I asked.

"He's twenty-eight. He came to me about eight months ago
and said he felt he wasn't moving fast enough up the ladder. He

told me most of the kids who graduated in his class were already chief executives of their companies, and he didn't want to wait until he was thirty-two years old before he reached the top."

"Did you point out that you were only forty-nine years old?" I asked.

"I did mention it, and he said, 'No wonder you're burned out. Maybe it would be a good time to slow down and hand the torch to the yuppies who have the management skills that are required to deal with the future.' "

"Young Harvard MBAs don't mince words," I said. "Did you tell him that this business was your whole life, and your dream had always been for you and Roger to work as a team?"

"Yes, and he said that from a family standpoint he understood it, but as an executive of a corporation he had to think of the stockholders first."

"What stockholders? I thought you owned the store."

"I forgot to tell you. Roger took us public last year. He told me it was the only way he could raise enough capital to buy out Brooks Brothers."

"He's trying to buy Brooks Brothers?"

"Either that or Bloomingdale's. I didn't understand the details, except that he plans to use Roger Weinreb as a holding company to threaten takeovers of other companies. His roommate, who is twenty-seven, is now an investment banker who specializes in leveraged buyouts, whatever the hell that means."

"Okay, I can understand Roger wants to get ahead, but why would he change Efrem Weinreb and Son to Roger Weinreb and Father?"

"Roger said that if we wanted to be in the big time we had to change our image, and the name Efrem Weinreb was too closely associated in our customers' minds with the late seventies. I don't want to be too hard on him, though. He worked out a golden-parachute deal with me before we went public. He said I could stay on at my present salary as a consultant and have an office until I reached fifty-five, providing I didn't work for a competing store."

"Did he say you had to work in the stockroom?"

"No, that was my own choice. It's easier to work back here than to have to explain to everyone why we changed the name of the store."

"I think Roger's an ingrate."

"I don't blame him, and I don't blame Harvard. I understand the first thing they teach you at any top business school is that if you have to choose between net profits and your own flesh and blood, you go for the bottom line."

Goodbye, Old Paint

Everyone saw James Watt ride off into the sunset. Unfortunately, we didn't hear what he said to his horse.

As they climbed up the winding trail he said, "Well, Old Paint, our work is over. I knew it would only be a matter of time before the Nazis, the commies, and the environmentalists got my job. I'm not saying it doesn't hurt. I had great plans for this country from sea to shining sea. But I knew the Beach Boys would finish me off sooner or later."

Watt reached the top of the trail and looked out over the massive mountain range.

"I had great visions for this land, Paint. I wanted every American to have a strip mine he could call his own. I wanted to sell off the wilderness areas and make them into thriving real estate developments which produced jobs and taxes.

"I dreamed someday we could cut down all the forests to provide wood for the lumber people who love this country as much as I do. I wanted to drill into the deep brown earth and offshore blue waters for gas and oil, to supply our fuel needs for the next fifty years.

"I longed to take America's most valuable heritage and protect it from the bird lovers and the Indians and the Democrats who don't believe in progress and economic growth. I needed time to sell off the outer continental shelf.

"Just think, Paint, if I'd had a few more years we would have had bulldozers down there in the valley, oil rigs in the hills, and all of that snow on the mountain could have been turned into acid rain.

"I dreamed that everyone who entered a national park would be charged a fee for setting up a tent, and fishing in a trout stream.

"I was going to build motels and souvenir shops so that the park service would pay for itself. No more would the wilderness become a free lunch for every black, woman, Jew, and cripple."

Watt and his horse started down the trail. He was singing, "I'm an old cowhand who wanted to give away this land."

He stopped by a mountain spring. "Look at that spring there, Paint. Nobody uses it. Nobody even knows it's there. If I were still Secretary of the Interior, I would dump hazardous chemical wastes into it, where they wouldn't do any harm to anyone. You see those deer over there? They're eating federal foliage. Even they think they're entitled to a free lunch."

Old Paint neighed. Watt rubbed the horse's nose. "But don't worry, fellow. We lost the battle but we didn't lose the war. I'll go back to private life as a lobbyist and a fund-raiser fighting for what I believe in. There are thousands of patriotic Americans out there willing to pay a thousand dollars a plate to fight for their oil and gas leases. Now that I'm no longer part of the administration, I can say what's on my mind. We'll beat the reds, the pinkos, and secular humanists yet."

Suddenly a man on another horse came riding over the hill.

"Why, it's Bill Clark. What are you doing out here, Bill?"

"The President has appointed me the new Secretary of the Interior."

"I'll be darned. You don't look like a secretary of the interior."

"I've been searching for you everywhere, Jim. I'm trying to find out what land you sold off and what land still belongs to us."

"I'll draw a map for you here in the dirt. Now you don't have to worry about California anymore, but the government is still stuck with Montana. We've got two coal bids on the Grand Tetons and we're still waiting to hear from the oil companies about the Chesapeake Bay. . . . Down here in the wetlands of Florida the real estate developers have an option, and. . . ."

Where Did They Go Wrong?

This is not an easy time for many of my friends raised in the good old liberal tradition. Events are moving too fast, and they don't know what is happening to them.

I dropped in on Fred and Mira Staunchley the other night and could sense the tension in the air.

"What's wrong?" I asked Fred.

"Tommy came home for the week and announced that he's voting for Reagan."

"I don't believe it!" I cried. "He's only twenty-two years old."

"He says all the kids in his political science class are voting Republican," Mira said.

"That explains it. He's being subjected to peer pressure," I told them. "Where does he go to school?"

"Berkeley, California," Fred replied.

"Did he give any good reasons why he had gone conservative?"

"None that made sense to us. He said he would have a much better opportunity getting a job with a large corporation if he voted Republican. He mumbled something about it being a dog-eat-dog world, and he had to think of his future if he ever hoped to get in the upper-income brackets before he was thirty."

"He was such a good child before he went off to college," Mira said.

"Maybe he's just putting on an act to shock you," I suggested.

"It's no act," Fred said. "Mira found this under his pillow this morning."

"What is it?"

In Search of Excellence: Lessons From America's Best-Run Companies. When she confronted him with it he just shrugged his shoulders and said if he was going to scratch and claw his way up the ladder, he had to know what big business was doing."

"I don't know what we did wrong," Mira said. "We taught him to have concern for the poor and disenfranchised. We took him to antinuclear demonstrations. He led a boycott of California lettuce when he was in high school. We had such high hopes for him. Our dream was someday he would be arrested for protesting a toxic waste dump."

"And he turned his back on everything you believe in?"

"Not only that. He said we were bleeding hearts and didn't understand the real world. He told us there would always be poor people, and there were a lot worse things than a nuclear arms race. As far as the environment was concerned, he said he would have nothing to do with a movement that was impeding the economic growth of the United States."

"Did he tell you where he stood on school prayer?"

"He said we were a nation under God and there was nothing wrong with children praying before they started their classes. Then he gave us ten minutes on having a Supreme Court that would not always come down on the side of the criminal."

"It sounds like this has not been one of your better weeks," I said. "Where is Tommy now?"

"He's upstairs watching Louis Rukeyser's 'Wall Street Week in Review.' "

"That's heavy," I said.

"It isn't the worst of it. Mira found four empty bottles of Perrier under his bed this morning."

"Maybe it's a cry for help. Have you suggested he see a psychiatrist?"

"He refuses to go because he says if he gets a job with a conglomerate he'll be passed over for chief executive officer if they find out he had a mental health problem."

"I can feel for you," I told them. "But there are worse things in the world than having a kid who votes for Reagan and George Bush."

Fred said bitterly, "Name one."

Why Not to Vote

Many people did not vote on Election Day. When they are asked why they didn't, they might be stuck for an answer. So as a public service we offer some excuses that even the League of Women Voters wouldn't quarrel with.

"I've never stood in line for anything in my life."

"My spouse voted so our family is covered."

"I was going to vote, but I was afraid if I took the time to do it the supermarket would close before I got there."

"If you vote they know where they can find you for jury duty."

"I don't have to vote because all my friends are aware of how I stand on the issues."

"You never can find a parking place around a school on Election Day."

"If I stopped off to vote in the morning I'd be caught in the rush hour traffic."

"I get claustrophobia in a voting booth."

"I overslept after watching Monday Night Football."

"I watched all three presidential debates. I figure I've done enough for my country."

"I'll vote after I get out of college when it has some meaning for me."

"The last time I voted for a president, the other guy won. It certainly taught me a lesson."

"I have tennis elbow and it hurts when I pull a lever."

"I may not have voted, but I did something much more important. I wrote out a check to my Congressman and told him exactly what I wanted him to do for me."

"My mother sent me an absentee ballot, but she forgot to send a stamp."

"How do they expect you to vote your conscience when they close the bars on Election Day?"

"In our precinct we have to vote in the school gymnasium and the smell will kill you."

"It was such a beautiful day so I decided to play golf instead."

"Every time I vote in November I get a rotten cold."

"If everyone voted, there would be no one left to keep the politicians honest."

"I can see the people in the Philippines wanting a free election. But we have one. So what's the big deal in the US if you vote or not?"

"We have this car pool, and two guys were for Reagan and two guys were for Mondale. So we said the hell with it, as we'd only cancel out each other's vote."

"We were having our traditional election night party and I had to stay home and clean the house."

"I'm unemployed, and if I showed up to vote people would have thought I was a sore loser."

"I know a couple who voted in the last election, and someone broke into their apartment and stole their television and every piece of silverware they owned."

"I wouldn't be where I am today if I spent all my time hanging around polling places."

"When you close the curtain in a voting booth, everyone can see your legs."

The Ratings Game

I walked into Sullivan's house and found him in a serious conversation with his twelve-year-old son, David.

"Am I interrupting anything?" I asked.

"No," replied Sullivan. "We were just discussing going to a movie together. What would you like to see, David?"

"I'll leave it up to you, Father," David said. "If you think a film is too violent or has sexual content not suitable for someone of my age, then I would hope you would not let me see it."

Sullivan was very perplexed. "You're not helping me much."

"The decision is not mine to make. After all, you're my parent, and you know what is best for me."

Sullivan picked up the newspaper with the theater listings.

"How can I tell what is in the movies if I haven't seen them?" he said.

"You must be guided by the Motion Picture Association ratings. At my tender age I certainly would not expect you to take me to a film with an R rating, since it would contain improper language, excessive violence, or even nudity that we both would find morally offensive."

Sullivan said, "Yeah, I guess you're right."

"We can also eliminate X-rated movies since you couldn't take me to one even if you wanted to."

"Who said anything about taking you to an X-rated movie?"

"I was just making it easier for you to select the right film for me. You can forget the G category, as we'd both be bored, even if we could find one," David said.

"So what we're looking for is a PG, or Parental Guidance, film?" Sullivan said.

"That would be a good place to start. Of course, there is a new rating, PG-13, which is a warning to you that there is more violence and sex in it than a PG film, but not enough to rate an R."

"Would you like to see a PG-13 picture?"

"The question is not whether I would like to see one, but whether you and Mother would want me to view it," David replied. "It's a grown-up decision that, as a child, I don't feel I should be part of."

"Every film in this paper sounds like either a sophomoric college joke or a stupid comic strip adventure. What kind of guidance can I get from that?" Sullivan complained.

David said, "You can't blame the motion picture producers. Adults don't go to the movies, and therefore Hollywood no longer has to pander to their tastes."

"Where the heck did you hear that?" Sullivan wanted to know.

"I saw Jack Valenti on the 'Today' show and he said it while defending the rating system," David replied.

"What else did he say?"

"The PG-13 rating places an even larger guidance responsibility on the parent. You, in effect, Dad, are the final arbiter about how much violence or sexual permissiveness I will be exposed to in my developing years."

I could see Sullivan was losing his patience. "If it was up to me, I wouldn't let you see any of these idiotic movies," he said, throwing down the paper.

"I may not agree with your assessment of the current crop of summer films, but as a twelve-year-old, I respect your right as a parent to protect me from them."

"Here's five bucks," said Sullivan. "Go see anything you want."

"Thank you, Father," David said.

"What are you going to see?" I asked David as we left Sullivan steaming in the living room.

"*Indiana Jones,*" he whispered to me. "We go through this charade every week."

The White House Noisemaker

I spoke to a man who has one of the most important positions in the administration. His job is to stand on the lawn when President and Mrs. Reagan are leaving the White House by helicopter.

"I actually work for Larry Speakes, the Press Secretary," the man told me, "but my duties keep me outside."

"What do you do?"

"My job is to make sure that the President's copter motors are going full blast, so that the press can't ask him any questions."

"That's a very responsible position," I admitted. "How do you do it?"

"I station myself right here next to the helipad. The press is over there behind those ropes. When the helicopter lands on the lawn, I get in radio contact with it. As the President walks out, I tell the pilot how much thrust to give the engines so that the copter will drown out the yelling reporters. In that way the President can just smile and shrug his shoulders, as if to say it isn't his fault if he can't understand what they're saying."

"I've seen your work on TV," I said admiringly.

"We've got it down to an art. The only one we haven't been able to silence is Sam Donaldson of ABC-TV. No matter how much noise we make, Donaldson manages to get his question heard above it."

"What's his secret?"

"He has developed a higher pitch to his voice than we can give the motors. It's uncanny. We've tried every type of engine to drown him out, but nothing seems to work. Everyone knows that no matter how loud the copter is roaring, the President is going to have to answer one question from Sam, even if it's just a simple yes or no."

"That doesn't seem too high a price to pay to get off for a weekend at Camp David."

"It all depends what the question is. As you know, the President has a slight hearing problem, so there are times when he should say no and he says yes, and other times he says yes when he should say no. Whenever I see the President is going to reply to a Sam Donaldson question, my job is to make sure that the helicopter pilot gives the bird full throttle so no one can understand the answer."

"Wouldn't it be easier for the President to leave the White House without the press being there on the lawn?"

"It might be, but this is the only chance Mr. Reagan has to be seen by the public. If we didn't allow the TV cameras to cover his departure and arrival from the White House, everyone might think he's in the Cabinet Room taking a nap."

"Do you do anything else besides rev up the President's helicopter on the White House lawn?"

"Of course ... I'm also in charge of making sure that Air Force One never shuts off its engines when the President is descending from the plane. It would be disastrous for Mr. Reagan if the engines were quiet when he stepped on the tarmac and reporters started throwing questions at him."

"I imagine even Sam Donaldson can't compete against the four jet engines of Air Force One."

"That's the amazing thing. Somehow Donaldson has learned to throw his voice so that he can even be heard over the noise of a Boeing 707. It's gotten so bad that the President automatically yells yes or no when he sees Sam in the crowd."

"Donaldson must drive him crazy."

"You would think so. But the strange thing is that when the President comes out of the White House to board his helicopter, and Sam isn't there, Mr. Reagan gets very upset and confused because he doesn't know whether to shout something to the press or not."

I said, "I admire the President for being able to walk out on the White House lawn with the engines going full blast, and not only field a question from Sam Donaldson, but hold on to Nancy's arm and board his copter all at the same time."

The man smiled. "They don't call Ronald Reagan the Great Communicator for nothing."

The Computer Is Down

The most frightening words in the English language are, "Our computer is down." You hear it more and more as you go about trying to conduct your business.

The other day I was at the airport attempting to buy a ticket to Washington and the attendant said, "I'm sorry, I can't sell you a ticket. Our computer is down."

"What do you mean your computer is down? Is it depressed?"

"No, it can't be depressed. That's why it's down."

"So if your computer is down just write me out a ticket."

"I can't write you out a ticket. The computer is the only one allowed to issue tickets for the plane." I looked down the counter, and every passenger agent was just standing there drinking coffee and staring into a blank screen.

"What do all you people do?"

"We give the computer the information about your trip, and then it tells us whether you can fly with us or not."

"So when it goes down, you go down with it."

"That's very good, sir. I haven't heard it put that way before."

"How long will the computer be down?" I wanted to know.

"I have no idea. Sometimes it's down for ten minutes, sometimes for two hours. There is no way we can find out without asking the computer, and since it's down it won't answer us."

"Don't you have a backup computer when the main computer goes down?"

"I doubt it. Do you know what one of these things costs?"

"Let's forget the computer. What about your planes? They're still flying, aren't they?"

"I couldn't tell without asking the computer, and as I told you—"

"I know, it's down. Maybe I could just go to the gate and ask the pilot if he's flying to Washington," I suggested.

"I wouldn't know what gate to send you to."

"I'll try them all," I said.

"Even if the pilot was going to Washington, he couldn't take you if you didn't have a ticket."

"Why don't I give you the money and you could give me a receipt and I could show that to the pilot as proof that I had paid?"

"We wouldn't know what to charge you. The computer is the only one who keeps track of air fares, because they change every hour."

"How about my credit card?"

"That's even worse. When our computer is down, it can't notify the credit card computer to charge the fare to your account."

"Is there any other airline flying to Washington within the next few hours?"

"I wouldn't know," he said, pointing to the dark screen. "Only IT knows."

"And at the moment IT don't know nothing."

"IT knows it," he said defensively, "IT just can't tell me."

By this time there were quite a few people standing in lines. The word soon spread to other travelers that the computer was down. Nobody knew exactly what this meant, but some people went white, some people started to cry, and still others kicked their luggage.

A man in a red blazer came out. "Please don't get excited. Wichita has been notified."

"What's Wichita got to do with it?" I asked.

"That's where our main computer went down. But as soon as it gets over its glitch, it's going to buy everyone who missed his plane a free drink."

The Great
Loophole Industry

Anyone who comes to Washington these days may notice that there are new office buildings going up all over town. The visitor might be wondering why there's an office boom when the President has sworn to cut back on government bureaucracy.

I asked one of Washington's leading builders what kind of firms were renting all the space.

He said, "For the most part anybody involved in the loophole business."

"What loophole business?"

"Didn't you know that Washington has the largest loophole industry in the world?"

I confessed my ignorance.

"Congress passes laws, and regulatory agencies try to enforce them. Then many of the people you see going in and out of the offices downtown have to find legal loopholes to satisfy the private sector, who would just as soon not abide by the rules."

"You mean there are thousands of people in Washington who are paid to do nothing but thwart the will of Congress?"

"That's the way the town works," he said. "There's hardly a law or regulation that doesn't have a loophole in it, and it's worth millions for anyone in American business to have someone find them."

"Give me an example."

"Let's say that the EPA has a regulation ruling that you can't dump toxic waste on a Boy Scout campground. The loophole might be located in what constitutes a toxic waste, or what constitutes a Boy Scout campground, or you could find it in the definition of the word dump.

"You could also raise the point that Congress, in passing the law, never intended to include Boy Scout campgrounds when it gave the EPA authority to regulate toxic wastes."

"So once the loophole is found, the information is passed on to the people who are dumping the poison, and they can legally keep doing it until Congress closes the loophole?"

"Yes. But while some professionals devote themselves to finding loopholes, other firms are paid to lobby to keep the loophole open. If they do their job, it takes Congress years to close a loophole."

"What if there are no loopholes in a law?"

"There are firms who specialize in creating loopholes where none exist. The best example is every time a tax reform bill comes up on the Hill, thousands of lawyers and lobbyists go to work to see that there is a loophole for their particular client to crawl through. I would say that making loopholes for tax laws accounts for fifty percent of Washington's loophole industry."

The builder continued. "Now, not everyone in those offices works on finding and making loopholes in the nation's laws. There are many gainfully employed in closing loopholes that are already on the books."

"Why would they want to close a loophole?"

"Suppose there is now a loophole in the banking laws which makes it possible for big New York, Chicago, and California banks to put the smaller banks around the country out of business. The small banks will then hire a loophole expert to close the loophole so that the big guys can't do it."

"Then Washington's loophole people work both sides of the street."

"Of course. That's what makes it such a profitable industry. There are those who find loopholes, those who manufacture loopholes, and then there are those who are paid to close them. You need an awful lot of office space to make the American capitalist system work."

"Where do the companies find the people with the expertise to do all this?"

"They usually hire an ex-congressman or someone from the IRS or a government regulatory commission. As former guardians of the public interest, they know every loophole in the book."

PART SEVEN

A MILLION-DOLLAR BABY

A Million-Dollar
Baby

There was a great deal of excitement in our neighborhood last week. The first house advertised to sell at over a million dollars was put up for sale.

Most of the homes in our area were built in the forties and fifties and originally sold for thirty to fifty thousand dollars. Over the years they have increased in value, but no one ever dreamed that one of them would ever be advertised for a million.

Trembling, who reported the news to me said, "I knew someone would break the six-figure barrier sooner or later, but I never thought it would be Ed Hurwitz."

"I can't believe Hurwitz is asking a million for his lean-to. I don't think he paid more than sixty-three thousand for it ten years ago."

"I saw the ad in the paper this morning. It said, 'Historical mini-estate, located in one of the most prestigious neighborhoods in Washington. A once-in-a-lifetime opportunity for that special affluent family seeking more from a home than just a place to live. Offered at $1,450,000. Within walking distance of the Swedish Embassy.' "

I said, "It's a joke. It has to be a joke."

"Oh, yeah? You should see the lineup of cars in front of the house. You would think T. Boone Pickens was coming to dinner."

Out of curiosity we decided to wander over to Hurwitz's house. Sure enough there were Mercedes Benzes, BMWs, Jaguars, Lincolns, and chauffeured Cadillacs parked all along the street. Women in fur coats stood in line waiting to get in, and Hurwitz passed out a mimeographed sheet describing the features of the house. This included "antique lighting fixtures, a wet bar in the basement, contemporary library with original moldings, and a state-of-the-art laundry room."

"What a turnout," I said to Hurwitz.

"It even surprised me," he said, "but not the real estate agent. She said the only way to keep out the bargain-hunters and attract the upper-bracket crowd is to ask for more than a million dollars for your house."

"Aren't they disappointed when they arrive?"

"They don't seem to be," Hurwitz said. "They figure if you're asking over a million there's got to be more to it than they can see. Besides, people who can pay prices like that want to gut the structure anyway, and spend another million to make it 'livable.' One of the big attractions of this place is they can throw out everything in the house and not feel guilty about it."

Hurwitz took Trembling and me inside.

"You didn't even paint it," I said.

"Why paint it? Whoever is going to buy it will only *repaint* it. Women's eyes light up when they see this joint, and they can hardly wait to call their decorator. The one thing I learned in selling a house for a million bucks is the less you offer somebody the more chance you have of getting them to buy it."

We went into the kitchen. There was a 1960 gas stove, a 1970 refrigerator, a scarred wooden table, two chairs, and a spice shelf that Hurwitz had gotten with Green Stamps.

One of the women said to the other, "It's utterly charming. You don't see kitchens like this anymore."

The second woman said, "It's a dream. You can start from scratch and do anything you want with it."

"That's true of the bathroom, too," Hurwitz told them.

When we got back into the living room I said, "I wouldn't believe it if I hadn't seen it with my own eyes. The people are actually salivating to buy this hunk of junk."

Hurwitz seemed offended. "It may be a hunk of junk to you, but for the people who came here today it's the dream they've worked for all of their lives."

"Hey, wait a minute," Trembling said. "If you get one million four for this wreck, that means all our homes in the neighborhood will be reassessed for tax purposes and we'll be paying for your scam."

"Don't blame me," Hurwitz said. "I originally asked a hundred thousand for the house and had no bites. Now that I'm asking for a million, I can't keep people from kicking down the door."

I Love You, But . . .

Whether we want to admit it or not, there are serious emotional problems in the new man-woman relationships.

Peter Gastonernough, a young friend, asked me a very strange question the other day. "Do you think I'm a wimp?"

"I don't believe so. Why do you ask?"

"My girlfriend thinks I am."

"Why does she think that?"

"Because she says I'm indecisive and I don't know what she wants."

"Did you ask her what _she_ wanted?"

"Yes, and she said if I didn't know what she wanted then I must be a wimp."

"You have a problem. Do you have any idea of the way she wants you to behave?"

"I think she wants me to be strong and assertive and masculine."

"Have you tried it?"

"Every time I do, she says I don't treat her as an equal. She maintains that the days of pushing women around are over. She wants me to respect her feelings."

"Have you told her you do?"

"Yes, and then she calls me a wimp."

"Are you sure this is the girl for you?"

"We're very much in love, but there is a lot more going on than I bargained for. It's not easy being a man today," he said.

"We're all aware of that. Perhaps you should tell her your feelings and the problems you have satisfying her."

"If I told her my feelings, she would think I was a weak person."

"Well, she already thinks you're a wimp, so you really don't have too much to lose."

"I could lose her respect."

"How did you get into this mess in the first place?"

"I think it had something to do with consciousness raising. When we first met she said I was nothing but a macho jock, and that if I didn't change my attitude she'd never see me again. So I made an effort to change. When she wanted to do something, we did it. When I wanted to do something, I left the decision to her. At first she liked the role I was playing, but pretty soon she got ticked off and asked why she had to make all the decisions for both of us."

"That could have been a signal. Women may pretend they like it, but they're much happier when someone makes a decision for them."

"I'm aware of that. But I spoiled her. Now when I make a decision, she gets mad and says it's only fair that since we're partners she should have as much of a say as I do."

"Maybe she said it but didn't mean it."

"I asked her if she really meant what she was saying, and she told me she was tired of always being questioned."

"On the basis of our conversation, she seems to enjoy making life miserable for you."

"I don't think so. I believe she's as confused as I am. It's not easy being a woman these days."

"We all know that. Why don't you take the bull by the horns and go back to being the macho jock you were before?"

"I don't think she'd stand for it. She's very much into being a liberated woman."

"Which means?"

"Even if she accepted it, her girlfriends would never forgive her."

"There has to be something between macho and wimp," I said. "What happened to the new liberated man?"

"We cry a lot."

Knock, Knock,
Who's There?

A man knocked on the door of the White House the other night and the President, in his pajamas, answered it.

"Yes?" Mr. Reagan said.

"I'm from the Visa card company, and you owe us two hundred and ten billion dollars. We were wondering when you planned to start paying on it."

"Two hundred and ten billion? I thought it was only one hundred and seventy billion," the President said.

"That's what you told everyone during the election campaign. But it turns out it's two hundred and ten, give or take five billion. You've been using your credit card for the past four years, and I think it's time you acknowledged the debt."

"Who is it?" Mrs. Reagan called from the top of the stairs.

"It's a man from the Visa credit card company who says we owe him two hundred and ten billion dollars."

"That's ridiculous," Mrs. Reagan said. "I only bought two suits at Adolfo's."

The Visa man said, "These were not for personal purchases. They are government related. I have all the receipts here. Defense, Social Security, Medicare, Human Services, and entitlements. We can't stay in business if people just keep using plastic and don't honor their debts."

"Don't worry about getting paid. My tax advisers are now working on a plan to see that you get your money."

"How do they propose to do that?"

"We're cutting back on spending, reforming the tax structure, and lowering interest rates."

Mrs. Reagan yelled from the top of the stairs, "Tell him we didn't run up the bill, Congress did."

The Visa man heard her. "The card is made out in your name, Mr. Reagan. Whether you like it or not, you're responsible."

"Don't worry, we'll borrow the money to pay you," the President said.

"Do you realize how much interest you're going to pay on two hundred and ten billion?"

"My staff deals with minor details like that," the President replied.

"Mr. Reagan, the reason we gave you a Gold Visa card is that in 1980, we considered you a good credit risk. You made a big deal that Jimmy Carter was in debt to us for ninety billion, and you promised if you got his card you wouldn't owe us *anything* by 1984. Now you've more than doubled his debt, and we're getting very nervous."

Mrs. Reagan shouted, "Tell him if he doesn't want our business anymore, we'll use an American Express credit card."

The Visa man yelled back, "American Express wouldn't touch you with a ten-foot pole."

"I don't think that this is the time or place to discuss how much we owe you," the President said. "Why don't you come to my office in the morning?"

"Because your staff won't let me in," the Visa man said. "Every time I ask to see you, they tell me you're taking a nap. I don't like to make night calls, but that is the only time I get to speak to the principals who are in hock up to their ears."

"Okay, so maybe I spent more than I should have. But if you let me keep my card, I'll cut back on all my spending, and I assure you by 1988, I won't owe you more than one hundred billion. Would that be in your ballpark?"

"We don't seem to have any choice, do we?" the Visa man said.

The President shut the door and went upstairs.

Mrs. Reagan said, "I think that was very rude of the credit card people to wake us up and tell us we owed them two hundred and ten billion dollars. It could ruin our sleep."

"Not mine," the President said.

Getting the Short Form

A business reporter came rushing into my office. "Did you hear the news? President Reagan is leaning toward a flat tax."

"That's good," I said. "What's a flat tax?"

"A fair tax, a balanced tax, a simple tax, and a tax that you would be proud to bring home to your mother."

"What's the catch?"

"You may pay less of a percentage of your income to the government, but you won't be allowed to deduct anything except mortgage interest on your primary residence."

"That's bad. Without second-home interest deductions we can all say goodbye to Florida. Will the new tax reform plan cut down on the budget deficit?"

"No, it has nothing to do with deficits. They call it 'revenue neutral.' It won't bring in any more money to the Treasury, but they claim it will be much fairer for the poor people."

"That's good," I said.

"Not necessarily. The poor people depend on private charity to keep their heads above water. Under the flat tax, anyone can deduct up to two percent of their gross income for charitable donations. Very few people give more than two percent of their gross to charity. So with all the cutbacks in government services that Reagan has proposed, the private sector won't be able to take up the slack to provide a safety net for the poor. Hospitals, universities, foundations, and all cultural institutions are in the same boat."

"So much for trickle-down economics. Tell me something good about this new idea."

"Corporation loopholes will be closed. You won't be able to depreciate any of your investments and there will be no more capital gains. Everything will be considered ordinary income."

"That sounds good."

"Don't be too sure. If companies can't get tax benefits for investing in the economy, they might put their money in Treasury notes, which the government has to issue to pay off the two-hundred-ten-billion-dollar deficit."

"Why is that bad?"

"If the companies don't build new plants or upgrade their equipment, they won't be able to provide jobs for the people.

Besides, without loopholes there is no incentive for venture capital, which is supposed to create the industries of tomorrow."

"Therefore although the flat tax is fairer, many people won't have salaries to pay it."

"There's also a provision in the reform bill that the cities and states can no longer sell certain tax-free bonds to keep public services from falling apart. If they can't raise bond money for local projects, the cities and states will have to raise taxes which are also no longer deductible from your federal form."

"What other goodies do they have in the proposal?"

"The three-martini lunch will be a thing of the past."

"That's good. I never felt like going back to work after three martinis."

"What's bad about it is that every type of business entertainment will no longer be deductible, and thousands of restaurants, hotels, theaters, taxis, sports arenas, and travel-related services will go down the tube. You could easily have millions of people pounding the streets."

"That does sound pretty scary."

"There is no reason to be frightened. Reagan will never get the flat tax through in its present form."

"That's good."

"It could be bad. While they're jawboning about it in Congress for two years, the economy could be stopped dead in its tracks. The longer business is confused, the more chance you have of a truly deep recession."

"You really made my day," I said.

"Don't complain. During the presidential campaign Reagan never promised the people a rose garden."

"He sure as hell did. Why do you think he was reelected?"

Fun in
New Jersey

A recent state Supreme Court ruling in New Jersey has been making life very difficult for people who are giving parties. The court ruled that the party givers could be held responsible if one of their guests left the premises in an inebriated state and hurt someone in an accident.

The burden on the host and hostess is more than most Jersey residents can stand.

I attended the twenty-fifth wedding anniversary of the Richard Faheys in their home in East Orange, New Jersey, not long after the new ruling had taken effect.

There were mountains of delicious food, an anniversary cake, and a bar off in the corner.

"Well, Fahey," I said, "this is really a great occasion. I think I'll have a drink."

He looked at me sharply. "How many have you had already?"

"Just one," I said.

He took out his notebook and wrote something in it.

"What are you doing?"

"I'm keeping track of all the guests. Your limit is three," he replied.

"Why three?"

"We checked out all our guests before the party. Reports from Washington indicate three drinks are all you can handle."

"But I'm not driving. I came with Mike Clark."

Fahey looked in his book. "I'm glad you told me. Clark is only good for four glasses of wine before he goes blotto. Excuse me. I just saw Dale Denton over there take his second glass of champagne. What kind of party does he think we're throwing?"

I walked over to Jonah Shacknai. "How's it going?" I asked him.

"Okay. I'm leaving."

"So early? We haven't had dinner yet."

"I had two scotch and waters and Fahey told the bartender to cut me off. I don't intend to suck ice cubes for the rest of the night."

"It must be tough going to a party in New Jersey," I said.

"We had better ones before the state Supreme Court ruling. You see that beautiful girl over there? I'm told she goes crazy when she has five vodka tonics."

"Well, you're a bachelor. Why don't you get to know her?"

"Fahey won't let her have more than three, so I'd just be wasting my time."

Mrs. Fahey came by. "Is everyone having a good time?"

"Sort of," I said.

She looked in her notebook and then said, "Can I freshen your drink?"

"I'd rather wait for my last one after dinner," I said.

"That's a good idea. There is no reason to peak too early."

I happened to pass the bar and found Fahey in an agitated state. He was checking all the bottles.

"What's going on?" I asked him.

"My bar inventory doesn't jibe with my records. People have been lying to me on how many drinks they've consumed."

"Relax, Fahey. It's your twenty-fifth anniversary."

"That's easy for you to say. You don't have to worry about being sued."

Finally dinner was served. Instead of wine we toasted the happy couple with Perrier. I took my final drink for the road and got my coat to leave. In the hallway I noted several guests sitting in a row of chairs.

"What are they waiting for?" I asked Fahey.

He said in disgust, "They couldn't pass the breathalizer tests so they're going to have to sit there all night."

The
Cabbage Patch Doll

It wasn't meant to be that way, but Christmas has become a nightmare for parents who feel they must prove their undying love for their children. The only way some fathers and mothers know how to do it is to provide them with the "in" toy of the year.

This was the case when Broadstreet came into my office perspiring and shaking.

"Help me," he said.

"That's what I'm here for," I told him gently. "What do you need?"

"I have to get my hands on a Cabbage Patch doll for my daughter this Christmas."

"Are you crazy? If you need a green card for an illegal alien I can get you one. If you want a billion-dollar defense contract from the air force I can fix it for you. If you'd like to go on the next space shuttle flight I'll get you a seat. But where am I going to find a Cabbage Patch doll in late December?"

"You're my last resort. I've been to every toy store on the East Coast. I've advertised in the newspapers. I even tried to break into the Coleco toy factory in Connecticut. In all cases I came up empty. I can't face my Jessica on Christmas morning if there isn't a Cabbage Patch doll under the tree."

"A lot of fathers will have the same problem this year," I told him.

"I don't care about other fathers. All I worry about is Jessica. If I don't produce a Cabbage Patch doll, she'll never believe anything I say again." He put his head in his hands. "I've failed as a parent."

"You're not a failure," I told Broadstreet. "The system has *failed* you. Jessica can't hold you responsible because the toy manufacturer didn't produce enough dolls for Christmas."

"It's not just Jessica that I'm worried about. Every night when I come home, my wife Deborah is waiting for me at the door and she hisses, 'Did you get one?' When I shake my head I see nothing but fear and loathing in her eyes."

"Does she say anything?"

"No, but I can read what's going on in her head when we're eating dinner in silence. She's saying, 'I could have married a hundred successful guys, and I had to choose one who couldn't even provide his child with a Cabbage Patch Kid.' "

"You're just imagining things," I told him. "She's probably thinking, 'I wish I could share his pain.' "

"You don't know Deborah. Four of her girlfriends already have Cabbage Patch dolls stashed in their closets for Christmas. They don't say it out loud, but Deborah knows they pity her for having married beneath herself."

"Broadstreet, if you don't get a Cabbage Patch Kid for your daughter, you're not going to be accused of child abuse. Maybe it's as good a time as any for Jessica to learn that she can't have everything in life she asks for."

"Would you like to tell that to a four-year-old girl on Christmas morning?"

"I guess not. Are you sure you've tried every resource available? I read in the newspaper the other day that if you deposit fifty thousand dollars for ten years with the Old Faithful Savings and Loan, they'll give you a Cabbage Patch Kid absolutely free."

"I saw the same ad. They ran out of dolls the first day. Someone also ran an advertisement for a two-million-dollar house in Georgetown, and said they'd throw in a Silver Cloud Rolls-Royce and a Cabbage Patch doll in the deal. They had to call out the police when six hundred people showed up. I'm desperate. That's why I came to you."

"All right," I said. "I'll make one call for you to the White House. They owe me a lot of favors."

I rang up one of the President's top gofers. When I hung up, Broadstreet said, "What did he say?"

"He told me to forget it. The Reagans can't even get a Cabbage Patch doll for their grandchild."

They Really Care, But . . .

NEW YORK CITY —They say that people in New York are reluctant to get involved.

This is a bad rap. People who live in the Big Apple will get involved if they believe something unusual is going on.

I realized how oblivious New Yorkers are to their environment while walking up Lexington Avenue with a friend named Arthur Stevens. We were hemmed in by giant skyscrapers, and everything looked gray.

"Don't you miss the sun?" I asked him.

"What sun?" he wanted to know.

"You know, the thing that lights the sky in the daytime. It's up there somewhere above the glass buildings."

"If God wanted New Yorkers to have sun, he would have never sold the air rights to Manhattan," Stevens said.

We couldn't continue the conversation because twelve jack-hammers were going full blast in the street.

A half block later I said, "I don't understand how you people can take the noise."

"I don't hear any noise," Stevens said.

"Doesn't the constant din of jackhammers, wrecking balls, and automobile horns get on your nerves?"

"It probably would if I thought about it."

"What do you think about when you're walking in New York?"

"Most of the time I think to myself, 'I hope a bank or brokerage firm in one of those skyscrapers doesn't go broke.' "

"Why do you think about that?"

"I'd hate to have a vice president on the thirty-fifth floor fall on me just as I was passing by."

We walked around mountains of plastic bags filled with refuse.

"Do you ever think about garbage?" I asked him.

"What garbage?" he wanted to know.

"The stuff in those large green bags on the curb."

"You could have fooled me," he said. "I thought they were Christmas bushes the merchants put out to decorate the sidewalks."

"I'm just a tourist," I said, "and I don't want to be critical of New York. But there is a lot more going on here than you people are aware of."

"Give me an example."

"A man on roller skates just grabbed that lady's purse."

"How do you know he did it?"

"He was wearing a ski mask. Should we call a cop?"

"Are you crazy? If New Yorkers called a cop every time a guy on roller skates snatched a purse, no one would ever get home for dinner."

"Don't you care about the lady?"

"Of course I care about the lady. But when you live in the Big

Apple you have to make choices. Mine right now is whether I want to deal with her purse problem or get something for dinner. Let's stop in the delicatessen."

"A large pizza," Stevens said to the man behind the counter. The man replied in a foreign tongue.

"I think he's speaking to you in a calypso patois, probably indigenous to Haiti," I said.

"Is that what it is. I've been coming here for ten months, and every time I ask for pizza someone gives me a loaf of pumpernickel bread."

"Why do you patronize this place if no one speaks English?"

"It's only a block from my apartment."

"Aren't you tired of eating nothing but bread for dinner?"

"Now that you mention it, yes, but like most New Yorkers, by the time I get home I'm too bushed to argue with a guy over the difference between pumpernickel and pizza."

The Wrong House Call

You may be wondering why Santa Claus did not make it to every house this year. He ran into some bad luck.

The old boy was right on schedule until he got to my doctor's house. My doctor happened to be up late reading *The New England Journal of Medicine* to his wife, as he does every Christmas Eve. When Saint Nick slid down the chimney, my doctor looked up and said, "I'm not seeing patients tonight. Dr. Pincus is taking my calls."

"I'm not here as a patient. I came to drop off some presents for your kids."

"Why are you puffing so hard?" my doctor asked him.

"I have a tight schedule," Santa said. "And besides, this bag is loaded with so many transformers and home computers, it's breaking my back."

My doctor said, "You're awfully fat for someone carrying a bag that heavy. Do you mind getting on the scale?"

Santa got red in the face. "I just look heavy because of this outfit I'm wearing. I really only weigh two hundred fifty pounds."

My doctor pulled a book down from his shelf. "According to the latest life-insurance tables your ideal body weight should be one eighty-five."

"I'm going on a diet right after Christmas," Santa said.

"You better take off your clothes and let me check you out. Go behind the screen."

Santa came out in his BVDs.

"I don't like the look of that red nose. How much drinking do you do?" my doctor asked.

"I just take a few snorters in the sleigh to keep warm."

"You drink while you're driving?"

"I do, but my reindeer don't. Ho-ho-ho."

My doctor held his stethoscope to Santa's chest.

"Say that again?"

"Ho-ho-ho."

"I detect the beginnings of a bronchial condition. You may have picked up carcinogenic substances sliding down all those chimneys. I'm going to send you to the emergency room at Georgetown Hospital for a pulmonary test."

"I was just there making a delivery to the children's ward," Santa said. "The emergency room is packed with people because no doctor will come out on Christmas Eve. Look, I feel great. Have you ever seen anyone so merry and bright? I'm laughing all the time."

"Laughing could be a clue to endogenous anxiety. People who laugh and chortle incessantly are filled with inner tensions. A person like yourself, who is trying to please everybody all of the

271

time, has to be under tremendous stress, and the denial of it eventually takes its toll. How much exercise do you do?"

"A lot when I'm climbing in and out of chimneys."

"But you have no regular walking or jogging program the rest of the year?"

"You ever tried jogging around the North Pole? You can freeze your fanny off."

"All right, Mr. Claus, you can put your clothes on again. But before you do, I'm going to give it to you straight. If you don't lose weight, and if you continue carrying a bag on your back, you're going to wind up with either a stroke or a hernia. You better go home now and get some rest until your tests come back from the lab."

Santa Claus arrived at the North Pole at two o'clock in the morning, and Mrs. Claus asked him in horror, "What are you doing home so early?"

"Some doctor told me I'm in terrible shape."

"But what should I do with all the toys that are still on the sled? They have to be delivered by morning."

Santa stretched out on the bed and sighed. "Call Federal Express."

No More
Soviet R & D

At the end of the year I always have a three-vodka-martini lunch with my mole from the Soviet embassy in Washington. His code name is Nutcracker.

"So tell me, what's new in the Kremlin?" I asked him.

"We cutting defense research budget by seventy-five percent," he said.

"Come on, Nutcracker, planting KGB disinformation with me will get you nowhere."

"Is true. Politburo made decision early this year to stop developing new weapons because they were getting too expensive."

"So how do they expect to keep up the arms race if they don't spend trillions of rubles for research and development?"

"Is simple. We plan to let Americans spend money to do scientific dirty work and then we buy it from you."

"You don't think the United States is going to sell the Soviet Union our military weapon secrets?"

"Not directly from manufacturer, but we can always go through the middleman."

"What middleman?"

"Somebody who works for defense contractor and wants to make little extra money to achieve American dream."

"What exactly do you meant by that?"

"Take Stealth bomber. You people spent billions of dollars to develop airplane that could escape Soviet radar. We had choice of spending twice as much to find answer, or buy plans from one of your people in California. We found engineer who delivered blueprints to us for twenty-five thousand dollars. Was a lot of money, but still cheaper than starting from scratch and building Stealth bomber of our own."

"That's dirty pool," I said. "In an arms race each side is expected to pay top dollar for developing its own weapons. It's not fair of Soviets to make us do all the work and then go out to California and buy the system for a song."

"Sue us for patent infringement," Nutcracker said. "Comrade, I will tell you dark secret. Russian computers lousy, and if we had to depend on them for new weapons, we would have dropped out of arms race long ago. The only thing keep Russian war machine going is American know-how.

"How do you find these middlemen who sell our secrets?"

"Is easy. We plug into credit rating system on cheap Apple computer and find California defense worker who can't make payments on house. Then we go to him and pay mortgage in exchange for plans to guidance system for MX missile."

"Why have you concentrated on California?"

"Because nobody can pay his mortgage in California."

"You would think the Soviets would have too much national pride to reproduce a weapons system Americans have worked on for years."

"Is not question of pride. Is question of cost. Soviet taxpayers getting tired of paying so much money for defense. If Moscow can deliver bigger rumble for a ruble, Soviet peoples don't care who came up with idea first."

"Is twenty-five thousand dollars the highest price the Kremlin will pay for an American weapons system?"

"That's all Moscow has allotted in R & D military budget for 1985. But if someone wants to sell us secrets of Star Wars, we would go to fifty thousand, even if we had to take money out of Soviet school-lunch program."

A Test
for the President

"The Rising Tide of Mediocrity threatens our very future as a nation." Thus sayeth the report by the National Commission on Excellence in Education.

Here are few statistics they uncovered: There are twenty-three million functionally illiterate adults in the country, and 13 percent of all seventeen-year olds cannot read, write, or comprehend. The average teacher in America makes $17,000 a year and must moonlight to stay out of the poorhouse. There are severe shortages of instructors in math, science, and foreign languages. Half of those now teaching these subjects are not qualified to do so.

President Reagan, in his radio address, blamed the US government's role in the past twenty years for the country's educational problems. If parents would just get involved in their children's learning process, and we turned our education back to the local communities, all would be well again, the President said. He was adamant that the government not increase its activities in education for any reason.

If anyone needs remedial education right now, it's the President of the United States.

"All right, Mr. President. Here is a graph. The red line shows where the Soviets are in education, and the blue line shows where we are. Note that the blue line is going down every year and the red line is going up. What does that mean for the nation?"

"American parents aren't doing their job."

"It could mean that. It could also mean that the country is not spending enough on education to meet the Soviet threat. Now, Mr. President, here is another chart. It indicates that if we keep turning out people not equipped in the sciences, commerce, or technology, we will soon be overtaken by our competitors throughout the world. As the nation's leader, what should you do about it?"

"Work for a constitutional amendment to bring back prayers in the schools."

"I'm not certain that that is the correct answer. Would you consider raising teachers' salaries and getting more qualified instructors to make sure our students are equipped to deal with the tasks that lie ahead?"

"Are you crazy? I need every dollar I can get for defense. Bigger budgets for education are not the answer."

"But where are you going to get the people to build your weapons and learn how to use them if they are illiterate?"

"I don't know the answer to that one. Go on to the next question."

"Do you know what it costs the country in unemployment, welfare, and crime because Americans can't read and write?"

"I didn't know I was supposed to study that."

"Don't you think it's your duty as president to be concerned about the quality of education in the United States? Isn't it a question of national security and survival?"

"I've advocated tax breaks for parents who want to send their kids to private schools."

"That isn't the right answer, Mr. President. You have to consider the illiteracy bomb in this country with the same seriousness you consider the threat from Central America."

"You don't expect me to appear before a Joint Session of Congress just because Americans can't read and write?"

"It could eventually become a bigger threat than El Salvador."

"If I did that, Congress would take away my tax cut. Are you seriously asking me to choose between the education of our children and a ten-percent tax cut?"

"Mr. President, your homework assignment was to read the report of the National Commission on Excellence in Education last night. Apparently you watched television instead."

"It's not my fault. I didn't know I was going to have a test today."

The Moderates Are Coming

It's been thirty years since the Great Red Hunter, Senator Joe McCarthy, announced that the State Department was filled with communists, commiesymps, pinkos, and fellow travelers.

That was in the early fifties and things have changed. As far as the Republican right wing is concerned, we have nothing to fear from commies in the State Department anymore. The real threats to the nation today are the "moderates," who have infiltrated the President's own family.

It's a very serious situation according to my conservative friends. .

Simon Simple, the leading right-wing columnist in the nation, told me, "Secretary George Shultz is reshuffling the department, and purging all the hard-liners, and replacing them with moderates so he can take control of the foreign policy of the country."

"Why would a secretary of state want to do that?" I asked.

"Because he's a closet pragmatist."

"Those are strong charges," I said. "I hope you have evidence to back them up."

"I do. Shultz wants to replace one third of Reagan's politically appointed ambassadors with foreign service professionals, and he plans to substitute six hard-line assistant secretaries with State Department experts."

"Maybe he just wants to beef up his staff."

"Here is the list. The majority of Shultz's appointees are reasonable people who would sell out the country."

"That's a heck of a story. If they got control of Foggy Bottom they could force diplomatic solutions to military problems. Does the President know what's going on?"

"For the moment he's sticking by Shultz, but the conservatives are not going to stand by and see this country's hard-line policy go down the drain. We didn't reelect Reagan to make an arms control treaty or keep us from getting militarily involved in Central America."

"It would be a disaster to purge ideological presidential appointees with State Department professionals," I agreed. "It could lead to another détente, or worse still, a nuclear freeze. I can't believe Shultz would do this if he didn't have friends in the White House."

"That's just it. The moderates in the White House are behind the whole thing."

"Are you trying to tell me that there are moderates in the White House too? Who are they?"

"Jim Baker, Mike Deaver, George Bush, just to name a few."

"I never thought of them as moderates."

"Why do you think they refused UN Ambassador Jeane Kirkpatrick a key job?"

"She said it was because they were male chauvinist pigs."

"You can be a male chauvinist pig and moderate as well."

"What are the conservatives going to do about it?"

"We're calling for a Senate Investigation to root out all the moderates and pragmatists in government. Anyone who can't pass the conservative ideological litmus test will be hounded out of office."

"I hope it's televised. I'd like to see what a moderate in the Reagan administration really looks like."

"Don't worry, you'll see all of them. Not only will they have to testify under oath whether they are moderates or not, but they'll have to give the names of other moderates in their cell. If they refuse they'll be held in contempt of Congress."

"It could be the beginning of another witch hunt," I said excitedly. "We haven't had a good one since Joe McCarthy was alive."

Simon smiled. "May he rest in peace."

The Georgetown
Vigilantes

After noting the positive reaction of citizens to the shooting of four thugs by a vigilante in the New York City subway, a bunch of us in Washington decided to form our own vigilante organization to see that justice was served in the nation's capital.

There are tough gun laws in the District of Columbia, so we drove over to Virginia, where you can buy anything you want from a .22 Saturday Night Special snub-nosed revolver to a Uzi semiautomatic machine gun.

I chose a .38 Smith & Wesson because it fits snugly under my coat and reminds me of the old westerns when the good guys constantly drove the bad guys out of town.

Our vigilante group didn't have long to wait. Schneider had been mugged the night before and he said he could identify the guys who did it. We went with him to a Georgetown bar and he pointed them out to us.

"Are you sure they're the ones?" I asked him.

"Of course I'm sure," he said. "The big guy is wearing a raincoat just like the one I owned."

That was good enough for us. So we took the three men out of the bar and shot them.

The police were furious that we had done their jobs for them. But the public was delighted and we became folk heroes overnight.

The next time we went out was when a Seven-Eleven in the neighborhood was held up.

The clerk in the store said the stickup man wore a Halloween mask, but he had a hunch it was a taxi driver who lived down the street.

We routed the cabbie out of bed and brought him down for identification. The clerk said, "It could be him."

"Wait a minute," Pester said. "We have to be certain, because as vigilantes we don't want to hurt an innocent man. You said the guy was wearing a Halloween mask. What kind of mask was it?"

"It was a Darth Vader mask."

We sent Pittman to get a mask at the costume shop. Then we put it on the cabdriver.

The clerk said excitedly, "That's the guy!"

"You're sure?"

The clerk replied, "I never forget a face."

So we took the cabbie out in the alley and broke his legs.

After that we were dubbed "The Magnificent Seven-Eleven" and more people were rooting for us than they were the Redskins.

The liberal press wrote bleeding-heart editorials accusing us of being nothing more than hooligans, and the Mayor went on television to condemn us. It didn't matter, because the criminals were now more afraid of us than they were of the police.

Christmas night Alvin told us, "I just got a tip that there are a bunch of drug dealers holed up in a house in Northwest Washington."

"Let's burn it down to teach all the drug dealers in town a lesson."

We hopped in our van with ten gallons of gasoline and drove to the address the tipster gave Alvin. We threw the liquid all over the house and set it on fire. A father and mother and three children came pouring out of the front door. The father screamed, "What the hell are you doing?"

"Teaching you drug dealers a lesson."

"I'm not a drug dealer! I'm a postman."

"Is this your address?" Alvin asked, showing him the one the tipster had written down.

The postman looked at it and said, "No, you dumb SOBs! That's in *Southwest* Washington, not Northwest. You guys burned down the wrong house!"

"Don't get all shook up, pal," I said. "Even vigilantes make a mistake once in a while."

The Rainmaker

Well, everyone seems to be back in town, not only the winners, but the losers in last November's election. The victors have taken their seats in the House and Senate, and the losers have taken theirs in one of Washington's one hundred thousand prestigious law firms.

Ex-Congressman Turtleback is one of the losers, if you call making $350,000 a year with Tort & Tort a losing proposition.

"I thought you'd go back to Wistful County after you lost your seat," I said.

"You ever been in Wistful County?" Turtleback asked me.

"Can't say that I have," I admitted. "All I know about it is what you said on the floor of the House—that it was America's biblical Garden of Eden."

"I'm not on the floor anymore, and Wistful County is the pits. I'm not just saying that because I lost the election after serving the people there for twenty years. It was the pits when I first came to Congress, and it's the pits now."

"Did you ever practice law before you got elected to public office?"

"No, and I don't intend to practice it now. I'm going to be the rainmaker at Tort and Tort."

"What's a rainmaker?"

"The fellow that makes it rain new business on the firm because of the people he knows. I may be out of office, but I still have friends who owe me a few favors."

"Then you're going to be an influence peddler."

"Never. My job is to provide advice and consent to the private sector which can't operate under the oppressive laws passed by a vindictive, antibusiness Congress," he said. "Clients will come to me not because of the influence I still wield, but because of my expertise in getting around the overbearing rules and regulations I demanded when I served the people."

"I can see where Tort and Tort would want you to be a partner in their firm," I said. "Will you also provide lobbying services?"

"You can't be a rainmaker in Washington if you are not willing to stand up for the things your clients believe in. The reason ex-congressmen and ex-senators are in demand by Washington law firms is that we have access to our former colleagues on the floor, not to mention the use of the congressional dining rooms and the gym. It's amazing how much law you can practice when you're doing Jane Fonda exercises with the chairman of a House or Senate committee."

"And they don't treat you any differently because you are no longer a member of Congress?"

"They treat you better, because now that you're with a big law firm, you are a potential source of funds for their future political campaigns."

"What about the administration? How do they look on you?"

"Kindly. If you were a former Republican congressman, they want to make it up to you for losing your election. And if you were a former Democratic congressman they are so delighted that you are no longer in opposition that they'll go overboard to show they don't hold grudges."

"You can't say Washington doesn't take care of its own."

"Had I known then what I know now, I would have lost an election ten years ago," he said.

The phone rang and Turtleback picked it up. "Willy, how are you? How are things at Wistful Tools? . . . You don't say? The navy refuses to pay you for the Snail Darter tool kit? . . . They claim you overcharged them by ten million dollars? No problem, Willy, we'll not only get your money, but we'll get an apology from the Pentagon." Turtleback hit the Tort & Tort timer on his desk and then said, "Tell me the story."

After twenty minutes he hung up, and winked at me, and started humming "Singing in the Rain."

Two Modest Proposals

In the world of nuclear arms, missiles do not kill people, nations kill people.

Therefore at the start of the new arms negotiations it's time both the Soviet Union and the United States take a new approach to the question of disarmament.

Instead of working for the reduction of offensive and defensive nuclear weapons, we should negotiate limits on how many times each superpower may kill a person in the event of an all-out war.

At the moment it is believed that the US and the Soviets have stockpiled enough weapons to destroy each others' citizens ten times over.

The first step then is to produce an agreement that would reduce the nuclear arsenals in both countries to the point where they could only kill every American and Soviet citizen *five* times.

Cutting the KR (Kill Ratio) in half won't be easy, but it is possible to persuade the superpowers to agree to it, particularly when it can be argued that you only have to kill a person *twice* to make your point in an all-out holocaust. With a Kill Ratio of five, both sides would still have a margin of safety in case their missiles malfunction or fail to hit their targets.

The US military will argue that the Soviets may sign a treaty agreeing to kill every American only five times, and then cheat, by stashing away enough weapons to kill them seven times.

The Soviet military could balk at cutting the KR in half on the grounds that while the US might reduce its weapons, they are still at a disadvantage because if we refuse to include West European warheads in the count, each USSR citizen could still be killed eight times.

At this point the negotiators in Geneva would have to resort to compromise.

The Americans could address the US military fears by insisting on on-site inspection of both nuclear stockpiles. If it were found that the Soviet weapons on hand had enough power to kill the Americans more than the agreed upon KR of five, the US could abrogate the treaty and proceed to build new weapons that would kill every Soviet citizen fifteen times.

In exchange for on-site inspection, we would include the West European nukes in our KR, and reduce American stockpiles until both the US and West European KR came out to five.

If the Kill Ratio formula is unacceptable, there is no reason for the superpowers to leave the bargaining table.

Another solution might be to work out a fair agreement on how many people each side may be permitted to wipe out in the event of a war. Neither country would have to reduce its arsenal, but would be limited to firing only enough missiles to waste one hundred million people on the other's territory.

The obvious question is, who would monitor the pact to see that the superpowers did not bag more than their limit? This could be done by the International Red Cross, who would have access to all the stricken areas. If either side went over the one-hundred-million ballpark figure, the other would then be permitted to match them body for body.

With the limits set by the treaty, it would not only be a waste of money for the superpowers to continue the arms race, but there would be an incentive to reduce their nuclear arsenals accordingly.

I have no illusions that either the Kill Ratio reduction proposal, or the one-hundred-million limit on casualties can be successfully negotiated overnight.

I'm throwing them on the table as a starting point in the new discussions. When it comes to serious disarmament talks you have to start somewhere.

Switch

The President was adjusting quite well to all the musical chairs in the White House staff, but even he wasn't prepared for the big one.

One night Nancy Reagan said to him, "I'd like to swap jobs with Secretary of Heath and Human Services Margaret Heckler."

"How can you do that? You're the best First Lady a President ever had."

"I'm burned out, Ronnie. After giving all those luncheons and dinners for heads of state, and making all those official appearances, I feel I need a new challenge. At least as a Cabinet officer I won't have to smile all the time. Ronnie, my cheekbones hurt."

"But," the President protested, "I'm losing Deaver, Baker, and Meese. You're the only one left from the old gang. With them gone, who can I confide in?"

"Margaret Heckler is well qualified to be the First Lady. She knows the inner workings of government and she's a quick study. Besides, Ronnie, it's not as if I'm leaving Washington. I'll only be a few blocks away, and I'll come over any time you want to talk."

"Gee whiz, Nancy, I just don't think it would work. If you leave me now, with all the other staff changes, the American people will get upset. They sleep better knowing that you're in the White House."

"I was afraid you'd try to talk me out of it. But I have to think of my own career. There is no future in being a lame duck First Lady. As Secretary of HHS I'll have a high profile, and I won't have to deal with all the power plays in the White House anymore. I'm sick and tired of everyone coming to me and asking me to put in a good word with you for all the silly ideas they have."

"You don't understand, Nancy. I can afford to lose Deaver, Baker, and Meese, but who is going to look adoringly at me when I make a speech?"

"I'm sure Margaret Heckler can do that. We've talked it over, and I explained what the duties of First Lady entail, and she said as far as she was concerned there wasn't one she couldn't handle."

"You mean you talked it over with her before you talked it over with me?" the President said.

"I knew if I asked you first you might raise an objection. I got the idea when Donald Regan asked Jim Baker if he wanted to swap jobs. If Regan had gone to you first he could have been turned down."

"Suppose I put you on the National Security Council? Would you stay then?"

"I'd rather be in charge of Health and Human Services. I've proved myself as First Lady, and after four years there are no surprises."

"I can't believe anyone who has the ear of the President of the

United States would want to throw it all away for a Cabinet position. Do you realize you're the first person who sees me in the morning and the last person who sees me at night?"

"I know that, Ronnie. But as First Lady, I'm still perceived as nothing more than your wife. As a liberated woman, I want to be appreciated for myself."

"But you promised if I were reelected you'd remain on board as First Lady of the country for the next four years. You're indispensable to me."

"No one is indispensable to the President of the United States. And you can prove that by letting me switch with Margaret Heckler."

"I'm going to have to sleep on this one," the President said.

"Why don't you do that? And while you're at it, remember, it could be worse."

"How's that?"

"I could have offered to swap with Jeane Kirkpatrick."

The Selling
of the President

Now that the selling of the presidential inauguration has proved so successful, can the selling of the presidency be far behind?

The inauguration committee copyrighted the inaugural logo and licensed all rights to souvenir companies as well as corporations which could then advertise they were the "official company" of the presidential inauguration.

Obviously the committee got the idea from the Los Angeles Olympics. Inaugurations do cost money, but my fear is that the people who organized the presidential festivities won't stop there. They may soon start selling the rights to the presidency.

"White House Licensing Committee."

"This is the Fruitcake Cereal Company. We'd like to become the official cereal company to the President."

"We're sorry, those rights have already been spoken for. Do you make any other products?"

"We're the largest cupcake manufacturer in America."

"Well, cupcakes haven't been spoken for yet. We can let you have the presidential seal of approval for a million dollars."

"Will the President do our commercials?"

"He can't do that. But we'll give you permission to hang a tasteful cupcake banner behind him in the East Room when he's holding his press conferences."

"We'll take it. Send the contracts to us right away."

"Thank you . . . . White House Licensing Committee."

"This is the president of the Real Instant Coffee Company. We wish to sign on as the official coffee supplier to the White House."

"What did you have in mind?"

"We want to produce one TV commercial showing Margaret Thatcher drinking our coffee at a state dinner and expressing her surprise that it was an instant brand and did not come out of a coffeepot."

"I don't see any problem with that, but let me check it out with the White House chef and get back to you. . . . White House Licensing Committee."

"This is the Cartilage Sneaker Company. Has anyone put in a bid yet for the official President's running shoes?"

"No, it's still up for grabs."

"Good. All we ask in exchange is that the President and his wife wear our sneakers when they're running for the helicopter to take them to Camp David."

"I don't think we could promise you that. The First Lady has never publicly worn sneakers in her life. But we could get Vice

President George Bush to wear them as he's flying off to attend a state funeral."

"We don't want Bush, we want the President and his wife. If you can't deliver them forget it."

"Sorry about that. . . . White House Licensing Committee."

"This is the Yakamura Film Company. We want to become the official film company to the White House."

"It will cost you."

"We don't care what it costs. But we'd have to be assured that the White House photographers will only use Yakamura film when they take pictures of the President."

"We can't do that because we have no control over the White House photographers. But what we can do for you is make sure that those photographers using Yakamura film will get the best places up front to shoot from while they're snapping away at the President."

"Put us down for the license."

"Will do. . . . White House Licensing Committee."

"I'm a lawyer representing the Fourth of July Souvenir Company. The Secret Service visited my client yesterday and informed him he couldn't put the American flag on his beer mugs anymore."

"That's correct. We now hold the copyright on the Stars and Stripes. But for a small royalty your client can have exclusive beer-mug rights to the American flag for the next four years."

Dinner for Two

I read in a *Newsweek* story on yuppies that when credit card companies found women were not responding to their overwhelmingly male television commercials, they decided to launch ad campaigns which feature up-to-date activities such as a woman taking a man out to dinner to break in *her* card.

I've seen the ads on TV and I've been impressed with them. But I've always wondered what happens after the girl shows her charge card to the good-looking guy in the lobby of the skyscraper, and they go off to a very expensive restaurant.

The maître d'hôtel presents the menus.

Woman with credit card to male guest: What is your pleasure?

He: Why don't you order for the both of us?

She: Pasta verde with pesto sauce, steak Diane, soufflé potatoes, endive salad with the house dressing, and a bottle of the nouveau Beaujolais, slightly chilled. Kiwi soufflé for dessert.

He: You certainly know your food.

She: You have to if you're on the fast track.

He: I usually don't go to dinner with married women.

She: Come on, loosen up. We're out to have a fun evening.

He: I just didn't want you to get any ideas because you're buying me a meal that it will lead to something later on.

She: What kind of upwardly mobile person do you think I am? Have some more wine. Let's drink to having it all and having it now.

He: Having what now?

She: Did anyone ever tell you that you have beautiful eyes? Talk to me a little about yourself.

He: It's nothing exciting. I was raised in Iowa and came to the Big Apple to make a name in advertising.

She: I have some influential friends on Madison Avenue that might help you. They all owe me favors. Here's my card.

He: Please don't do that.

She: Do what?

He: Hold my hand. I'm not that kind of guy.

She: What kind is that?

He: You know. Someone who sleeps around with any woman who has a gold credit card.

She: Let me refill your glass.

He: You're trying to get me drunk so I won't know what I'm doing.

She: How can you say that? I wouldn't be a vice president of marketing if people didn't trust me.

He: Let's talk about your husband. What kind of person is he?

She: Let's just say he doesn't understand me. He's boring. All he wants to talk about is having children.

He: And you don't want children?

She: They don't issue gold credit cards to women who buy Pampers.

He: Please take your hand off my knee.

She: I was trying to find my napkin. Here, have another glass of wine with your steak Diane. Do you find me attractive?

He: Very much. But can't we just have a nice dinner and be friends?

She: We are friends. I genuinely like you for your mind. What health club do you go to?

He: I'm starting to feel tipsy. Maybe you better take me home.

She: If that's what you want. We could have a nightcap at your place.

He: No way. I told you not to get any ideas about the evening.

She: But we're the "me" generation, and we have the whole night ahead of us.

He: I vowed never to get involved with a married woman.

She: Why on earth not?

He: Because I don't want to be the "other man," waiting for the phone to ring while you're buying your husband dinner with your gold credit card.

Is Ed Meese Worth It?

"Hear ye, hear ye. In the case of the American taxpayers versus Ed Meese's lawyers, the court is now in session."

"Proceed."

"Your honor, as counsel for the American taxpayers I hold in my hand a bill for legal services for seven hundred and twenty-one thousand dollars. We believe this is too high a price to pay to insure that the next Attorney General of the United States is not a crook."

"Objection."

"Sustained. Counsel will stick with the facts."

"The facts, your honor, are that Mr. Meese's attorneys charged my clients two hundred and fifty dollars an hour to defend him against charges of conflict of interest in helping get government jobs for individuals who loaned him money. We feel these fees are totally out of line with President Reagan's vow to cut spending in the government."

"Objection, your honor. President Reagan's political promises have nothing to do with my client's legal fees."

"Sustained. Counsel will refrain from mentioning Mr. Reagan unless it has something to do with the case."

"There isn't a lawyer in America worth two hundred and fifty an hour, your honor . . ."

"Objection, your honor. Counsel has no right to decide what lawyers are worth."

"Let's see where he's going with his argument."

"The Justice Department policy—a policy I hope Mr. Meese will continue—has a ceiling of seventy-five dollars an hour on what a private lawyer can charge in a government case. Why doesn't it apply in this case?"

"Your honor. The Ethics in Government Act, under which Mr. Meese was investigated, places no restrictions on hourly rates. If a self-respecting lawyer in Washington charged less than two-fifty an hour he would become the laughing stock of the capital."

"It is so noted. Counsel for the taxpayers will continue."

"Thank you, sir. American taxpayers resent the fact that Mr. Meese's attorneys are socking it to them. I wonder if learned counsel would submit a bill for seven hundred and twenty-one thousand dollars if they knew Mr. Meese was paying it out of his own pocket."

"Objection. That is a theoretical question."

"Sustained."

"Your honor, counsel for Mr. Meese has charged my clients two hundred and fifty dollars an hour for conversations with the press over a period of five and one half months. Why should the taxpayer pay for attorneys' meetings with reporters?"

"I can answer that, your honor. Mr. Meese was being tried in the press as well as investigated by the special prosecutor. It was necessary to insure accurate reporting of allegations against him or else Meese would take over the Justice Department under a dark cloud. It's in the taxpayers' interest to have a US Attorney General who is squeaky clean."

"Your honor, just because Mr. Meese was cleared of criminal charges against him doesn't necessarily make him qualified to be Attorney General. What about his bad judgment?"

"Objection. Mr. Meese's bad judgment has nothing to do with our legal bill."

"Your honor, I say it does. If Mr. Meese didn't show such extraordinarily bad judgment in the first place, the taxpayer would not be stuck for seven hundred and twenty-one thousand dollars."

PART EIGHT

HELPING THE FARMER

Helping
the Farmer

President Reagan, in last week's radio address, said the government has done everything it can for the farmer. It is now time for others to pitch in and do more, "from officials at the state level to banks, private groups, and individuals in the community."

I wasn't quite sure what I, as an individual, could do to help the farmer, so I drove out to Culpeper, Virginia.

"Hi, Farmer Brown. President Reagan told me I should pitch in and help you. What exactly can I do?"

"You can buy my farm."

"I don't know much about farming."

"Shucks, there's nothing to it. All you have to do is get up at five, milk the cows, feed the hogs, and see how many chickens died in the night from the frost. Any fool can do that."

"When do you get to play golf or tennis?"

"After you till the soil, plant your seed, spread fertilizer, spray for bugs, and dig furrows for irrigation."

"Don't you ever get into town?"

"Sure. You get to go once, maybe twice a week, to meet with your banker and explain to him why you can't meet the payments on your loan."

"Dave Stockman says the reason you farmers owe so much money to the banks is you keep speculating in land and buying new equipment to make windfall profits at the expense of the American taxpayer."

"Dave's a good old boy, but he knows as much about farming as he does about drawing up a balanced budget."

"It wasn't just Stockman. President Reagan said the same thing. The reason you're in so much trouble is you bet on inflation and you were wrong. Didn't you hear him Saturday morning?"

"I meant to. But since it was the weekend I decided to relax and dig fence holes, repair the barn, cut down timber, wash my horse, and sit up with a sick calf. I'll let you have the farm real cheap."

"How much money can I make?"

"You can make a bundle—provided the bugs don't get your corn, the subzero temperatures don't freeze your tomatoes, your cows don't get pneumonia, the dollar gets weaker, and the Russians are starving to death."

"You don't make it sound like much fun."

"It's a lot of fun if you're a gambler. What other business offers you a chance to bet your house on the crap table once a year?"

"The people in Washington say the reason you farmers are living on the edge is that you're always producing too much food and the taxpayers are stuck with the bill."

"I can't quarrel with that. We're just dumb people who know how to grow things, but we don't know how to market them. The ideal situation for America is if we farmers didn't grow enough food and made everyone pay through the nose. Then instead of the taxpayer having to give us price supports, we could charge him fifteen dollars for a pound of potatoes. I'm sure those smart fellows in Washington will be able to figure out a way of causing a food shortage in the country so we could get a fair price for our crops. You should buy my farm now while it's dirt cheap. Then when Washington works out a plan there will be so few farms left you can get six dollars for a quart of raw milk on the open market."

"It sounds tempting. But I'm not sure I want to be a farmer. Even if you make a lot of money it doesn't sound like you have much time to enjoy it. Isn't there some other way I can help you?"

"Well if you're going back to Washington you can take this corncob with you and tell David Stockman to stick it in his ear."

The Auto Vigilantes

The vigilante movement is really catching on in the United States. I had read about vigilantes on the subways, and vigilantes in the streets, but I didn't realize they had also taken to their automobiles.

Bart Urp, an unusually mild-mannered man, revealed to me as we drove to work that he carries a gun just in case another driver tries to cut him off or take his parking place

"You wouldn't *use* the gun?" I asked him.

"Of course I would. If another car attacks me, what choice do I have?"

"But you're taking the law into your own hands."

Bart said, "So be it. The police aren't interested in protecting innocent drivers from the criminals, so we have to do it ourselves. Look at that taxi driver over there. He's trying to get into my lane."

"There's construction work going on in his lane."

299

"Tough luck for him. One more move and he's going to get it right between the eyes."

"You've read him all wrong," I protested. "He has his signal on and all he is asking to do is get in your lane."

"Three weeks ago a dame tried to cut in front of me, and I rammed into her back bumper. She skidded on ice for half a block. You should have seen the look of terror on her face as she realized that someone had finally decided to fight back. She'll never mess with a law-abiding citizen again."

"I can't believe you, Bart. You've turned into an animal."

"You'd turn into one too if you had to drive to work during rush hour. It isn't safe to be on the streets. Where are the cops to protect us?"

"From what?" I asked.

"That school bus over there, for one. The driver's looking at me funny."

"He's looking at you funny because you still have your gun in your hand. I know our traffic system isn't perfect, but you're never going to make it better by shooting a school bus driver."

"I may not shoot him," Bart said, "but I can scare the hell out of him."

A car shot out from a side street and Bart put everything he had into his horn. "Did you see what he did? He went through a stop sign."

I shouted, "It's not your problem, Bart!"

"If not mine then whose; if not now then when?" he cried. "I'll give him one shot across his hood. If he doesn't stop, the next bullet blows up the gas tank."

I grabbed the gun. "Not while I'm in this car."

Bart looked at me. "So you're one of them."

"Them?"

"The bleeding hearts who don't care about all the drivers out in the street ready to kill, rape, and pillage the community."

"Vigilantes are not going to save us from bad drivers," I said. "Everyone thinks the person behind the wheel of another car doesn't know how to drive, and we all have fantasies about knocking them off. But if we were able to fulfill those wishes, we would wipe out half the population in America."

"You can save that drivel for your column," Bart said. "Once people know you're not going to let them pass you without a fight, they'll think twice about giving you the horn."

"Unless they also have a gun in their car," I said. "When will all the killing end?"

Bart said, "When the cops start protecting us from people on the road who shouldn't be there. There isn't a driver in America who isn't a vigilante in his heart."

How Green Is My Mail

Ever since the oil crisis back in the seventies, I've had a fantasy that someday I would drill a well in my backyard and hit the biggest gusher this side of Kuwait.

I made the mistake of telling my dream to a banker friend named Eyal Shapira.

"There's an oil glut now and you'd be better off capping the well and sitting on it until the prices go up," he said.

"But what about my fantasy? I need the money right now."

"Why don't you make a bid on an oil company?"

"How can I make money buying an oil company if there is an oil glut?"

"You won't make your fortune on oil. You'll make it attempting to take over the company."

"I'm listening."

"Name an oil company, any oil company."

"Phillips Petroleum out of Bartlesville, Oklahoma."

"That's a good one. T. Boone Pickens made a pass at them and failed."

"Well if he couldn't buy it how can I?"

"You *don't* want to buy it. You want to announce you're buying it. In today's world of high finance the easy money is made not from producing oil, but from producing threats."

"I don't see how I can make dough from threatening to buy an oil company."

"Haven't you ever heard of greenmail?"

"What's greenmail?" I asked.

"It's like blackmail, only it's legal. Now this is what you've got to do. You announce your intention of taking over Phillips for nine billion dollars."

"Wait a minute, where do I get nine billion dollars?"

"From the banks, you dumbbell."

"What do I put up as collateral?"

"The Phillips Petroleum Company. If you sold off all its assets it would be worth fifteen billion."

"But I don't own Phillips yet. How can I put it up as collateral?"

"It doesn't matter if you own it or not at this stage. The bank doesn't have to give you money. All it has to do is promise to provide it for you if you win the takeover. In the meantime you can buy up enough stock to become a threat. Once the word is out that you're serious about the takeover, you can demand an inflated price for your shares in exchange for promising *not* to raid Phillips again."

"I don't want to do anything illegal in my fantasy," I warned my friend.

"Everything I've told you is legal. That's the beauty of today's takeovers. You don't have to produce anything, or employ people, or worry about Japan. All you have to do is make nasty noises and you can walk away with a fortune."

"What kind of money are we talking about?"

"The last guy who tried to take over Phillips is ahead some-where between fifty and one hundred million dollars, and he didn't have to find one cup of oil."

Shapira continued, "Just think. If, in your fantasy, you become a greenmailer instead of an oil driller, you could have the management of any petroleum company on their knees. That to me is a *real* American dream."

"I'm in Heaven"

Attention, earthlings. It won't be long before you can "bury" your loved ones in outer space. Deke Slayton, a former astronaut, is working with a consortium of companies that will orbit the ashes of a deceased person nineteen hundred miles above the earth. Funeral services should begin in late 1986.

The Department of Transportation has enthusiastically approved the plan and said, "it represents a creative response to the President's initiative to encourage the commercial use of space."

As I understand it, the remains of your Uncle Sidney will be compressed by a secret process in a special two-inch-tall, lipstick-shaped, titanium capsule, which will then be placed into a three-hundred-pound shiny sphere, along with the ashes of 10,330 of the recently departed. The sphere will be launched into the heavens, where it's guaranteed to remain in orbit for at least sixty-three million years, or you get your money back.

While Mr. Slayton's consortium will provide the rocket and the capsule, they prefer to leave actual sales and arrangements to funeral directors and undertakers around the country.

This might lead to some problems.

"Please have a chair."

"Thank you. I would like to cremate my Uncle Sidney and put him in celestial orbit."

"You're in luck. We have a launch next month, and we can reserve a place for him."

"Wonderful. I noticed in your advertisement that the price for the service was three thousand nine hundred dollars."

"That's the base cost just to get him up there. Did you love your Uncle Sidney?"

"Very much."

"Then I wouldn't advise you to put his ashes in the standard titanium capsule."

"Why not?"

"I'm not supposed to tell you this, but although the containers are advertised to last for sixty-five million years, some of them fall apart after thirty million. You wouldn't want your uncle's ashes all over the sky, would you?"

"I guess not."

"Then I'd recommend this upgraded From Here to Eternity model. Notice the outside is twice as strong as titanium, and the inside is lined with French satin."

"How much is it?"

"It's only nine hundred dollars more, but if you insist on the cheap tacky one, I'm sure your uncle would understand."

"No, no. I'll take the From Here to Eternity capsule. Will that do it?"

"There is the placement of the ash container in the sphere. I assume you would want your Uncle Sidney as close to the skin as possible, facing toward the earth."

"Certainly."

"Then there is a premium charge of six hundred dollars to guarantee his ashes won't be thrown in the middle with all the economy-class passengers. Will you want to bid a fond adieu to your loved one as he is launched into space?"

"Of course."

"We can give you a package tour to Cape Canaveral with complimentary breakfast before liftoff, at a group rate of fifteen hundred dollars per person."

"Sending Uncle Sidney up into orbit is costing me more than I planned on."

"But it's worth it. Every time you look up to the heavens, you will see your Uncle Sidney and know he is smiling down on you because you booked him first class."

The Uncle Doctrine

When President Reagan was asked if he intended to overthrow the Sandinista government in Nicaragua, the President replied he wouldn't if they said uncle.

"What does he mean by that?" I asked my reliable State Department source.

"Remember when you were a boy and you wrestled another kid to the ground? The first one who cried uncle lost. Then the winner got up without breaking the loser's arm."

"What has that got to do with Nicaragua?"

"It's our new foreign policy. We're willing to let any country exist as long as it cries uncle."

"How do you get Nicaragua to cry uncle?"

"The best way is to support the 'freedom fighters' who are trying to overthrow the government there. Since Congress is reluctant to put up the money to make the Sandinistas scream uncle, the President is taking his case to the American people. He and Secretary of State George Schultz have warned that if Congress won't support this country's Uncle Doctrine, then we may wind up in an endless darkness of communist tyranny."

"If our policy is to make totalitarian countries cry uncle, why don't we overthrow the government of Chile?"

"We can't go into Chile because the military regime there is on our side. Nicaragua, on the other hand, fits the ideological profile and is just the right size, provided we give their freedom fighters the strength to wrestle the present government to the ground."

"Why don't we make South Korea cry uncle?"

"Because our Uncle Policy is only aimed at *communist* totalitarian governments that are not chosen by the people."

"What's the legal basis for making a government cry uncle if we don't like what they're doing?"

"The present policy is not predicated on legal grounds but moral ones. The President believes we have a moral duty to help people bring about freedom in their country and overthrow the tyranny from the left by covert force."

"What about tyranny from the right?"

"We only deal with tyranny from the right by quiet diplomacy. If we make a right-wing government say uncle publicly, it might be replaced by a left-wing government, and that is something we have to avoid at all costs."

"How much will it take to make the Nicaraguans cry uncle?"

"The President wants fourteen million dollars to help the freedom fighters make the Sandinistas throw in the towel."

"That doesn't sound like a lot of money. Does he really believe the Nicaraguans will cry uncle if we give the opposition fourteen million?"

"No, but it will get our feet wet. Once they use it up, then the President can go back to Congress and ask for some *real* money to overthrow the Managua government. If money doesn't do it, then we may have to send in American boys to do the job right. It won't be the first time American troops made the Nicaraguans say uncle."

"If we're going to go to that much trouble to overthrow a communist regime in our hemisphere, why don't we knock off Cuba?"

"Because if we tried to overthrow Castro it might bring in the Soviets. Then the question of who cries uncle first might be superfluous."

What a Mandate

Democratic Congressman Tender was chuckling.

"What's the joke?" I asked him as we stood on the steps of the Capitol after lunch.

"They're all coming up here to make their case, and get relief."

"Who is they?"

"The people who voted for Ronald Reagan in November because he promised to cut government spending without raising their taxes. The joke is everyone thought Reagan was talking about the other guy when it came to chopping off a federal program. The farmers voted for him because they believed he would eliminate urban transportation subsidies, the yuppies voted for him because they wanted him to cut agricultural price supports. The conservative students thought his economies had nothing to do with school tuition, and the Republican governors still can't believe the Gipper wants to do away with federal revenue sharing."

"But the President has to cut the budget deficit," I said.

"I didn't say he doesn't. All I'm saying is that everybody who voted for him, except for the defense contractors, didn't realize they were on Stockman's hit list. Come over to my office and see what's going on."

We wandered over to the Sam Rayburn Building. Tender pushed through the crowd to his office.

"I make them take a number like you do in a Baskin-Robbins Ice Cream Store." He rang for his secretary. "Who's out there this afternoon?"

She replied, "There is a delegation from the Fraternal Order of Retired Military Officers, the Contractors to Save Federal Highways, the Tax Shelter Institute of America, the Tobacco Growers United, the American Medical Association, the Veterans of Foreign Wars, the Brotherhood of Real Estate Brokers, the US Chamber of Commerce, and the entire state of South Dakota."

"Anybody waiting who voted for the Democrats?" Tender asked.

"Not that I know of. The Retired Military Officers are holding number 345 and are next."

"Send them in," Tender said.

The RMO delegation crowded into Tender's office. The spokesman said, "Congressman, are you going to allow cuts in our fighting men's pensions?"

"I hadn't thought about it until our Commander-in-Chief said it had to be done."

"It's an outrage. We had a contract with the American people that if we served our country we would be compensated for it. Now they're trying to break the faith and it's your duty to stop it!"

"Have you gentlemen taken this up with the Republicans?"

"They have to support the President on this. Our only chance is for the Democrats to stop it before it becomes a fact."

"I don't know why you are so shocked. The President has to cut everything across the board."

"Then why doesn't he cut the defense weapons budget? As retired military people we can assure you there's more waste there than anyplace in the government."

"I didn't think I'd ever hear you people say that."

"We wouldn't before Reagan announced he was going to cut

308

back on our pensions. Congressman, you're our only hope," the spokesman said with tears in his eyes.

Tender put his arm around the man. "I'll see what I can do."

After they left, Tender said, "This has been going on ever since President Reagan proposed his new budget. I know I shouldn't enjoy it, but we Democrats have so little to be happy about. It isn't our fault that the people gave the President a mandate and he gave them the sword."

University
of Champions

"Pressure for profits fuels cheating in college sports"—headline in *USA Today*.

Football coach Bobby Tawdry was livid. He had just been informed by the president of the University of Champions that his 1985 budget had been frozen.

"How do they expect me to get to a bowl game if they don't give me the tools to do it?" Tawdry asked his wife Delta.

"Why would he freeze your budget?" she asked him.

"He says he needs more money for his professors. They want to be paid the same rates as the football players."

"That's ridiculous. There isn't a top twenty school in America that could afford to pay professors what you pay your players. Did you point out that the team makes a profit while professors are just a drain on school finances?"

"Sure I did. And he said there's a new rule. I have to spend as much money on education as I do on athletics or the school will lose its accreditation. I said I'd like to see him tell that to an all-state lineman who won't take less than a hundred thousand dollars to play on the team."

"I hope that shook him up," Delta said.

"It should have. But then he went into a song and dance about how much money the athletic department was spending on steroids. He said it doesn't look good for a major university to be dispensing drugs to the football team. The next thing I expected him to do was tell me I have to play the kids without painkillers."

Delta was furious. "They all live in their ivory towers and have no idea what it takes to win a conference title! How do they think you can fill the stadium every Saturday afternoon without pills? Did you tell him if you didn't give your players steroids they would never be big enough to get a contract in pro football?"

"Yes, and he mumbled something about it wasn't the university's job to develop talent for professional sports. I told him, 'We're the little leagues for pro football. The only reason the kids put out a hundred percent is so they can get the attention of the NFL scouts in the stands.' "

"Did that shut him up?"

"It did about the steroids, but then he brought up student grades. He said he was still getting heat from the Conference about players not attending any classes last year. He told me the faculty has its back up, and recently voted not to pass anybody unless he came to school. Furthermore, he said I could no longer suit up a member of the team unless he could read and write. That really sent me through the roof. I told him, 'You're tying both my hands behind my back. Why don't you cut off my legs and be done with it?' "

"I'm amazed you kept your temper as long as you did," Delta said.

"Then I told him, 'I was hired to coach football to bring glory and recognition to the school. But I have to do it my way. If you freeze the money so I can't recruit the high school players, and if you put impossible drug and educational restrictions in my way, then I have no choice but to take my case to the alumni. Let them decide whether they want a winning team or one that plays by the NCAA rules and becomes the laughing stock of Saturday's TV game of the week.' "

"And he folded?" Delta said.

"He should have but he didn't. He said he was going to take it up with the board of trustees and ask for a vote of confidence. I warned him it was a mistake. When trustees have to choose between an administrator who is throwing away money on faculty salaries, and a winning football coach who is bringing in twenty million dollars a year, the school president doesn't have a prayer."

Wacko
in Washington

Does the fact that Washington has the most psychotherapists mean that there are more mentally deranged people here than anywhere else? The answer is probably yes.

Dr. Arnold Frisher, a noted psychiatrist who has been practicing in D.C. for forty years, and takes only the toughest cases, maintains that something happens to people after they stay in Washington awhile.

He said, "To put it in professional terms, fifty percent are nuttier than fruitcakes."

"How do you account for it?"

"Pressure, power, and politics. Although most of them are normal people when they come here, it doesn't take long for them to lose all sense of reality. Let me give you an example. I

have a patient who works for the Office of Management and
Budget. He makes twenty-eight thousand dollars a year. Every
time he comes to see me he says he has just chopped another billion dollars out of a government program. Then he bites his fin-
gernails."

"Would that make him crazy?"

"No. But on each visit he claims he's brought the money with
him and wants me to put it in my safe so Congress can't get their
mitts on it."

"It sounds as if he's suffering from exhaustion."

"That or guilt," Dr. Frisher said. "Six months ago he took a
wheelchair away from his eighty-year-old mother because he
said she wasn't entitled to it on Medicare."

"Why would he feel guilty about that?" I asked.

"She calls him every morning and tells him not to worry about
her because his father has offered to carry her to the supermarket
on his back."

"What other troubled patients do you see?"

"I have a senator who took five million dollars from political
action committees in the last election but still believes he's his
own man. Then there is a secretary of education who has a pho-
bia about college kids, a US Justice Department attorney for civil
rights who loathes civil rights, a newspaper reporter who be-
haves like an animal, a lobbyist who claims to have twenty congressmen sewn up in his pocket, and a CIA official who has to
continually wash his hands every time he testifies about Nicaragua."

"Is that it?"

"No. I have this high official in the White House who maintains he has a mandate to spend a trillion dollars on new weapons to keep the peace."

"That wouldn't make him gonzo. The White House did win
forty-nine states."

"My patient doesn't claim he has a mandate from the people—he says he has one from God."

"Haven't you ever had patients who talk to God?"

"Yes, but I have never had one who told me God wanted him to spend a trillion dollars. That's manic."

"At the same time, the way things seem to be going, a trillion dollars isn't too much to invest for security on earth."

"My patient doesn't want to spend it on earth. He wants to spend it in the sky."

"How is he going to do that?"

"He doesn't know. That is why he says he comes to me. He wants me to find the answer before people say he's flipped out."

"It sounds like a hopeless case. Why don't you fire him as a patient?"

"Because I think I have the solution. If I could hook up a network of lasers to ten hydrogen bombs and explode them just as the moon passed over the Soviet Union, I could create a nuclear winter which would negate a first-strike capability, and then the Russians would come to me and say, 'Ain't going to go to war no more, ain't going to go to war no more, ain't g-o-i-n-g to go to war no mooorrrrre.' "

Defending Defense

The biggest item in the General Dynamics billing dispute with the government is 4.5 million dollars for "public relations."

"What has public relations got to do with building submarines, planes, and tanks?" I asked the GD spokesman.

"If we didn't inform the people about the good job we were doing, we wouldn't get any reorders for new weapons. Whenever the taxpayer needs a Trident submarine, an F-16 fighter, or an M-1 tank, we want him to think General Dynamics."

"I can see the advantage from your standpoint. But I'm not clear why the taxpayer should be billed millions of dollars for your company's advertising and PR campaign."

He replied, "The average American doesn't know one billion-dollar system from another, and it is essential that he believes he is getting top-of-the-line merchandise for his money. The only way he will ever become a discriminating buyer and a connoisseur of fine weaponry is if he knows what defense contractors he can count on. That's why education through the media is so important."

"I don't quarrel with that," I said. "But you would think since you make so much money on your weapons, you would throw in your public relations costs for nothing."

"It's impossible to separate the price of our hardware from our PR costs. The consumer's faith in what we make is as important to this country's survival as the weapons themselves."

I then asked, "How does the taxpayer know the press releases he is paying for tell the entire story of what your company is doing for him?"

"Because we adhere rigorously to the 'Truth in Defense' contracting code. It prohibits us from advertising unsubstantiated claims about our weapons, deliberately underbidding to get a contract, and issuing false information concerning cost overruns. Under the code we have agreed to put a surgeon general's warning on all our products saying, 'This weapon could be dangerous to your health.' Without the code we contractors are nothing."

"I would like to ask you about some specific items which you people charged us for. Why the ten thousand F-16 necktie tacks?"

He said, "The F-16 is the finest fighter the company has ever built, and we felt our friends in and out of the Pentagon needed a tie clasp to remind them of it. With our markup they still cost less than a dollar apiece."

"I don't think the taxpayer objects to you giving gifts to any-

314

body. But there is still the question of who should have to pay for them."

"It is written in our contract that all tie tacks, cufflinks, and gifts to Admiral Rickover's wife may be listed as spare parts and included in the price of a weapon. That goes for baseball hats, necklaces, and special branding irons."

"I was going to ask about those branding irons. What do they have to do with the defense of the country?"

"Those branding irons were one of the most popular gifts we ever handed out. There are people all over Texas and Oklahoma who would have never heard of our fighter if they hadn't seen a steer with an F-16 logo on his butt."

"What other justification do you have for the Pentagon paying your public relations fees?"

"The obvious one is so we can defend ourselves in Congress and the media against charges that we are bilking the public. It would be criminal for an established defense contractor to pay those costs out of his own pocket."

Watching Gorbachev

The Soviet Watchers of Washington met last week in the Darkness at Noon Russian Tea Room to be briefed on Mikhail Sergeyevich Gorbachev's rise to the top of the USSR.

Professor Nicholai Dubokowsky, one of the leading Kremlinologists in this country, gave us the word. "Gorbachev may be around for at least thirty years, so you have to watch him very closely."

"What should we watch for?"

"Since he is only fifty-four years old, you should watch the way he stands when he's on the top of Lenin's Tomb. Remember, he is the first Soviet leader in ten years who can watch a parade without a Politburo member on each side holding on to his arms so he won't fall down. This has its good and bad implications. The fact that he can stand on his own two feet makes Gorbachev dangerous. At the same time we can expect more credibility from the Kremlin on their leader's health. Now when they announce he has a bad cold, we can all assume he *does* have a bad cold."

"Why is Gorbachev getting such a good press?"

"Because he speaks English and wears nice suits. One of the reasons Americans never trusted the Soviet leaders in the past was that they wore such tacky clothes. How could you discuss ways of avoiding World War Three with people who dressed in baggy pants and white socks? Gorbachev is a new breed of Russian. His suit coat fits, and his choice of shirts and ties is impeccable. He's the type of person you're not ashamed to be photographed with at a summit conference."

"Does the fact that he's a snappy dresser mean he's a more formidable adversary?"

"He could go either way. Khrushchev almost brought us to nuclear destruction by hammering his shoe on the podium at the United Nations. Gorbachev would never do this because he's afraid it would ruin his shine. But you still have to watch him very carefully. The fact that he doesn't drool all over the medals on his chest could be to NATO's disadvantage. With the others, you knew they weren't going to be around very long, so the West was willing to put up with their peccadillos for a year or two. With Gorbachev it will be at least three decades before he winds up in the Kremlin Wall."

"Do you think he will flaunt the fact he is only fifty-four years old in Reagan's face?"

"He has already. In a hand-delivered letter to President Reagan Gorbachev started by addressing it 'Dear Uncle Ronnie.' That threw the President for a loop. He doesn't even like his grandchildren to call him Grandpa."

"Vice President George Bush was watching Gorbachev throughout Chernenko's funeral. What was his impression of the man?"

"As you know, Mr. Bush has become an expert at watching Soviet leaders at Moscow funerals. He came back quite impressed. Mr. Bush thinks Gorbachev has the potential to become the first Soviet Yuppie Premier. The leader seems to enjoy the good things in life, and one of his priorities is to provide more of the same for his people. The Vice President believes if we can get Gorbachev to import more Perrier and buy more BMWs with stereo tape decks in them, the Soviets will lose their appetite for world conquest."

What about Mrs. Gorbachev? Should we spend much time watching her?"

"You have no choice. The press is now referring to her as another Jackie Kennedy. Mrs. Gorbachev could be a big help to the Soviet leader when he travels around the world. The thing to watch is his first trip to France. If he pulls a John Kennedy and says, 'I am the man who accompanied Raisa Gorbachev to Paris,' and it gets a big hand, we're in a lot more trouble than most people think."

Little
Red Riding Hood, Inc.

Once upon a time there was a sweet thing called Red Riding Hood, who owned Little Red Riding Hood, Inc., a small company that made children's dresses. One day she was walking down Wall Street when she met a great big wolf (Amalgamated Wolf).

"Where are you going, Red Riding Hood?" the wolf asked.

"To Grandmother Pizza's office with this new issue of stock which I hope will make her well."

The wolf thought to himself, "What a tasty morsel. I could eat Grandmother Pizza for breakfast and Red Riding Hood, Inc., for lunch."

The wolf then said, "Where are your grandmother's offices?"

And Red Riding Hood replied, "In the World Trade Center building."

The wolf then said, "Would you like to have a hot pretzel from the stand over there?"

"Why not? They are not expecting me at Grandmother's board meeting for a half hour."

Whilst Red Riding Hood was eating her pretzel and drinking her soda, the wolf sped off to the World Trade Center. He dashed into Grandmother Pizza's office and ate poor Grandmother up.

Then he pulled the curtains and sat in her leather chair.

Red Riding Hood was ushered in by the secretary.

"Good morning, Grandmother."

The wolf did not reply.

"Oh, Grandmother, what big ears you have."

"The better to hear all the merger rumors on the Street," the wolf replied.

"Oh, Grandmother, what big eyes you have."

"The better to read everyone's latest financial report."

"What big hands you've got."

"The better to grab all your assets with, my dear."

"Grandmother, what big teeth you have."

"The better to eat you with!" And with that the wolf sprang out of his chair and made a lunge for Red Riding Hood, who easily sidestepped him and knocked him to the floor.

"What are you doing?" the stunned wolf asked.

Red Riding Hood sat on the wolf's stomach and said, "I'm taking you over."

"You can't take me over," the wolf cried. "I'm five times bigger than you are."

"Size means nothing," Red Riding Hood said. "The only thing that counts is how much money I can raise to get control."

"Where could you find enough dough to buy a great big wolf?"

"I'll make a leveraged buyout. I'll cut off your head and sell it to a museum, your coat to a furrier, and your teeth to a key chain company. It's all here in the prospectus."

"The SEC will never let you do it."

"They haven't stopped anyone from swallowing anybody else up yet," Red Riding Hood retorted.

"Wait," the wolf said. "Why can't we make this a friendly takeover? Give me a golden parachute and I'll never try to eat you again."

"Sorry, but it's too late." And with that Red Riding Hood cut open the wolf's stomach and out popped her grandmother, who had a grin on her face.

The grandmother said, "It worked. I knew we could get control once he got fat and cocky."

Red Riding Hood said, "Where do you get that we stuff, Grandma? I'm spinning you off to Standard Oil of New Jersey."

President Reagan's
Secret

The secret of President Reagan's popularity is that he has the ability to make us feel good when we know we should feel bad.

His recent State of the Union speech was another triumph for the Gipper.

I have no idea how it played in Peoria, but from what I could tell it went over quite well in Washington.

"What did you think of the President's speech?" I asked a secretary in my building.

"I thought it was wonderful," she said. "He leveled with the American people."

"When did he do that?"

"When he asked the lady cadet from West Point to take a bow from the balcony."

"You felt that was the highlight of his address?" I inquired.

"That and when he asked the lady from Harlem to also take a bow because of what she had done for little babies."

"Yes, but what about the fact that the President glossed over the budget deficit and indicated that he wanted to proceed with the MX missile and Star Wars. Did you have any feelings on that?"

"Not really. I just thought Nancy looked beautiful in her red dress."

A young man working as an intern on my floor said, "I thought it was a good speech and it was about time someone came out for the poor people and the farmers and the urban centers and deregulation of the airlines, and the Peace Corps."

"Then you didn't get the impression that the President was avoiding the issue of how he expected to reduce the budget deficit without raising taxes?"

"Frankly, I wasn't listening that closely. All I know is what he told us. The country's in excellent shape now, and it's going to get even better if Congress passes all of Mr. Reagan's programs."

"That's a big if."

"Well, they sang 'Happy Birthday' to him."

"Was there anything about the speech you didn't like?"

"I was very annoyed when George Bush and Tip O'Neill kept talking while the President was speaking. They shouldn't have done that."

"Perhaps they weren't paying attention because the President had given the same speech before," I suggested.

"It doesn't matter if they heard it before. They should have pretended they didn't."

My third survey victim told me the thing she liked about the speech was the President's tie.

"Is there anything else you remember about it besides the President's tie?"

"No," she said. "Was I supposed to?"

"Forget the President's speech for a moment. What did you think of the Democratic reply?"

"What reply?"

"They put on their own reply to the President's State of the Union speech."

"I didn't hear it. I was watching 'Dynasty.' "

"Don't tell me you'd rather watch 'Dynasty' than hear the Democrats defend their party."

She said in disbelief, "Now you're putting me on."

Big House, Inc.

I always depend on Simon Wallin for inside information on the stock market.

The other day I got a call from him. "I have only one word to say to you," he whispered.

"I'm listening," I told him.

"Prisons."

"Prisons? What the hell kind of stock market tip is that?"

"Private prisons are soon going to be bigger than private hospitals. Incarceration is a growth industry, and I want you to get in on the ground floor. There's a new company just starting up called Big House, Inc."

"Come on. How are people going to make money on prisons?"

"Good management and tax breaks," Simon said. "There's an unbelievable demand for new prisons in every state in the union. The public wants criminals locked up, but they refuse to pay for the jailhouses. So they are giving out franchises to private entrepreneurs who have figured out a way of making money on the penal system."

"I don't get it. If the government is running in the red putting people away, how can the private sector get the system in the black?"

"It's the way prisons are financed. When the government builds a prison complex it has to borrow money from the public. If a private company builds it, then it becomes a tax shelter."

"They're going to lock up prisoners in tax shelters?"

"We're not going to put prisoners in tax shelters, we're putting investors in them."

"Okay, so I'm in a prison tax shelter. Now what happens?"

"Big House, Inc., leases it back to the government and gets a management contract to run it. We receive the depreciation on the prison as well as a daily fee for each prisoner we take care of."

"I'm not sure I want to make money on people who are locked up."

"You'll be doing the inmates a service because Big House, Inc., will treat the prison population much better than the bureaucrats treat them now. After all, they have a vested interest in the convicts' happiness. In order to make money they have to count on word-of-mouth. If former inmates start bad-mouthing Big House in the underworld, offenders will ask to be sent to the competition's prisons after they're caught."

"What about conflict of interest? Suppose a person is up for parole, and Big House doesn't want to give it to him because they'll be stuck with an empty bed. I would hate to deprive a man of his freedom just because I'm afraid of losing his business."

"You have nothing to worry about on that score. There's a waiting list for every prison in America. Most states are guaranteeing private-prison corporations one-hundred-and-five percent occupancy for the next twenty years."

"Won't prisoners be resentful that people are trying to make money on them?"

"Not when they realize private companies have a lot more to offer than public institutions. Big House is putting in the best security equipment money can buy. That way no one can break into a prison where they don't belong. We're also installing the latest athletic facilities, cable TV, workshops, and leisure activities. Their guards have been instructed to wish every prisoner a nice day. They have put 'How Did We Do?' questionnaires in all the cells, asking inmates to compare them with other prisons they've been in. Our business is to make the consumer, in this case the inmate, consider Big House a home away from home. That's the only way you get repeat business."

"It sounds awfully good on paper, but I still don't understand how, if they're going to provide all these services, Big House will still make a big profit on running a prison institution."

"It's quite simple," Simon said. "They're going to serve all the inmates airline food."

Robert Flack & Company

One of the better jobs in Washington these days is working for a public relations firm. There are hundreds of them all over the city, and anyone with a decent name in government can find a home at one—at triple his or her present salary.

There was a time when PR companies worked cheaply and secretly for their clients. Now they charge enormous fees and get their names in the newspapers as frequently as the people they're supposed to publicize.

What do PR firms in Washington do to earn their money? I dropped in on Robert Flack, founder of one of the hottest firms in the business. Among those listed as vice presidents on Flack's door are two retired assistant secretaries of state, the wife of a congressman, an ex-presidential advance man, a South American general, and the former Emperor of Tubistoland.

Flack's large penthouse office overlooks the White House.

"Boy," I said. "You have some view."

He smiled as he pointed out the window. "Some of the happiest days of my life were spent in the Rose Garden over there."

"I'll bet you miss it," I said.

He sighed. "It's only a stone's throw away, and the old man said I can smell the flowers anytime I want to. What can I do for you?"

"There's been a lot of stuff about Washington PR firms in the papers lately and I was curious. Why the high profile?"

"Well, first and foremost, we need clients who can afford our services. In order to get them we have to make sure everyone is aware that we know the right buttons to push. Excuse me just a moment. . . . Miss Blackwell, if Ed Meese calls tell him I'm still out to lunch. . . . What were you saying?"

"Is the client buying access to people in power?"

"Let's get this straight. I never mention my White House or Hill connections to get a client. I don't want them to think I can open any powerful doors for them just because I'm asking for a six-figure retainer."

"Then why do you have that autographed photo of Tip O'Neill on your desk?"

"It makes me feel good just to look at him."

"How about the one next to it of Nancy Reagan?"

"Nancy gave it to me, and I'm scared to death she's going to walk in here one day and not find it."

"Okay, so you don't use your government connections for your business. What do you do for your clients?"

"Hold it," he said. "Miss Blackwell, call Caspar Weinberger and tell him he looked great on the Ted Koppel show last night."

"You know Caspar Weinberger?" I asked.

"I never talk about anybody in Washington that I know," he said. "Back to my business. What we do is present our client's image in the best light. That does not mean we lie or are dishonest. But there are two sides to every story. Here's a perfect example," he said, holding up a photo of dead people lying in the street. "A foreign government retained us because American television kept showing their troops shooting demonstrators. We immediately put out the story that the only reason the people were shot was because demonstrations are forbidden in the country and the people were breaking the law."

"Didn't President Reagan say that about South Africa at his press conference?"

"We had nothing to do with that," he protested. "South Africa isn't our client."

"I didn't say it was. So what do you do besides make bad countries look good?"

"We don't make bad countries look good. We make *strong* countries look good. We also represent US industries under attack from the government, and create favorable climates for businessmen who are going to be indicted by a federal grand jury. We provide junkets for the media, and will even write their stories and film their TV news spots for them. America couldn't have an informed public without people like us."

"I believe it. Thanks for your time."

"Don't mention it. Oh, by the way, if you see Henry Kissinger out in the waiting room tell him I haven't fogotten he's there."

Happy Tax Day

My wife and I are not the sort of people who make a big deal about filling out our tax returns. As far as we're concerned it's just another rite of spring that has to be dealt with, like spreading mulch on the lawn and manure in the rose garden.

Not long ago, as we have done for so many years, we cleared off the dining room table, sat down with all our forms, the checkbook, a bottle of champagne and two glasses, donned funny paper hats, and went to work.

First we counted all our blessings and put them in Column A. Then we counted all our losses and put them in Column B.

After that we got down to the serious business of designating where our tax dollars should go.

"Do you want to give a billion three for the MX missile this year?" I asked her as I poured her a glass of champagne.

"Why not?" she said, drinking it down in one gulp. "What other way is there of sending a message to Moscow?"

"I like it when you take a tough stand," I said. "Besides, if the missile doesn't work we can always write it off as a bargaining chip. How much should we give to the B-1 bomber program?"

"Beats me," she said, as she threw confetti at me. "I haven't bought a bomber in years."

"We'll give them two billion, six. If it's too much, the Pentagon can always send back whatever is left over. How do you feel about making a payment to Lockheed Aircraft?"

"Are they the ones who overcharged us six hundred and forty dollars for a toilet seat?"

"Yes, but they said it was an accounting mistake and promised never to do it again."

"All right, but I don't want to give anything to General Dynamics because they tried to stick us with their dog kennel bill."

"If we don't give to General Dynamics how can we justify paying General Electric a hundred and sixty-eight million for their overcharges on spare parts?"

She blew on her noisemaker. "Because we need their stuff to defend the free world. Pay them, but enclose a nasty note telling them any more overruns come out of their pockets, not ours."

"You want to make a financial contribution to Star Wars?" I asked her.

"What kind of money are we talking about?"

"A billion dollars to get it off the ground," I told her.

"Let's do it. Especially since it takes so little to make Caspar Weinberger happy," she said.

"Are we supporting federally guaranteed student loans?" I asked.

"I hope not. I understand the kids take their money and go out and buy convertibles and stereo equipment with it."

"College students spend money like drunken farmers," I agreed.

"Don't give anything to Aid to Dependent Families. David Stockman says we can't afford it," she warned me.

"I trust David Stockman ever since he told schoolchildren there was no such thing as a free lunch."

My wife finished off the bottle. "We're doing pretty good for people who don't have an accountant."

"There is only one more item. Do you have any objection if I send in two hundred and fifty billion dollars to pay the interest on the national debt?"

"Why should I?" she giggled. "That's what our money's for. What have we got left in our checking account now?"

I added up all the disbursements in Column C, and wrote the balance in Column D.

"We have nine ninety-five," I told her.

"Great," she said, putting on a Groucho Marx mustache. "Let's go out and buy another bottle of champagne."

What Is an Editor?

The American Society of Newspaper Editors held their annual convention in Washington, D.C., and as usual everyone was overjoyed to see them.

What, you may ask, do these high-powered newspaper editors do when they aren't stroking each other at an editors' convention?

Everyone seems to have his or her own idea.

Here are some varied impressions, which depend on where you are sitting.

The Editor (as he sees himself): A slightly aging Robert Redford, maybe five pounds overweight. It wasn't his choice, but someone has to be the "captain of the ship." It's lonely at the top. God, is it lonely at the top! You don't know who your real friends are anymore. Because you're tough but fair, you're always getting a bad rap. The editorial staff thinks you're constantly knuckling under to the business side of the paper. And the business side is always giving you a hard time for wasting the paper's valuable space on editorial content. They can't pay you enough for the aggravation you take. You'd go back to the police beat tomorrow if you could just keep your present salary and still eat in the executive dining room.

The Editor (as seen by his wife): She never sees him, except at two in the morning when she wakes to hand him the phone.

The Editor (as seen by the reporter): Editors have two heads, no heart, and eyes in the back of their pointy heads. For some reason, which the reporter can't fathom, the editor either ignores the reporter all the time or is constantly on his or her back. The editor has his favorites and assigns them the best stories. He wouldn't recognize *real* talent if it were staring him in the face. The best way to keep your job is to have as few dealings with him as you possibly can. Editors used to tear up your story with a black crayon in front of your eyes—now they do it on the computer in their office, and there's nothing you can do but stare at the monitor and bash your head against the screen.

The Editor (as seen by the reader): Wears shirtsleeves in the office and polyester suits with unmatched pants and jackets to dinner parties. Either looks like Jason Robards or Ed Asner, depending on whether you saw *All the President's Men* or watched "Lou Grant" on television. He is responsible for all the bad news in the paper, especially the unfair and libelous articles about the reader's (A) political party, (B) religious affiliation, or (C) favorite sports team. The editor is held accountable not only for printing the news, but also for the news itself. He has too much power and you can't wait to see him cut down to size.

The Editor (as seen by the publisher): Never is around when there is a crisis. Is responsible for four million dollars in libel suits now pending in courts, not to mention the legal fees which the paper will have to pay, win or lose. The editor's entire operation is a drain on the paper's finances. All he wants to do is spend money that isn't his and print news that nobody wants to read. Has no sense of how much flak the publisher has to take from his friends and business associates for some stupid story the editor let through.

The Editor (as seen by the syndicated columnist who appears in his paper): Forthright, brave, intelligent, and honorable, the editor is not only a credit to his profession and his race, but the one indispensable person in a free and thriving democratic society.

His main job is to make crucial decisions. For example, this article may have been submitted to him and he had to decide whether it should appear in a family newspaper.

If the editor said, "No way," then you wouldn't be reading it right now. But since you're reading it, you have to assume one of two things. Your paper has an editor with a sense of humor or yesterday was his day off.

It's the Real Thing

There are only three great Master Coca-Cola Tasters in the world. One is Beauregard Cokely from Marmaduke, Georgia. Beau has been producing and bottling the finest vintage Coca-Cola in the South for the past forty years.

His palate is so sensitive that I have seen him perform a blindfold test where he was able to distinguish between unmarked bottles of Coca-Cola, Dr Pepper, Seven-Up, and Miller's Lite Beer.

I have attended four-star banquets where Beau, by just holding his glass up to the light, was able to tell the year a Coke was bottled, the district it came from, and, what was more astounding, the first name of the truck driver who delivered it to the supermarket.

It was no wonder that when Coca-Cola announced it would introduce a new formula for its drink last week that I sought out Beau to discover exactly what was going on.

I found him in his famous Coke cellar at Château Lafite Atlanta with his wife and daughter. The three of them were hip deep in a large vat, stomping on juicy red cola grapes in their bare feet.

Beau climbed out of the vat and greeted me warmly. Then he bent over, opened a spigot, and poured some cola syrup into a tin cup. He sniffed it, sipped it, swilled it around in his mouth, and spat it out. "Stomp a littler harder," he yelled up to his wife. "It's not sweet enough."

He handed me the cup. "What do you think?"

I tasted it and also spat. "It shows extraordinary promise, and it's honesty can't be questioned," I told him.

Beau nodded. "I believe that 1985 could be one of the great vintage years for Coca-Cola. You would have to go back to the glorious reds of thirty-one and thirty-five to match this one for body and bouquet. The sun has finally shone on Georgia."

"Is it true that after ninety-nine years Coca-Cola has a new taste?"

"We haven't *changed* the taste. We've *improved* its virility. In place of the light, dry, bubbly that has been our trademark, we're producing a mature, full-bodied, more distinctive cola."

He went over to a Coke case marked 1984. "Taste the difference between this and the eighty-five," he said.

I did. "Now that you mention it, the eighty-four does seem to lack breeding."

"Of course it lacks breeding. To give Coke back its nobility, we've made this year's vintage rounder, smoother, and bolder. We're allowing the cola to mature in its six-pack a week longer, and the bubbles to breathe in the can. We want our customers to be part of an entirely new soft-drink experience."

"Rumor has it that you are just pandering to the Pepsi generation," I said.

Beau was furious. "It's an insult to mention Coke in the same breath with Pepsi-Cola. Pepsi consists of nothing but carbonated water, sugar, caramel color, phosphoric acid, caffeine, citric acid, and natural flavorings. Coke, on the other hand, is the real thing. It will always be the pause that refreshes, because every American knows things always go better with Coke."

Beau's wife and daughter were leaning over the side watching us. He looked up and yelled at them, "Who told you to stop stomping?" They went back to jumping up and down.

I said, "Beau, could you tell me what the Coke formula is all about?"

"I'm sworn to secrecy."

"All right. Just nod your head if I'm right or wrong. Would it have anything to do with making the syrup with your bare feet?"

Beau kicked me out through the cellar door.

"What did you do that for?" I asked.

He said, "You're getting too close to the secret for comfort."